D0122329

HOW COMPANIES SUCCEED IN SOCIAL BUSINESS

CASE STUDIES AND LESSONS FROM ADOBE, CISCO, UNISYS, AND 18 MORE BRANDS

Shawn Santos

Editor-in-Chief: Amy Neidlinger
Acquisitions Editor: Charlotte C. Maiorana
Operations Specialist: Jodi Kemper
Cover Designer: Chuti Prasertsith
Managing Editor: Kristy Hart
Project Editor: Deadline Driven Publishing
Copy Editor: Apostrophe Editing
Proofreader: Deadline Driven Publishing
Indexer: Angie Martin
Compositor: Jake McFarland
Manufacturing Buyer: Dan Uhrig

For information about buying this title in bulk quantities, or for special sales opportunities (which may include electronic versions; custom cover designs; and content particular to your business, training goals, marketing focus, or branding interests), please contact our corporate sales department at corpsales@pearsoned.com or (800) 382-3419.

For government sales inquiries, please contact governmentsales@pearsoned.com.

For questions about sales outside the U.S., please contact international@pearsoned.com.

Company and product names mentioned herein are the trademarks or registered trademarks of their respective owners.

Printed in the United States of America

Second Printing, May 2015

ISBN-10: 0-13-403648-4
ISBN-13: 978-0-13-403648-9

Pearson Education LTD.
Pearson Education Australia PTY, Limited.
Pearson Education Singapore, Pte. Ltd.
Pearson Education Asia, Ltd.
Pearson Education Canada, Ltd.
Pearson Educación de Mexico, S.A. de C.V.
Pearson Education—Japan
Pearson Education Malaysia, Pte. Ltd.

Library of Congress Control Number: 2014952637

To my amazing wife, Aran. Your love and support inspires everything I do. You care about others far more than yourself, and it is that caring that has made this book possible—thank you. You are brilliant, compassionate, and not a day goes by that you don't make me laugh. You're my dream girl, and quite simply, you're the best thing that has ever happened to me. I brim with excitement when I think about continuing our life's adventure together. We can pickle that!

To my pack: Cody, Zeppelin, and Buster. What good boys! You are my shadows and my best friends. You've made me so proud—what an adventure it has been.

To my son, Julian. Even though I've only known you for 6 months, I can already tell you're a special guy. I love our inside jokes and seeing you develop your personality and interact with your surroundings. If you could only cut back on all the pooping!

To my mom, Tanya Gylfe. The world is a better place because of you. You are the most kind and thoughtful person anyone could ever aspire to, and your courage in the face of hardship is nothing less than inspirational. You are beautiful and loving, and you have taught me to be a better person. I am who I am because of you, and I hope I continue to make you proud.

To my closest friends (you know who you are… or so you think). I love that you see the world differently. You make me laugh at things I shouldn't be laughing at, and I love how you help me take life a little less seriously.

And finally, to all of the people who came together to make this book a success. From my brilliant co-authors, to my publisher, editors, and even the business and legal teams—I sincerely thank you! I am honored and humbled that you believe in me and my ideas.

Contents

Foreword

Why was this book written? This is an interesting question to start a foreword. After all, all books are written for the purpose of sharing the knowledge and expertise of the author with a varied audience—at least the business books are, like the one you are holding in your hands.

Do we need another book on social business? Are there not enough already out there? True, a lot has been written and said about social business. A lot has been written by gurus, ninjas, and rock stars—people with limited knowledge of the concept of business, but likely with some background in social networks and collaboration. These rock stars wanted to share their early experiences with social business. A few other books on social business were written by people who went through a process, who knew about business and some about social, and who wanted to document their experiences. A few more were written by charlatans with little more than a good English education and the ability to quickly write a book to capitalize on hype.

Alas, none of those books are like this one. But I don't want to get ahead of myself here—let me start at the beginning. Social business—not the operation of a business for the good of society, but rather the ability to integrate social channels and networks with the operations of a traditional business—is relatively new. It can be traced a couple of decades if you look at the components (collaboration tools, communities, listening to customers, and so on), but it was not before the onslaught of online communities in the past ten years or so that the concept began to carry weight in businesses.

As with any other technology or enterprise software tools, the hype grew quickly and to deafening levels. There were so many people who were experts (see two paragraphs above to identify those who were brave enough to write a book about it) and so many vendors that delivered social business solutions that organizations were overwhelmed. As it often happens, overwhelmed organizations don't adopt a concept; they wait until it starts to climb what Gartner calls "the slope of enlightenment," the point where we begin to understand the value that the technology or concept can have for the business.

And that brings us to the three reasons why this book needed to be written:

- The time is now to learn how to do social business properly. This book is a compilation of chapters from some of the most notable business people who have succeeded in traditional organizations at moving them toward social business. These are real-life examples and lessons learned from people who took the concept and slowly helped their organizations become social businesses (although, most of those businesses are still moving toward it—it is a journey, not a destination).

As we move closer to the moment when we know what to do, how to do it, and when to do social business, well, we need a guide who will help us understand the issues, the gotchas along the way. The people who wrote these chapters have captured that knowledge from their own experiences and they are sharing those valuable lessons to shorten the time you have to spend understanding social business and how to make it work for your organization.

- This is not simply a book, it is a curation of very smart content. Shawn Santos spent a lot of time working with organizations that wanted to migrate to social business and with practitioners doing it. He learned who the real "pioneers" of the social frontier were and who knew what they were doing. He saw success and failure at many levels and at different scales. He understands from this experience who is qualified to talk about it—and he brings them together in a curated stream of intelligently displayed how-to examples of what works for social business.

The beauty of curation, however, is that not only the best can be displayed. Some of the bad experiences and lessons learned (especially those that you say "I will never do that again") are also displayed. Although none of the writers showcased write about their failure specifically, a lot of the content debunks the traditional "understanding" of what social business is and how it works.

- This book was written to be used in many ways. The concept of social business is complex and does not apply equally to all. There is a need to adapt it to your organization and that need has many facets: Executives need to support the initiatives, finance must provide the resources, managers must ensure it works with the current processes (rather, the reimagined ones when adding social features), and workers need to understand the WIIFM concept (what's in it for me, of course).

All these people can expect to find something that will fulfill their needs in this book.

Of course, saying that social business is complicated is exactly what you'd expect a foreword to say; after all, the idea is to convince you of the need for this tome. In the case of social business, the myriad components and the complexity of each mean this is not about convincing you to take it seriously. If you are looking at this book, you likely know how serious it is.

Among the many outcomes for this book, I hope you understand better what social business is and what is not and how it can help your organization.

- Create better engagement with your customers by bringing better data to understand what they need and want—and to let you decide how to better serve those needs and wants.

- Generate a more collaborative, open environment where you and your customers can co-create value in any way you and them define value.

- Collect data and information about your products, your performance, your operations, your customers, and your entire ecosystems, and put that data to good use to replace archaic, traditional performance-based metrics with effectiveness-based metrics that correlate to strategic objectives for your organization.

- Find the best people, inside and outside of your company who can help your customers get what they want and need.

- Change your business from on inside-out, company-centric model to an outside-in, customer-centric model where all involved parties (from suppliers to prospects) can find better value that meets their expectations.

- Create a true collaborative, social business focused on the value it creates from social interactions, not on the vanity metrics of number of friends or number of eyeballs in a specific content.

The previous items are a brief summary of the benefits you will find when transforming your business into a social business. You will find more and more benefits as you move into it, and the transformation will take a life of its own.

You need a place to start in this journey—this books will do that.

Esteban Kolsky
Founder, ThinkJar

Contributing Authors

Shawn Santos, Director of Solution Design, ServiceSource (Chapter 1)

Cory Edwards, Head of Social Business Center of Excellence, Adobe (Chapter 2)

Sara Del Grande, Senior Manager, Customer Interaction Network, Cisco (Chapter 3)

Gloria Burke, Chief Knowledge Officer and Global Portfolio Leader, Unisys Unified Social Business Practice (Chapter 4)

Shar Govindan, Director, Social Learning, Bentley (Chapter 5)

David Shimberg, Director of Global Services Marketing, BMC (Chapter 6)

John Ragsdale, VP of Technology & Social Research, TSIA (Chapter 7)

Nestor Portillo, Global Social Media Marketing Manager, Cisco (Chapter 8)

Jerome Pineau, Director of Social Strategy Consulting, Lithium (Chapter 9)

Lewis Bertolucci, Head of Social Media, Humana (Chapter 10)

Regina Estes, Former Director of Internet & Remote Services, Xerox (Chapter 11)

Sandra Puglisi, Manager of Customer Tools and Social Media, Xerox (Chapter 11)

Lynn Llewellyn, Sr. Director of Knowledge Management, ServiceNow (Chapter 12)

Genevieve Gonnigan, Former Social Care Manager, Infor (Chapter 13)

Michelle Kostya, Customer Success Executive, Hootsuite (Chapter 14)

Caty Kobe, Head of Training, FeverBee (Chapter 15)

Francoise Tourniaire, Principal, FT Works (Chapter 16)

Annie Tsai, Chief Customer Officer, DoubleDutch (Chapter 17)

Holly Nielsen, Social Media Leader, IBM (Chapter 18)

Christopher David Kaufman, Social, Mobile, & IoT Business Strategy, Oracle (Chapter 19)

Charlie Treadwell, Director of Global Social Media, Symantec (Chapter 20)

Erik Qualman, Author of *Socialnomics* (Chapter 21)

Esteban Kolsky, Founder, ThinkJar (Foreword)

Preface

Shawn Santos

Why You Should Care About This Book

My first forays into social media mirrored many of my Gen X peers: modem-powered experimentation with AOL and SixDegrees in the late-1990s, followed by much more regular use of Friendster and MySpace a few years later.

At the time, social networking was simply a distraction, a fun distraction that seemed to be sucking more of us in everyday, but a distraction none-the-less. It was never very serious, and I don't believe that any of us really thought about using these tools to connect with businesses, start a revolution, or change anything other than our profile pics.

It wasn't until a few years later that I first heard the term "Web 2.0," which described a shift in technology where the web was transitioning from static pages to dynamic applications that allowed users to collaborate with each other. In 2004, Tim O'Reilly argued that the trend towards user-generated content could be harnessed by businesses to create value. That's when I began to take notice.

The early- and mid-2000's was an exciting time to be in technology. People remember it as a turbulent time brought on by the dot-com bubble. It was. Billions of dollars were lost on Wall Street and Silicon Valley, companies folded, people lost their jobs, and some even lost their houses. And while the dot-com era will forever be remembered for its reckless investing, few seem to realize that after the bubble burst, the tech industry responded by gathering itself around building something of real value on the back of the irrational exuberance of the dot-coms. It's true that much of the invested capital was lost during this time, however, there was plenty of capital—and throngs of very smart people—that found its way into the development of better software, servers, and databases that would become the very foundation of Web 2.0.

Yes, this was an exciting time. First, of course, people were concerned about losing their jobs. But it was also exciting because, at least towards the end of the bubble, people were gravitating to where value was being created. I was working at Agilent Technologies near the end of the bubble, and during that time I had the opportunity to work on innovative initiatives focused on creating customer value through peer collaboration. Far different from the hype of dot-com applications, we were using simple online forum technologies in an Enterprise company to help customers "help themselves" (while cutting much-needed costs at the same time). As I observed "Web 2.0's" transition into "Social Media," I transitioned from Enterprise Technology to value-creation on the agency side.

After a few more transitions and lessons learned along the way, I found myself working for a research boutique and trade association called Technology Services Industry Association (TSIA). Here I had responsibility for our global program portfolio, and it was here where the seeds for this book began to take hold.

Central among TSIA programs is a research practice focusing on critical areas of tech services—customer support, professional services, services revenue generation, support technologies, and so on. In late 2007, after noting sweeping changes in the adoption and spending on social media and community initiatives by tech companies, we launched a research practice focused on the intersection of social media and technology services. We invited our member companies in to research and collaborate with us, forming the first "Social Media Roundtable" for the tech services industry, with members spanning Cisco, NetApp, Microsoft, Bentley, BMC, VMware, Yahoo!, HP, IBM, Xerox, Oracle, and many other brands.

The program was considered "extremely valuable" among members, not only from the data points, white papers, and perspectives generated through research and benchmarking, but especially for the collaboration element— there is a lot of value in learning from people who have faced similar challenges to what you're facing, and people love to share and gain strategies forged from battle-hardened industry lessons.

The idea for this book stemmed from these collaborations[1], and the notion that getting these stories out there has the potential to help others in our shoes, ultimately helping to build better social businesses along the way. And because social businesses tend to be more profitable, have more customer and employee satisfaction, helping to build them just might help the economy as well—even just a little.

I don't think there is another publication like this out there. There's nothing that explores the intersection of social media, customer service, and marketing from the "real-life" perspectives of numerous dynamic individuals who have directly helped shape the social business strategies—and results—inside some

---

1 A special "thank you" to Shar Govindan for the inspiration.

of the world's leading companies. The authors of this book are probably a lot like you, and I hope that their willingness to open up and discuss not only what has worked, but what hasn't worked so well, will resonate with your view of the world, and help you drive meaningful results inside of your company.

But there is also a selfish reason for publishing this book. While it's true that I see a lot of value being created in, and from, social businesses, from my perspective as a consumer, I *personally* like dealing with social businesses—I want more companies to care more, to respond and create value, and to make it easy—even fun—to do business with.

Unfortunately though, even today this is rarely the case. Most companies have rushed into social media without considering much more than the shiny new tools themselves, and executives and customers alike have been stung by the not-so-sweet outcomes. Have you ever been pleased to find your favorite company on Twitter or Facebook, only to be slapped in the face with a complete lack of a response after asking a simple question? I have—countless times. And not necessarily by the "corner store" from which a high level of social media responsiveness may not be expected. I've been stung by big brands, brands that I have been a loyal customer to, and some that are even considered social media "darlings" by the gurus—by asking straightforward questions that are simply ignored. Questions like "I lost my pre-paid coffee card, what should I do?" or "my flight has been canceled, is it better to re-book online or go back through security to the ticket counter?"

But I have also been guilty of directly or indirectly posting occasional feedback about a company's offerings or policies publically—not in a troll-like fashion, but more with a hope that companies are using the many tools they have at their disposal for monitoring the airwaves to understand the collective voice of their customers and adjust their go-to-market strategies accordingly. And deep-down, like other humans, I suppose I am looking for a simple acknowledgement of my concerns as well. Any type of "we appreciate your feedback" will do, but it rarely comes, which only serves to amplify the negative feelings of whatever the initial concern was.

With a lot of brands, you have to wonder—why are you even using social media? For many, using these tools—or rather, using them incorrectly—has the propensity to do more harm than good.

We're more than a decade into social, and I still consider it a fluke if a company responds to my direct or indirect comments online. However, last week I did get a response from a Tweet directed to my mobile carrier. I asked what my options are if I crack the screen on my iPhone. The person on the other end

Tweeted that he was in marketing, not support, and wouldn't be able to help me. In this case, I might have felt better being ignored.

Selfishly, I want companies to do better. I want better experiences with the companies I choose to do business with. My peers want better experiences. And every generation that will come after us will demand it. As business leaders, we are constantly looking for ways to make our customers more successful and our organizations more profitable. In order to achieve success in an era that is rapidly and inevitably transforming with exciting new technologies, and perhaps more importantly, new customer expectations, leaders must inspire fundamental changes in how we collaborate internally and with customers. The most successful transformations will not be led by technology, they will be led by a shift in company mindset—defined by a culture of caring, responsiveness, transparency, value-creation and authenticity.

We have brought you this book to help you create a better social business. And while a single resource can never have all the answers, you can be confident that the insights presented herein have their roots in actual practices and strategies in place at leading technology companies, and are presented by the very individuals who have successfully managed them through a rapidly evolving landscape of technologies and corporate mindsets.

Building a social business can be hard. We've learned first-hand that collaboration, sharing and learning from others can offer significant advantages over going it alone. I sincerely hope you enjoy reading our stories and find value in our approaches. We appreciate your support and always welcome your feedback! We wish you the best of luck in transforming your company into a truly social business.

Shawn Santos
@ShawnSantos

1

The Building Blocks of Social Business: Leveraging the Power of New Media and Human Connections to Grow Business Value

Shawn Santos

What Is a Social Business?

First, it might be helpful if I told you what a social business is not. A social business is not simply one that has deployed the latest social media tools, and a social business certainly does not conduct itself with the customer-avoidance service strategies and ad nauseam marketing messages that have become the norm over the past couple of decades. On the contrary, a social business is one that has fundamentally shifted the way it connects with people, inspiring meaningful, authentic—and sometimes even profitable—collaboration among employees, prospects, and customers.

The most important element of a social business is not its ability to switch on the latest technologies, but its ability to inspire and motivate people. Sure, cool technology helps—we weren't talking about social businesses before Twitter and friends came along—but social media and community technologies are simply the tools that help build the house; they are not the foundation that social business is built upon.

Social businesses do something that previous generations of business leaders could only dream of—they break down inefficiencies within organizations and create personal relationships that inspire loyalty to the brand.

And although I'm not imploring every business to drop everything and jump headlong into social media for the sake of social media, leaders must begin to recognize and adapt to changes in the market, changes to online behavior, and changes to customer expectations.

Author and entrepreneur Seth Godin noted, "Change almost never fails because it's too early. It almost always fails because it's too late." It's up to us to identify how these sweeping changes in online behavior can impact our businesses and inspire a transformation that treats this paradigm shift as an opportunity, not a threat.

For the enterprise business-to-business (B2B) companies that have shied away from social in the past, citing that it's more of a business-to-consumer (B2C) thing, I would argue that people continue to evolve how and where they prefer to access information, unquestionably leaning toward peer-to-peer (P2P) sources regardless of industry vertical. In the new era of social, the lines between B2B and B2C have already begun to blur—when it comes to online collaboration and accessing information, people are caring less and less about whether your company sells business products or consumer products, or even whether you happen to work in marketing or support. No matter what type of business or functional group you're in, it's hard to ignore the benefits of fostering real-time knowledge sharing and meaningful human connections.

And even for those companies whose recurring revenue from service contracts has become critical for maintaining overall company revenue and margins (where customers pay upward of 20 percent of the product price annually to maintain a support contract), social business should be looked at as an opportunity to bolster these important revenue streams—not by replacing traditional for-pay support services—but by adding additional value streams that nurture customer loyalty with proactive outreach and timely, informative responses focused on ensuring customers get quick answers to simple questions (such as login assistance and help with features and functionality), as well as how and where customers can access more complex for-pay support—so the value of their support contracts are realized.

What We Can Learn from a 9 Year Old

Why should business leaders pay attention to social media, and why now? Because social media has ushered in one of the biggest revolutions of mass communication and collaboration that the world has ever seen. To illustrate, here's a story about a brilliant, young girl named Martha Payne (see Figure 1.1).

In many ways, Martha is an ordinary girl who does ordinary things. She enjoys camping, playing netball (she's Scottish), and Jura, her Labrador.

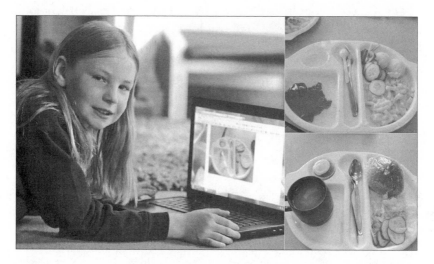

Figure 1.1   Martha Payne, founder of "NeverSeconds" school lunch blog

But unlike most pre-teenage girls, she has also raised hundreds of thousands of dollars to help feed needy kids in Africa, gets millions of visitors to her blog, hangs out with celebrity chefs, and has won numerous prestigious awards. (One time she was even toasted by Scotland's first Minster in the Great Hall of Edinburgh Castle.)

And believe it or not, all this fame began with a single photo of her school lunch that she uploaded to her own blog.[1]

She was just 9 years old when she created the blog, "NeverSeconds," as a school writing project with the help of her father, but it quickly gained a local following as other students, parents, teachers, and administrators heard about it. Then, after celebrity chef and school meals advocate Jamie Oliver tweeted, "Shocking but inspirational blog. Keep going, big love from Jamie," the blog went viral.

---

1 Wikipedia. "NeverSeconds," http://en.wikipedia.org/wiki/NeverSeconds.

Like a restaurant review, NeverSeconds rates Martha's school lunches for quality, health, "number of mouthfuls," and, just as appetizing as it sounds, "pieces of hair." Here's a sample:

> FRIDAY MAY 18: I chose a chicken grill [that] on the old menu was called a chicken burger but it is exactly the same.
>
> One of my peas was black. I had a black-eyed pea! If you look closely, [it's] the one in the middle.
>
> I love the sticky icing the school puts on its sponges.
>
> Food-o-meter - 9/10
>
> Mouthfuls - 44, I left the black pea.
>
> Health Rating - 4/10
>
> Pieces of hair - 0

In just more than a month after launching NeverSeconds, the blog gained 3 million hits. Then, she started collaborating with kids across the globe by featuring photos of school lunches sent to her by children as far away as Japan, Taiwan, and the United States. When someone left a comment on Martha's blog that said she was lucky even to get a meal at lunch, she responded with the comment, "You're right. That's why my friends and I set up a charity to raise money for Mary's Meals," a nonprofit that provides daily meals in schools to impoverished kids in Africa, to not only nourish them, but using mealtime to attract them to the classroom where they can get a basic education as well.

After several guest appearances on TV and radio as well as being invited to become the subject of a documentary, the unthinkable happened. She posted her "Goodbye."

> *"This morning in math I got taken out of class by my head teacher and taken to her office. I was told that I could not take any more photos of my school dinners because of a headline in a newspaper today.*
>
> *"I only write my blog not newspapers and I am sad I am no longer allowed to take photos. I will miss sharing and rating my school dinners and I'll miss seeing the dinners you send me too. I don't think I will be able to finish raising enough money for a kitchen for Mary's Meals either."*

Can you guess how Martha's legions of fans responded? If you guessed anything like "people went bezerk," you'd be putting it lightly.[2]

Locally, nationally, and internationally, blogs, Facebook, and Twitter were blowing up with calls for swift and decisive action. The human rights group Big Brother Watch called the act "an authoritarian infringement on her civil liberties."

The school council responded by issuing a rather harsh press release defending its decision, with statements like "the information presented in [NeverSeconds] misrepresented the options and choices available to pupils," and "the photographic images uploaded appear to only represent a fraction of the choices available to pupils, so a decision has been made by the Council to stop photos being taken in the school canteen."[3]

That didn't seem to go over very well either—the council's defiant, static press release dramatically fanned the flames of the growing social media firestorm. Under pressure, it finally took an intervention by representatives of the Scottish National Party to reverse the decision and withdraw the ban on pictures from the school dining hall.[4]

There was a lot of celebration, and Martha quickly became the most popular kid in school. But even more important, she was allowed to keep doing her thing—helping kids across the globe not only eat better, but also, eat at all.

The 5th Revolution in Mass Communications

What made Martha's school council—irritated with bad school lunch reviews and subsequent bad press—think it could get away with simply shutting her down? I believe the council thought it could get away with it because that's the way things have always been—people and organizations have *always* gotten away with these types of power

---

2 *Wired Magazine.* "9-Year Old Who Changed School Lunches Silenced by Politicians," http://www.wired.com/2012/06/neverseconds-shut-down/.

3 TwitLonger @peterwalker99 Initial statement by school council, http://www.twit-longer.com/show/hrom1r.

4 Statement on school meals from Argyll and Bute Council, http://www.argyll-bute.gov.uk/news/2012/jun/statement-school-meals-argyll-and-bute-council.

plays. The power has always rested with school councils, governments, corporations, police departments, and the like—telling you what to think, buy, and do.

But social media has enabled a momentous shift in the balance of power, and this type of democratization will only continue. The council failed to realize that social media is the great enabler of broadcasting thoughts, ideas, and even dissent, which has shifted much of the power from the few to the many. And what it especially didn't realize was that its decision to censor Martha would cause what is referred to as the Streisand Effect, where attempts to cover up or otherwise censor information can backfire and end up publicizing the information more broadly (named after American singer and actor Barbara Streisand, who tried to quash publicity and photos of her Malibu home, which resulted in far greater publicity of it[5]).

The widespread use of social media is the driving force behind fundamental changes taking place in business and society—from school lunch programs, to enterprise go-to-market strategies, and even terrorist recruiting tactics.[6] Internet technology thought-leader Clay Shirky writes, "We are living in the middle of the largest increase in expressive capacity in the history of the human race."

That's a big statement. After all, it's a reasonable assertion that only four innovations in the history of humans have truly revolutionized communications: 1) the printing press as the first true mass communications device, 2) the telegraph and telephone for "pigeon-less" two-way long-distance communications, 3) the capture of images and sound, and 4) the ability to send images and sound through the air in the form of radio and TV.[7]

5 *The Economist.* "What is the Streisand Effect?" http://www.economist.com/blogs/economist-explains/2013/04/economist-explains-what-streisand-effect.

6 *The New York Times.* "ISIS Displaying a Deft Command of Varied Media," http://www.nytimes.com/2014/08/31/world/middleeast/isis-displaying-a-deft-command-of-varied-media.html?smid=nytcore-iphone-share&smprod=nytcore-iphone&_r=0.

7 TechnoTouch. "Technological Milestones," http://www.technotouch.com/TechMilestones.htm.

And although these innovations are nothing short of revolutionary, Clay Shirky points out that there has always been something of a disconnect. The technologies that enable mass communication—print, television, and so on—simply do not work for conversations, and the technologies that are good for conversations—telephone and telegraph—do not work for mass communication.

For example, if you wanted to talk to someone other than your neighbor, start tapping out your Morse code or start cranking the telephone dial to reach an operator. If you wanted to get your message out to a large audience, you better know someone with access to a printing press.

Internet and social technologies are truly revolutionary because they bridge the gaps of these disconnects, enabling everyday people to effortlessly connect and share with vast audiences. What's more, as Shirky points out, is that as traditional media and modalities move onto the web, the web itself becomes the all-inclusive platform for all types of media—photos, sound, TV, movies, and print. Even phone calls have migrated to the web, and not only can audiences consume this information, they can also interact with it, share it, rate it, and talk about it.

But more important, so much more than the technologies themselves have changed. Perceptions about who to trust, and how and where to access information have changed. We are no longer in the broadcast era in which companies and governments urge you to sit back and listen; communications have shifted from static one-sided messages to dynamic social interactions, creating challenges for some business leaders and opportunities for others.

Until recently, most content and information was produced and controlled by companies, news organizations, governments, and similar entities. Those days are gone forever—today, everyone has their own microphone, film studio, and printing press connected to vast social networks. In *Can't Buy Me Like,* authors Garfield and Levy state, "Once, corporations and brands could operate behind nearly impregnable fortifications. Now there is hardly an event that takes place—especially an ugly one—that doesn't become exposed to one and all, immediately and in perpetuity." Everyone online should be looked at not as a submissive consumer of content, but like Martha, quite possibly a producer and promoter of content as well. As business leaders, it's up to us to understand—and capitalize on—these new dynamics.

Adapting to the Inevitable

In the new era of social, business leaders might feel conflicted between staying the course with traditional marketing and customer care strategies that might not feel like they're pulling quite like they used to, or jumping on the social media bandwagon, where business outcomes might appear soft, return-on-investment (ROI) elusive, and control seems to slip away.

Love it or hate it, our staff and customers are living and breathing social in every day. But we shouldn't get too wrapped up with Facebook vs. Twitter. From my perspective, although the technology du jour can be interesting, it's often the least interesting component of what makes social media interesting for business. That said, technological innovations that inspire pervasive connectivity will continue to evolve at a frantic pace. It's that inevitability (and subsequent changes in people's behavior and expectations) that we must adapt to.

Take "The Internet of Things," which quite simply refers to embedding web-accessible devices in "things" like climate control units, drones, and surveillance systems. This rapidly evolving technology spawned from simple RFID tagging for routing and inventory management circa 2000, to today, where we have the ability to monitor and control everything from home appliances to building facilities via the web.

Although a fridge that reminds you to pick up some more rice milk when your watch tells it you are at the store might seem far off, according to Gartner Research, there will be nearly 26 billion devices on the Internet of Things by 2020,[8] and in a recent study by Pew Research Internet Project, 83 percent of technology executives agree that in the Internet of Things, embedded and wearable computing will have widespread impacts by 2025.[9]

---

8 Gartner, Press Release December 12, 2013, http://www.gartner.com/newsroom/id/2636073.

9 Pew Research Internet Project. "The Internet of Things Will Thrive by 2015," May 14, 2014, http://www.pewinternet.org/2014/05/14/main-report-an-in-depth-look-at-expert-responses/.

We know that technologies and online behavior will continue to become more and more social. We also know that innovations that connect everything to everyone will continue to the point that they become ubiquitous—even taken for granted—by society. The most compelling argument for leaning into the era of social business doesn't come from weighing pros and cons, but rather, an unwavering acknowledgment that social technologies, behaviors, and expectations are here to stay. The question for business leaders then becomes, "How can we adapt the nuances of our business to the opportunities—and inevitability—of social?"

Social Business Requires a Change of Mindset

Social business can be difficult for some companies to embrace because it fundamentally changes time-honored approaches to marketing, customer care, voice of the customer, and other company functions.

Twenty years ago, companies started hiding behind automated "Interactive Voice Response" phone systems and obscured company contact information with the goal of reducing the amount of customer contact, and therefore, their operational costs. Back then, most executives viewed the support center as a cost center, not a driver of value and loyalty. These efficiency-only plays have created much customer dissatisfaction over the years, but it was only through the widespread adoption of social media that forward-looking executives actually started to pay attention—considering the dangerous potential for customers airing their frustrations in a very public way, as well as the benefits associated with driving more loyalty through value-laden personal interactions.

"It's always been about the individualized relationship," says Scott Olrich, chief marketing officer of Responsys, in *Can't Buy Me Like*. "A century or so back, the local corner shop lived or died based on the relationships they built…. As new means of mass communications emerged, companies used their increased reach to try to advertise their way out of that responsibility. But today every aspect of the company's behavior is on public display. A relationship-first approach to every customer interaction has again become that imperative."[10]

---

10 Garfield, Bob and Doug Levy, *Can't Buy Me Like: How Authentic Customer Connections Drive Superior Results*, Portfolio/Penguin, 2013.

If you're considering a move into (or further into) social business, a fundamental shift in corporate mindset needs to occur. This is not a question of Twitter versus Instagram, but a shift away from traditional broadcast-era marketing campaigns and efficiency-only customer care strategies to those that nurture individual relationships.

Take Zappos as an example. This is a company whose gross sales went from $1.6 million in 2000 to $1 billion in 2008[11]—a change of 499,900 percent over 8 years—with virtually no advertising budget.[12] In *Delivering Happiness: A Path to Profits, Passion and Purpose*, CEO Tony Hsieh illustrates that the number-one driver of growth at Zappos is repeat customers and word of mouth. One of the primary drivers of success was the diversion of the majority of its advertising dollars into progressive, relationship-oriented customer experience and customer care strategies, such as free shipping both ways and a 365-day return policy. Interestingly, Hsieh considers these not as a cost of sale, but a cost of marketing—that's right: great service as marketing.

What's more, Zappos' customer care center is staffed 24/7 with reps who are *genuinely thrilled* to talk with you, and in contrast to some companies' actions to obfuscate customer interaction behind IVF systems or several layers deep on the website, Zappos actively promotes the *accessibility* of these reps—the customer service phone number is displayed prominently on the top of every web page. Why? Because Hsieh considers it an *opportunity* to engage customers, "You have the customer's undivided attention for five to 10 minutes, and if you get the interaction right, what we've found is that the customer remembers the experience for a very long time and tells his or her friends about it."

"Too many companies think of their call centers as an expense to minimize," says Hsieh. "We believe that it's a huge untapped opportunity for most companies, not only because it can result in word-of-mouth marketing, but because of its potential to increase the lifetime value of the customer."

But Hsieh's enlightened customer experience mindset doesn't end there. Hsieh encourages staff at all levels to use social media to put a

---

11 Mitchell, Dan. "Shoe Seller's Secret of Success." *The New York Times*. May 24, 2008.

12 Garfield, Bob and Doug Levy, *Can't Buy Me Like: How Authentic Customer Connections Drive Superior Results*, Portfolio/Penguin, 2013.

human face on Zappos, deemphasizing technology, while emphasizing authenticity and casual exchanges. Zappos has four primary channels:

- **Twitter**: In an effort to humanize the Zappos experience, the staff is encouraged to engage in a casual manner rather than simply promote products or the brand. Hsieh also encourages customers on Twitter to not only give positive feedback, but also negative feedback as well.[13] And unlike some of the brands who close their eyes to the importance of online responsiveness, try mentioning Zappos in a tweet directly or indirectly. You may be pleasantly surprised.

- **Facebook**: With nearly 2 million likes, you might expect Zappos' direct customer interaction to be lost among the multitude. Quite the contrary. In a recent visit, I couldn't find a customer comment that was not responded to by Zappos, and the sharing of valuable content, contests, resources, and simple observations is just as prevalent as answering customer inquiries.

- **YouTube**: Zappos' video content provides another means to connect with customers (and even potential employees) by putting a human face on the company. The videos showcase the Zappos work culture, behind the scenes clips, comedic employee skits, as well as customer contests, and many of their organic employee videos have gone viral among customers.

- **Blogs**: Zappos blogs cover both timely corporate content from c-level executives, as well as customer-oriented blogs highlighting fashion products and trends.

Although it's true that this shift in mindset involves thinking differently about how to leverage new forms of media, the fundamental transformation involves a willingness among staff and executives to take individual ownership to connect with customers, and the realization that frequent personal interactions create relationships, and it is essentially that which builds the foundation of social business.

That said, it's critical to note that we can't talk about the power of company/customer relationship building without realizing that every meaningful relationship with a customer begins with a meaningful

---

13 Chafkin, Max. "The Zappos Way of Managing." *Inc. Magazine*, May 1, 2009.

company/employee relationship. Relationship building—and social business—starts at home.

If your company doesn't have what it takes to be considered a "Best Place to Work," you're going to have a difficult time becoming a social business. Why? It takes internal advocates to build external advocates, and it takes enthusiasm emanating from within the brand to be evident outside the brand. This critical shift in mindset starts at the top. Executives looking to build a social business should begin by building employee pride and loyalty—the goal is to have your staff talking positively about you wherever it goes—from blogs to the ball park.

And although it's true that Zappos gets plenty of kudos for what many consider to be an enlightened social media strategy, its positive social media outcomes have far more to do with the company's culture of sharing, authenticity, and pride than a carefully orchestrated plan to leverage the latest technologies. Zappos' success in social business is simply an off-shoot of its shift in corporate mindset; from efficiency plays to a culture of caring.

As mentioned previously, Zappos reps are *thrilled* to talk with you, 24/7—on the phone, via Twitter, and at a conference...you name it. This is not a coincidence. The company is considered by many to be the prototype for employee advocates, which CEO Tony Hsieh has championed as a part of what he calls his "Happiness Framework,"[14] which has four components:

- **Control of skill development and earnings**: Before they implemented the framework, reps were given raises once a year with no real control of how much they could earn or when they could earn the increases. The Happiness Framework is based on meritocracy, where reps can complete any number of 20 different skill set certifications, with potential pay increases attached to each. Hsieh has found that reps are much happier being in control of their own pay and skill development.

- **Frequent career advancement opportunities**: Similar to the previous approach with earnings milestones, employees at Zappos

14 Hsieh, Tony. "Delivering Happiness: A Path to Profits, Passion and Purpose," Hachette Book Group, 2010.

were given promotions once every 18 months. The new framework accommodated more frequent intervals for promotion potential—every 6 months—which gives employees a regular sense of career advancement.

- **Togetherness**: The company culture at Zappos is like a big Italian family. Employees are encouraged to speak their minds and help shape the culture; they are encouraged to attend company events and build relationships internally. This close-knit company culture has led to some of the most engaged employees in any industry.

- **Working for something bigger**: Zappos knows that a company with a vision beyond profits engenders employee loyalty, and ironically, long-term success in the market (that is, profitability). Ask a Zappos employee what she likes about Zappos, and you're likely to hear comments related to "company values," and "cares about its people," rather than, "doing great on Wall Street."

Not many companies are as far along as Zappos for sustaining a deep culture of social business. However, we can all look inside our own organizations to identify Zappos-like moments where this type of culture might be evolving organically so that we can learn from them and cultivate more of the same.

Recently I experienced an organic Zappos-like moment at the company I currently work for, ServiceSource, and our team is considering creative ways to harness more of the same. In my role as strategic partner to the outside sales team, we hosted executives from a prospect company in our office in Nashville, TN, one of our global sales centers, to demonstrate the dynamics of our recurring revenue optimization software and managed services offerings. This particular prospect represented a large, multiyear partnership opportunity that was global in nature, and as such, we asked some of our top global executives to attend. The executive meetings were fruitful and the prospect was genuinely engaged but really wanted to "walk the floor" of the sales center and talk to the people who are the engines behind our offerings. I have to say that our passionate and knowledgeable "on the ground" employees were the real stars of the show, and the time that was spent with them understanding the ins-and-outs of our offerings in an authentic, transparent environment went a long way in establishing trust, building personal relationships, and in my opinion, helping to close an important partnership.

Another recent example is when ServiceSource marketing executives recognized both the pride and competitiveness inherent to our global sales centers, and developed a simple Chatter campaign called #MyOfficeRocks, where individuals from different centers would post why their home office is particularly cool, humorous, effective, or valuable to the community—basically, why their office is a great place to work—and win prizes for the most compelling examples. Figure 1.2 shows representatives from the Dublin office proudly volunteering in the community, and other offices posted group photos wearing company colors, participating in fundraisers, or on exercise bikes in their on-site gym sporting self-made #MyOfficeRocks t-shirts. This simple campaign has gone a long way to both showcase and cultivate a budding social business.

Figure 1.2   ServiceSource Chatter campaign #MyOfficeRocks

When considering approaches to social business, many people want to talk first about the tools, often at the expense of the true change agent—internal and external relationship building. Relationships are the foundation of social business, and developing them requires a fundamental shift in mindset, starting with turning your employees into advocates and continuing with pouring passion and care into every customer interaction.

Harnessing Advocates to Create Community

In Malcolm Gladwell's 2010 *New Yorker* article, "Small Change: Why the Revolution Will Not Be Tweeted," he asserts that social media, on its own, is only a passive motivator. It can be great for asking people for relatively "soft" acknowledgment of what you're doing—for example, lazily toggling a "like" button—but it doesn't have the same "offline" leverage to inspire someone to rescue a shelter animal.

Without a true community built on relationships and shared passion, social media can be only marginally effective in achieving positive business outcomes. If your audience can consume your message in a moment or two without exerting themselves too much, they might click the "like" button, retweet the content you put so much into, or maybe, just maybe—when the stars are aligned just perfectly—post a helpful reply.

But the fickle nature of social media without community won't likely motivate people to donate to your cause, volunteer for charity, or even lend technical expertise to others. In short, if you build it, they might come, but they probably won't stick around for long or do anything particularly helpful.

Sustaining participation in social media without a sense of community is problematic at best. We need to give a reality check to the over-inflated sense of importance we give social media tools, and understand what it means to build community rather than simply turn on a new channel. This isn't to say that social media isn't powerful or meaningful or cannot help facilitate community; it can. But social media only facilitates community—it doesn't create it.

We know that advocates and frequent personal interactions create relationships, and relationships coupled with a shared purpose create community. This is essentially a continuum—from advocates, to interactions, to relationships, to community—and along it, the value of each type of engagement grows (likes versus blog posts) as participants develop a greater sense of purpose, belongingness, and accountability while contributing richer and richer content, more and more frequently. For example, the value of advocate-produced video content and blog posts might be considered more valuable than forum replies, and forum replies are usually worth more than likes and retweets.

As we consider the vastness of our potential audience, executives might question whether we will become victims of our own success. For example, is it possible for us to manage 10,000 conversations per day on our own? Not likely. Therefore, it's imperative that we understand how to scale our efforts with effective community-building strategies so our communities can thrive and support themselves.

It's All About Your Advocates: Program Dynamics and Strategies

Advocate programs leverage recognition and other key motivators to encourage desired behaviors among select members of your communities. It's up to you to decide what those desired behaviors are—whether it's happy customers blogging about how passionate they are about your products, responsive subject matter experts who are fanatical about providing technical help to others, or anything in between. It's also up to you to understand what will truly motivate your customers (and even employees) to blossom into advocates. (Check out two great chapters in this book on advocates and influencers: Hootsuite's Michelle Kostya with "Arming Your Advocates," Chapter 14, and Cisco's Nestor Portillo with "The Silent Revolution," Chapter 8).

There are some powerful statistics to support your company's investment in building a world-class advocate program, for example:

- McKinsey & Company found that peer advocacy generates more than twice the sales as paid advertising does.[15]

- Deloitte and 22squared showed that 1 in 3 people come to a brand through a recommendation, and customers referred by other customers have a 37 percent higher retention rate.[16]

---

15 McKinsey & Company, "A New Way to Measure Word of Mouth Marketing," 2010, http://www.mckinsey.com/insights/marketing_sales/a_new_way_to_measure_word-of-mouth_marketing.

16 Deloitte and 22squared, "Brand Advocacy and Social Media," 2009 GMA conference, http://www.slideshare.net/brandonmurphy/brand-advocacy-and-social-media-2009-gma-conference.

- Deloitte also showed that advocates spend 2 times more than average customers and recommend or share 2 to 4 times more than an average customer.[17]

- Fred Reichheld found that a 12 percent increase in brand advocacy generates an average increase of 2 times in revenue growth rate and boosts market share.[18]

But the most salient fact in accepting the benefits of brand advocates is that people simply don't trust companies; they trust each other. And now more than ever, people have adopted powerful platforms that they are leveraging to share opinions and information across vast networks, with or without your involvement. Trust has shifted to the participants in these networks, and as business leaders, we must recognize this shift and adapt in creative ways—most importantly, by encouraging our communities to share authentically and transparently, while incenting desired behaviors and rewarding our top contributors.

Although the business benefits of leveraging advocates can be similar, few advocate programs are themselves identical. The goals and needs of each company—even each organization within each company—can be different, and the core motivators of each community to participate can be different as well. Let's pretend, for a moment, that you don't work for Apple or Google, where the perception of legendary products and legendary workplaces themselves lead to the creation of legendary advocates (even without advocate programs). Let's say you work for a company that will benefit from a thoughtful approach to encouraging certain behaviors.

Here are seven key considerations for building a world-class advocate program.

#1 Get Internal Support, Anticipate Risks

"Go as far as you can see; when you get there, you'll be able to see farther."
—J. P. Morgan, American Financier

---

17 Deloitte referenced by Zuberance, http://zuberance.com/resources/resourcesStats. php#sthash.cb0Md83T.dpuf.

18 Reichheld, Fred. *The Ultimate Question: Driving Good Profits and True Growth* ([Nachdr.]. ed.). Boston, MA: Harvard Business School Press, 2006.

Step-wise, it's always a good idea to get your internal stakeholders involved by making them aware of the plan, benefits, and even risks of launching an advocate program—especially if you are considering more than recognizing top contributors in your branded communities, and leaning more toward external advocacy where participants are encouraged to talk about your brand in blogs and social networks. Getting internal buy-in is important because some executives might not be prepared for a new layer of company spokespeople, and being able to articulate the "whys" while anticipating the "what ifs" should be an imperative.

Although advocate-driven peer-to-peer technical support might lower the financial overhead of the organization, and the power of peer-to-peer endorsements might increase customer retention and purchasing, the question from your executives just might be, "at what cost?" The more an organization depends on others, the more the expectations placed on the brand might change. When people become more passionate about participating on the brand's behalf, they expect a relationship with that brand. You should anticipate questions from executives like, "Is it dangerous to have so many people acting as company advocates?" "Should we pay them?" And, "What are the risks associated with co-owning the brand?"

#2 Ask Them What They Want, and Build It Together

"I love the early process of asking questions about a story and deciding which questions matter most." —Diane Sawyer, American Journalist

If you think that your product isn't "sexy" enough for people to get excited about, you might be surprised—all you have to do is shift the lens to focus on what your customers are *doing* with your products and what aspects they are most passionate about to determine what to build community around. Don't build a community around your products, build it around your customers.

One of my favorite examples of an "unsexy" product surrounded by a vibrant community is the "Fiskateers"[19] community, created by word-

---

19 *Brains on Fire* "Fiskateers" case study, http://www.brainsonfire.com/work/fiskateers.html.

of-mouth agency Brains on Fire on behalf of its client, Fiskars—the 350-year-old company that makes those orange-handled scissors that everyone either owns or remembers. After brand loyalty at Fiskars dropped to a historic low, Fiskars did some brand research and found that there was little emotional connection between its products and its customers—Fiskars was described as the "milk and saltine crackers of its industry"—which isn't very sexy at all. However, they shifted the lens and focused not on a community around scissors, but what people do with scissors—namely crafting—and built one of the most energetic word-of-mouth inspired communities that I have come across. (For a sample of its enthusiasm, search for "Fiskateers" on YouTube.)

Every guide to social media will tell you to "listen" first, and that's great, but I believe most of these guides are referring to passive listening, for example, following your customers on Twitter and identifying trends. Although that's helpful, I recommend going a bit old school to *really* understand what your potential advocates are passionate about. That's right—talk to them.

Ask them what they want, what problems they're trying to solve, and what they're passionate about, and build a community with them around what you learn. For example, you can ask

- What aspects of working with your products are they most passionate about?

- What are their biggest pain points?

- What types of collaboration would make them more effective?

- What kind of content do they like to consume?

- How would showcasing their expertise or helping others advance them personally or professionally?

- What is their interest in helping to build it with you?

Talking to customers, listening to what they say, and asking them to build it with you not only positions your community to harness the passion of your advocates, but it creates a sense of shared ownership from the beginning. This sense of shared ownership is critical for seeding both early content *producers* and community *promoters* as well. Shared ownership means a sense of purpose and accountability, and that's the inspiration that will get them talking about it with friends and colleagues.

#3 Raise the Barrier to Entry

"I'd never join a club that would allow a person like me to become a member." —Woody Allen, film director

Sure, we love all our customers, but when it comes to inviting customers to participate as brand advocates, we should love some more than others. The point is, it's important to have a filter so that the advocates are admired for the accomplishment of gaining advocate status, and the risks associated with unwanted behavior from less-qualified candidates are reduced.

Begin the screening process with nominations from your staff—who do your engineers, salespeople, customer success, and marketing people think would be a good fit? Then survey your communities and ask community managers who the top contributors are (if that isn't already part of your reporting process). Also consider venturing outside your four walls and determine who in your industry has a presence at events, a respected blog, or an influential Twitter following.

And one more thing to consider: Asking the right people to participate is great, but asking them to demonstrate their commitment to participate *first* is ideal. This can be something as simple as filling out a simple profile on their skills and experience, and why they should be considered a good candidate. The goal isn't determining whether they can write a good essay; the goal is to determine whether they'll write one at all. If they don't bother jumping this low barrier, do you think they will bother jumping a higher one in their role as advocate?

#4 Make it Meaningful, Tangible (and Transparent)

"Be a yardstick of quality. Some people aren't used to an environment where excellence is expected." —Steve Jobs, Co-founder of Apple

Anyone who you'd consider making an "official" advocate is probably already an "unofficial" advocate, currently poking around the periphery of your online platforms. It's likely that these folks would be delighted to be acknowledged by you, so thanking them, sharing their insights, and promoting their work today will go a long way in formalizing the relationship a little further down the road. And when you do formalize your approach, there are numerous ways to incentivize advocates, depending on your company culture and a clear understanding of which specific motivators have the potential to be the most compelling to your unique audience.

A common approach is letting advocates demo your products before they are released to the public with the understanding that they will provide candid reviews. But recognizing them offline at events, as top contributors in online communities, and providing access to experts inside your company are all proven approaches as well. One recommendation is to simply ask them how they would like to be recognized and rewarded—you might be surprised at what you will learn.

It's also important to consider ways to bridge the online/offline divide with your advocates (for more on this topic, check out Chapter 5, "360^0 Social," authored by Shar Govindan). When is the last time a witty tweet swayed you more than an in-person conversation? My guess is never—the most powerful word of mouth happens offline, in bars, at conferences, and dare I say the water cooler. But that doesn't mean the vast reach of online networks isn't important; it means that web strategists need to find creative ways to connect people by integrating online and offline strategies.

There are different approaches to bridging this divide and making your communities more tangible. Many larger communities host conferences and events for their biggest supporters. This provides a reward for participating, the elevated status of being a top contributor and a unique opportunity to connect and collaborate with other subject matter experts in person. Those on a budget might consider simple thank-you gifts or even cards that recognize community participation, or invitations to special online events such as Q&A with key executives or engineers. The goal is to connect online and offline worlds to make the experience more tangible.

Whatever recognition or incentive program you choose, it's critical that all aspects of the program are kept transparent at all times, which means a policy should be clearly and publically articulated that states that relationships with the brand are disclosed.

The "Target Rounders" program[20] is a searing lesson in how clandestine advocate operations can backfire. The popular retailer encouraged customers—mostly college students—to promote the brand on Facebook, and it *also* told them to "keep it like a secret," while getting free CDs, store discounts, and other prizes for doing so. The corporate e-mail with the stealthy instructions was intercepted and posted online—everywhere—which created quite a backlash that lives on today in social media infamy. Of course, that was way back in 2007. Today, the pros at Target are teaching many of us how to do social. But what it taught us back then is to always be transparent with the relationships we have with our advocates, and it's never a good idea to pay advocates to promote you.

#5 Encourage Authenticity

"Truth is a point of view, but authenticity can't be faked."
—Peter Guber, American producer, executive, entrepreneur

The most successful word-of-mouth communities are built on trust, and the feeling that members can personally relate with one another. Both internal and external advocates should be encouraged to be real people when they communicate online. Training programs should teach advocates that successfully engaging in social media is more like chatting at a cocktail party than speaking at a conference. They should be encouraged *not* to blatantly advocate the brand and your offerings, but instead talk about what they did over the weekend, how their dog digested a pair of socks and threw up all over the rug, and even talk about other products and companies (in a positive light). Of course, potentially inflammatory topics like politics and religion should be avoided in public venues where diverse views are common.

---

20 *Star Tribune*, "Bloggers Seeing Red over Target's Little Secret." December 1, 2007, http://www.startribune.com/business/11987331.html.

#6 Gamify It

"[Gamification] is not a new concept…it's just that now we're beginning to create systems and technology to empower it."
—Bob Marsh, CEO, LevelEleven

Although the term itself might be reviled, its impact on spurring engagement in branded online communities is anything but. Gamification is a general term for applying the principals of games and healthy competition to online community participation, with the goal of motivating certain behaviors, for example, for contributing helpful replies in a support forum, and bolstering loyalty in trust with increased user-created content.

However, there is no one-size-fits-all approach to gamification—the goals and games are as diverse as the companies they support. It's only through a careful assessment of your business objectives along with a thoughtful consideration of the most likely community motivators that your gamification strategy will become a success.

For example, EngineYard, a platform as a service (PaaS) company for coding and deploying applications, had implemented a Zendesk knowledge base and community to increase the effectiveness of peer-to-peer support, only to find that the amount of customer-contributed content was initially far below expectations,[21] putting its investment at risk. EngineYard turned this around by incorporating unique badges (from gamification company Badgeville, see Figure 1.3) related to customers' abilities to accomplish different "missions" considered critical to community engagement—one for liking content, another for creating a topic, and more. Its gamification strategy ultimately paid off. The ensuing flood of user-generated content for its self-help portal led to 40 percent greater engagement in the forum, freed up staff with a 20 percent reduction in support ticket volume, leading to a 40 percent decrease in ticket response time and higher customer satisfaction.

Many companies also use gamification to identify and encourage top contributors, or as some call them, "Super Fans," which although accounting for only the top 0.5 percent of responders, are especially

---

21 Badgeville. EngineYard case study, http://badgeville.com/customer/case-study/engine-yard.

valued by companies because they account for a disproportionate volume of responses. For example, "KachiWachi," a Super Fan in the Logitech community, has posted an astonishing 50k helpful replies supporting one of its products.

Figure 1.3 EngineYard's Knowledge Base & Community

At Lenovo, a measly 30 Super Fans have contributed 1,200 accepted support solutions, which is 44 percent of all solutions available.[22] And Giffgaff, a mobile telecom provider in the UK, rewards helpful users with points that can reduce their monthly phone bills (a perfect example of tying business outcomes to solving customer pain points). Because of this unique approach, 100 percent of the questions that were previously answered by Giffgaff staff are now answered by the community.[23]

#7 Prepare to Take the Good with the Bad

"When the best leader's work is done the people say, 'We did it ourselves.'"
—Lao Tzu, Chinese Philosopher and Poet

---

22 Lithium. "The Lenovo Story," http://www.lithium.com/why-lithium/customer-success/lenovo.

23 Lithium. "Giffgaff case study," http://www.lithium.com/why-lithium/resource-center/solution/social-support/case-studies.

If we're asking advocates to be authentic, be themselves, and provide candid feedback, sometimes we are going to hear things that don't sound exactly like advocacy. It's okay, really. This type of unadulterated feedback—and what we do with it—is exactly the type of public discourse that will build credibility and trust in our communities. If you agree that poor customer experiences that are quickly redeemed with stellar customer service can create heightened customer loyalty, then you will also agree that how we deal with less-than-stellar feedback in public forums will reveal the human side of our companies, ultimately building new levels of trust and credibility.

And it's not only how we respond to individual comments, but it's also what we do with the feedback we receive. Companies that leverage negative feedback as opportunities to create a feedback loop with customer service, marketing, product development, and other groups will capitalize on timely and less-costly Voice of the Customer insights. And companies that complete the loop by circling back to the customer with mentions of how they are utilizing the feedback will make customers feel even more involved, appreciated, and willing to continue engaging with the brand on even deeper levels.

Yes, there might be risks in handing our customers the microphone, but if advocate programs are approached thoughtfully, there will be unimaginably greater reward. The point is that we can't talk about an effective community without talking about a sustainable community co-created with the people it aims to support. It's up to us to find out what our members are passionate about and what inspires them to participate, and built a community around that.

On Developing a Social Business Strategy

Social business isn't apps and tweets and status updates. That's social media. Social business is a shared passion for collaboration and caring that happens to leverage social media as a tool. Understanding how the tools work is the easy part. The challenge is overcoming the divide that separates traditional business mindsets from the blood, sweat, and tears of transforming into a social business.

Navigating this divide will be more difficult or less difficult, depending on your company culture. Because social business starts within the organization, you must be willing to understand and articulate its risks and benefits to executives to obtain stakeholder support. And the best way to get that support is through a carefully developed strategic plan. Here are three high-level considerations for building the foundation of your social business strategy.

#1 Align Your Business Goals with Creating Value for Your Customers

When social media entered the mainstream lexicon several years ago, many traditional marketers built strategies to capitalize on it. Unfortunately, these strategies often involved traditional ways of thinking about the use of new media to build awareness around a given company's products and services, and as such, the din of the hall became "social media is a new tool that lets us blast our message to thousands of people for free!" And although having goals tied explicitly to revenue generation, cost savings, or customer retention are often critical for sustaining long-term support of your social media programs, it's important to note that none of these goals will likely be realized unless you are successful at creating actual value in your community and eliminating pain points for customers.

When certain individuals think about potential business-use cases for social media in their companies, they have such a comprehensive understanding of the needs of their business, their customers' pain points, and the many ways to leverage social media that they can start correlating business objectives with customer needs right away. Does your business need to increase customer satisfaction? Check. Then focus your social media efforts on improving service quality (just an example). Does product development want new ideas and new sources of product feedback? Check. Then focus your social media efforts on crowd-sourced ideas and reward the most popular submissions. Do you need to reduce support costs and leverage knowledge from actual users? Check. Then co-create a support community and knowledge base with your customers.

For the rest of us, choosing the right objectives—those that are meaningful to both the business and customers—takes a little more due diligence.

Social media means different things to different people. It's a broad term, and it's also a broad category in terms of how certain aspects of it can be applied—it's certainly not a templated process that can be copiously applied to every situation because value drivers vary from one company to the next. When we're thinking about building a social media strategy, we have to start with the end in mind and ask ourselves what we want to accomplish for the business and how that relates to creating value or eliminating pain points for customers. The reverse approach works as well—look at how you can use social media to help customers, and then track potential successful outcomes back to specific business goals. For example, if you know that an upcoming product release will likely disrupt the day-to-day operations of a segment of your customer base, you might consider proactive social media outreach in advance, during and after the release, ensuring that the impact to customers is minimized. This could, of course, translate to the business goal of supporting higher levels of customer satisfaction during the transition.

We can't do everything that's possible with social. (And we shouldn't *want* to do everything.) Start focused, and simply ask, "What is the most important thing we can accomplish for our customers by leveraging social media?" I will wager that the answer to that question will equate to an important business goal as well.

Using Social Media to Ease Complex Change Management at VMware

A great example of a social media strategy that directly and preemptively addresses customer pain points (and, therefore, supports customer retention) is when VMware deployed a specific social media initiative to ease the pain of a complex change management initiative in its services organization.

VMware was undertaking a massive change in the way it presented and managed information by ripping out the guts of back-end systems that managed crucial data such as licensing, support, customer profiles, and more. It was also launching a new customer portal and anticipated that upward of 2.5 million customers were going to be impacted by the transition. To add, VMware would also need to support a large number of field staff globally who would also likely have questions.

VMware's goal was to make sure it quickly and effectively mediated any problems, and it planned to do so by leveraging social media. Its strategy had three key pillars:

- **First:** Arm VMware staff with the right knowledge about the changes, and give it somewhere to go to get questions answered in real time.

- **Second:** Be proactive about sharing externally, and use several social channels to share key details about the change.

- **Third:** Be proactive about listening—and responding—to customers in specific channels.

The only new social media tool it leveraged for this strategy was an internal support forum. The majority of the plan's strategic components had to do with tailoring processes for listening, responding, and proactive outreach using the tools it already had in place, from blogs to support forums to Twitter. This customer-focused social media strategy paid off by supporting the business goals of reducing call center activity and improving customer satisfaction through the complex roll-out.

After identifying where you can deliver value to customers using social media, it's important to also understand your customers' aptitude for adopting and using these tools. One example of a *failure* to do so is from a few years back, when a company called "Hoveround," which produces motorized scooters primarily for senior citizens with mobility issues, apparently launched a new Facebook page (see Figure 1.4) where customers—presumably seniors—were encouraged to "join need fanssssssssss!!!" This was at a time before a lot of senior citizens were even *familiar* with Facebook and, therefore, the strategy (and tactics) to engage them in this channel was clearly short-sighted and out of touch with their target demographic.

Adding to gaining a clear understanding of where your customers hang out online (Are they on Twitter? Do they blog? Are they members of other branded communities?), it's also important to understand what they do and how they "act" in those channels. You can think about understanding this social media aptitude as a continuum from basic actions to advanced actions, and ensure that your application of social media tools and desired behaviors and desired behaviors accommodates their relative social "maturity" level and propensity to interact with your media landscape in a meaningful way.

Figure 1.4 Out of touch and ineffective

Where do your customers and staff fall on the following social media activity continuum (from basic to advanced)?

- **Content consumption:** Watches online video and reads blogs and forums

- **Social networking presence:** Maintains a profile and presence in social media

- **Likes, retweets, and kudos:** Provides simple online acknowledgments

- **Ratings and reviews:** Posts experience-based feedback

- **Comments and replies:** Replies to blogs and forums
- **Content creation:** Creates original blog posts, wiki edits, and forum topic creation
- **Media creation:** Original video and podcast production

#2 Tear Down These Walls! Approach Social Business Cross-Functionally

Sooner or later, social business will break down organizational silos—whether you like it or not. Customers don't care whether marketing or support "owns" your online community. They don't care who runs your Facebook page or who manages your corporate Twitter account. If you have a marketing presence on social media and customers have a support question, they will find you, and they will ask their question to your marketing folks. This is your moment of truth: The customer might already be agitated. He might have significant online influence. He is asking you for help in a public way. Your marketing group is responsible for the platform. How will you respond?

For social media, "customer support is marketing, and marketing is customer support." That is, how you (or your advocates) respond to legitimate questions in these widely visible channels has the potential to connect with not only the question asker in meaningful ways, but also a vast silent audience as well. This audience will acknowledge your credibility and responsiveness—the simple fact that you care for and respond to your customers—which is much more powerful marketing than your latest press release.

And as far as "marketing is customer support" goes, organizations should be tightly aligned around the common goal of creating value for customers, not simply promoting their wares. At a minimum, successful social businesses have customer success, marketing, and support organizations working collaboratively on developing social media strategies to enable product and feature adoption, spearhead proactive outreach for addressing known support issues, and build awareness for valuable company resources. Sure, social media marketing can still be effective with the development and promotion of online contests and the like, but driving real value—with the input and collaboration from other functional groups—is the new imperative.

Many companies have resisted the notion of integrating the social media strategies and tactics from different functional groups. For example, several well-known brands have numerous distinct communities—one for support, another for product feedback and ideation, and yet another completely separate community for users to share tips and customizations. Although at the other end of the spectrum, marketing has spearheaded the companies' involvement in social, launching, say, a company Facebook page, with no plan or intention to respond to customer inquiries that fall outside of marketing's domain. This is a recipe for disaster. Even for the companies with numerous disparate communities, some have had the foresight to create engagement plans that describe response paths for different scenarios, for example, how to respond to support questions posted to the ideation community or how to deal with product feedback posted to the support community. But it begs the question, "Why the separation in the first place?"

That said, most situations are unique, and there might very well be a rationale for this separation. But in all cases, I would highly encourage the company to develop a cross-functional "Center of Excellence" to collaboratively arrive at the decision to integrate or separate, as well as define policy, outline triage plans for response escalations and potential fire storms, and develop a program that encourages participation and advocacy. (Check out Chapter 2, "The Reinvention of Social-by-Design Business," by Adobe's Cory Edwards for an in-depth view of the value of Centers of Excellence.)

The conversation today is all about inspiring meaningful engagement across the customer life cycle. If you agree that customer loyalty is the key to success in your business, you will probably also agree that a singular focus on one stage of the customer life cycle—say, presales—while neglecting others—say, post-sales—is *not* a formula for success. Both marketing and customer care play critical roles in social business. However, a true social business is a *culture* of customer care—not simply emanating from customer support—but one in which every employee is encouraged and inspired to delight customers with every interaction.

#3 Keep It Simple: An Optimized User Experience Is Key to Adoption

When it comes to the adoption of social media, optimizing the user experience is critical. The key to an optimized user experience is simplicity: ease of access, just the right feature set, and integration with existing technologies and work streams.

Today, we are beginning to see categorical evidence of the move to optimize the social user experience by integrating social into existing environments. For example, the following statistic might surprise you: The growth of standalone enterprise social software has *fallen* by approximately 50 percent over the past 2 years.[24]

Contrary to first impressions, the trend is not explained by businesses using enterprise collaboration software less, but because these collaboration tools are being embedded into existing applications and work streams (think Salesforce.com's Chatter), which is reducing the prevalence of the standalone tools. Peter Coffee, a VP in Salesforce.com's strategic research group, puts it this way, "It is like having a telephone room at the end of the hallway where you make your calls. (It doesn't happen that way.) The phone is infused into the way we get work done."

Another important development that further describes the shift to optimizing user experience was by Microsoft's purchase for $1.2 billion in 2012[25] of Yammer, an enterprise collaboration tool that works like Twitter. One month after Microsoft made the purchase, it announced that further development of Yammer was moving under the Office 365 team (responsible for the popular suite of Microsoft Office applications). To me, this speaks volumes to the notion that Microsoft is focused on integrating social capabilities to tools that many of us use on a daily basis—optimizing the user experience—and making access, adoption, and ultimately collaboration, that much easier.

Consider the integration of branded communities with website login, with knowledge base content, and with federated search. We want to

---

24 *The Wall Street Journal.* CIO Journal Blog. "As Facebook Goes Parabolic, Social Media Adoption at Work Is Slower Affair," http://blogs.wsj.com/cio/2014/07/24/as-facebook-goes-parabolic-social-media-adoption-at-work-is-slower-affair/.

25 Wikipedia. Yammer, http://en.wikipedia.org/wiki/Yammer.

make sure that customers know where to go and what to do for whatever the task at hand might be. The way most communities are set up—with separate logins, separate platforms, and scattered content—is confusing and inefficient for staff and customers alike.

Integrating technologies to enhance the user experience can sometimes be expensive or resource-intensive, but if thoughtfully planned and executed, a return on your investment is certainly possible. ROI from user-experience initiatives can take several shapes—from customer retention to call deflection through more engaged support communities. Microsoft measures "customer effort" as a precursor metric to community ROI: Their user experience-focused initiatives help users move easily among channels and find what they are looking for with less effort, which they equate to customer satisfaction and can subsequently measure as ROI.

Another forward-looking technology company starts its online support process not by abandoning users in a confusing tangle of community threads, but with a simple, prominent search box with results that auto-populate from both the knowledge base and community forums as the user types. If no relevant results are identified, the user has the one-click option of turning the search query into a new forum topic. If the question posed to the community is not responded to within 24 hours, it is automatically bumped to a distinct "needs assistance" area designated for the community's top advocates. In the instance that the question is not marked as "resolved" by the question originator after 48 hours, the forum post escalates into a support incident automatically.

This successful approach at optimizing the user experience integrates website login with community, community and knowledge base with search, top advocates with escalated topics, and support reps with twice-escalated topics. No system is perfect of course: Sometimes the forum questions are actually resolved in the community, but the originator simply neglects to mark it as resolved. However, the support reps see the subsequent follow-up as an opportunity to demonstrate their responsiveness, inquire about any other issues they can help with, and enhance the relationship through proactive outreach. But it doesn't end there. The community's "top advocates" are responsible for vetting the most helpful answers and best content, and when content ratings surpass a certain approval threshold, the content is automatically harvested and added to the knowledge base. This is a shining example of an optimized user experience.

Another fantastic story of optimizing the user experience is from the innovators at Enterasys Networks, who are credited as the first company to be successful with building "social machines."[26] Vala Afshar, who was then chief customer officer at Enterasys and always a consummate champion—and practitioner—of social business, invented a product called Intelligent Socially Aware & Automated Collaboration (ISAAC). Realizing the significant amount of time that his customers spent using social media, as well as the ubiquity of smartphones and tablets, he saw an opportunity to reduce the number of interfaces his customers needed to access by deploying a solution that enabled them to manage and control Enterasys' network products dynamically through social media such as Twitter, Facebook, LinkedIn, and Chatter by Salesforce.com.

ISAAC is essentially a social media interface that translates the complex language of systems to English, German, Japanese, and other languages, and not only posts updates in customers' preferred social media channels, but also enables them to communicate back to the machines—giving users both visibility and control of mission-critical systems, all within the applications they already use on a daily basis. There are few better examples of optimizing the user experience through platform innovations.

The ISAAC example is of course more Cadillac than Chevy, and most of us will be starting out trying to build the latter. With that in mind, it's important to do a type of user-experience mapping, where your team runs through specific customer use cases and tasks that are likely most common among your user base, for example, put yourself in your customers' shoes when they are searching for product reviews or help with certain features. Better yet, invite different types of customers (representative of various product lines, seniority, or level of familiarity with your platforms) to run through certain tasks, which will quickly expose pain points with content access, navigation, messaging, purpose differentiation for various applications, accessibility from mobile devices, and more.

---

26 Afshar, Vala and Brad Martin. "The Pursuit of Social Business Excellence," 2012.

Generally speaking, it's best to approach new community and social media initiatives as small and focused as possible, ensuring that every platform and every customization supports the goals of your business and eliminates pain points for customers, no more and no less. The excitement that often pervades sparkly new tools has given rise to many companies inundating their customers with too many places to go, too many things to do, and too few integrations, which only obscures clear paths to desired behavior.

How to Develop Meaningful Metrics and ROI

Nothing a company does is free. Somehow people seem to forget this when it comes to social media. Sure, setting up a Twitter account is free. Launching a snazzy Facebook page? Zero dollars. Even with certain community platforms, simple monitoring applications and analytics packages you'll see a $0 price tag. But social media takes *people* to make the *social* side of social media work, and more often than not, it takes "for pay" *technologies* to optimize the *media* side of social. And it *always* takes time, and everyone knows the old cliche....

So, contrary to what some people will say, most social media initiatives are not actually free. When it comes to putting a plan together for the first time, or doubling up on your recent momentum, it's important to realize that funding for new or improved service or marketing initiatives doesn't usually appear automagically. Getting resources allocated to your project means demonstrating business value with meaningful metrics, and more and more, we are asked to capture and prove the most elusive social media metric of all—ROI.

Like most things social, there is no single key performance indicator that will describe the success of all social media implementations—KPIs (Key Performance Indicators) will depend on your objectives, the behaviors you are trying to inspire, and the outcomes that are most meaningful to your business. Susan Etlinger, Altimeter Group's social data expert, said, "Everybody has data, what we need is meaning." What does having 10,000 Twitter followers tell you about your business? Nothing? Maybe something? Context is king here—data is only meaningful if it is intrinsically tied to what you are trying to accomplish.

One way companies can begin to think about success metrics is to consider a series of KPIs in three broad categories—awareness, interest, and action—which can be thought of in terms of three sections of a funnel that progressively increase in value, where

- **Awareness** is the broadest section of the funnel, which might be measured by your community's number of members, likes or followers, which could support a goal of expanding potential reach. On their own, awareness metrics are rarely viewed as a measure of business success.

- **Interest** is the middle section of the funnel, which represents significantly more business value than simple awareness metrics. Interest metrics are measures of engagement: forum posts and replies, likes, comments, retweets, media views, and downloads. These metrics tell us that people are engaged, that content is being shared, and that value is being created.

- **Action** is the narrowest section of the funnel, which represents the most business value and can be measured in different ways. From a marketing perspective, this usually means measuring conversions, that is, tracking a user's path from a social media interaction to a "microsite" or lead generation web page, to the submission of contact information or similar action.

  From a customer support perspective, this can involve tracking a user's path from the company website, search query, or social media interaction, to the company's support forum. It is what can be inferred from the user's next action that can be interesting:

  - The visits to the forum can be viewed as successful if users indicate their questions were "resolved." This information can be captured in a number of ways, including tracking the volume of new forum posts compared to those marked in the community as "resolved" or "answered my question" (or similar).

  - Of course, not every user that has her question successfully answered in the forum is going to remember to mark the question as resolved. And although you can certainly develop reasonable estimates of what percentage of successfully resolved forum posts are actually marked as such with follow-up surveys (which is one of the most popular methods), it is also helpful to triangulate your metrics to help support your assumptions.

As a quick aside, let's say you have a data point on new forum posts versus those marked as resolved. For example, you have 100 new forum posts, but only 50 are marked as resolved within 72 hours—a 50 percent resolution rate. Let's also assume that you've gone a step further and know from your survey results that 20 percent of users who had their questions resolved said they neglected to close the loop and mark the question as such. By interpreting these two data points, we can reasonably assume that we have a 70 percent resolution rate in our support forums. But you can build even more confidence in this finding by triangulating your interpretation of resolution rate with tracking where traffic flows on your online properties. For example, what percentage of your online forum users visit your Contact Us page after their forum session? If the answer hovers near 30 percent, it could support your assertion of a 70 percent resolution rate.

Think of the social metrics value funnel as a launch pad—it's more of a concept for framing an approach to metrics than a template. Clearly, there are countless ways to measure social—from content amplification to sentiment—that are as creative and unique as the businesses and business objectives they aim to support.

Many companies have developed their own unique measures of performance, like VMware, who has used the following three KPIs that are unique to their business goals: awareness, accessibility, and engagement.

- **VMware KPI: Awareness**

   Business goal: *Ensuring customers are aware of self-help content*
   What they measure:

   - "Social Network Effect": Percentage of Knowledge base (KB) visitors coming from social networks

   - "VMware Search Index": Percentage of KB visitors using VMware.com search engines

- **VMware KPI: Accessibility**

  Business goal: *Ensuring content is easy to consume*

  What they measure:

  - "Single Page View Index": Percentage of viewers that access no other VMware.com assets before or after viewing the article in a session

  - "Exit Index": Percentage of viewers who do not access any other VMware.com assets after viewing a KB article

- **VMware KPI: Engagement**

  Business goal: *Ensuring customers are interacting with or sharing content*

  What they measure:

  - "Twitter Engagement": Percentage of Twitter traffic about KB articles outside of VMware

  - "Ratings Rate": Percentage of KB visitors that interact with/rate content

The Elusive Question of ROI

To sustain corporate investment and top-down support of social media initiatives, we often need to reveal and clearly articulate positive business outcomes. Not coincidentally, positive business outcomes are most often tied to positive *customer* outcomes as well, where it can be demonstrated that customers are actively engaged, creating and receiving value, and ultimately more satisfied with your company operating as a social business than not.

However, even though positive customer outcomes and other interesting measures such as "reach" can be correlated to business outcomes, they can only be considered *precursors* to ROI—not a measure of ROI itself.

It should not be inferred that metrics other than ROI are not important to measuring impact to the company—they are. In addition to representing the mix of characters, themes, and subplots that develop your ROI story, even on their own, different internal stakeholders have different interests and uses for different metrics. This is a salient point: We need to provide the right metrics to the right audience.

For simplicity, we can segment audiences into three groups with different metrics requirements. Community managers are likely interested in media metrics, such as members, clicks, active visitors, top content, and contributors, whereas business managers are likely interested in customer metrics, which might include measures of community effectiveness, knowledge harvesting, and insights on the voice of the customer. Mention success in any of these areas to executives and you might be greeted with an initial curiosity, but that will quickly change to some form of, "So what?" Executives simply want to know how all the time, money, and company resources you are pouring into this unfamiliar concept called "social business" is paying off in terms that are meaningful to them—KPIs like customer loyalty, retention, and importantly, ROI.

ROI is a financial measure—it's all about the P&L—and should be interpreted only as such. For example, measures of customer satisfaction (CSAT) are critical for understanding the health of a business, but improving CSAT does not *explicitly* spell ROI unless you *explicitly* create a financial correlation between the two. Sure, we can *assume* that improving CSAT is good for business and likely equates to some amount of revenue retention or increase, but executives will want to know how much you invested to improve CSAT by X percent and how that X percent equates to dollars. When thinking about ROI, think in terms of the P&L.

Let's look at one of the more popular approaches to developing an ROI story for customer support.

Case Deflection

Case deflection is among the most-practiced measures of ROI, especially in technology companies with established communities. Oddly enough, this is essentially a measure of something that *didn't* happen. I touched on this concept earlier—some companies (not Zappos) try to measure the effectiveness of their communities in terms of reducing the amount of incidents opened with their call centers, which can be explicitly equated with cost-savings, and therefore, ROI.

There are at least two approaches to measuring case deflection. The first works to understand the impact of a *new* community or initiative on the volume of support cases. Generally speaking, the idea is that you launch a new initiative, wait for the impact, and then simply compare pre- and post-incident rates. If your incident rate drops after the launch of your community, there might be a correlation between the two. The problem is that you need to be patient while you wait for results to trend over time, but even more problematic, is that other organizations or initiatives could be responsible (or even claim responsibility) for your apparent success.

A more reliable measure of case deflection-based ROI has to do with obtaining direct feedback from customers who have indicated their support question was resolved in the community. To some, understanding the community's resolution rate might spell ROI, but it's only assumed ROI unless we make a direct correlation. That's why we need to determine whether the customer would have opened a support incident if it were not resolved in the forum. This type of information is almost always obtained through a simple, two-question survey:

- Did you resolve your issue in the community?

- If yes, would you have opened a case otherwise?

These simple surveys either "pop up" during the community session, or they are e-mailed to the customer after the session. And survey best practices apply—it's important not to inundate the same customers with the same survey on repeat visits (which is one of many reasons why customers should be encouraged to engage in auditable channels where you can track activity, contact history, and more). Remember that not every visit needs a survey. As with most surveys, it's important to accurately gauge sample size to reflect the impact of your entire population. I've observed many companies using a confidence level of 95 percent (also the standard in most quantitative research) with a margin of error of 5 percent. (These two boundaries equate to a statistically significant sample size of 370 respondents for a population of 10 k.)[27]

---

27 *CheckMarket*. Sample Size Calculator. https://www.checkmarket.com/market-research-resources/sample-size-calculator/

Cisco recently reported cost-savings due to case deflection of nearly $10 M over a 12-month period ending in January 2014,[28] and that ROI is expanding as the community gains momentum noting that cost-savings increased 48 percent over the last two quarters alone. Although Cisco has been reporting ROI from its various support communities for years, its recent success is the result of a new effort to change the way its engineers not only collaborate with each other, but also how they share valuable content with customers, *all in the same channel*. The 2-year-old community is called Tech Zone (built on the Lithium Technologies platform) and was recently recognized as the winner of the 2014 Groundswell Award for Employee Empowerment. As word of the community's success has spread, many different groups within Cisco are organizing to empower their engineers, connect them with customers and reap similar benefits, while their vast partner community and more and more customers are taking notice.

However, just because Cisco sees ROI in case deflection, it doesn't mean that's necessarily the right metric for everyone. If you remember our Zappos conversation, case deflection would likely be considered *negative* ROI by the likes of Tony Hsieh, as he views each customer contact as a moment of truth for both selling and relationship building. There are many methods to evaluate the effectiveness and value of your social media implementations—from metrics that describe the initiative's effectiveness at repurposing content, to describing how social can lead to a better understanding of the voice of the customer. But when it comes to true measures of ROI, it makes sense to correlate outcomes with tangible financial results—noting how your initiative has generated revenue or saved costs.

Final Thoughts

Much of the hype that has permeated social media discussions over the past several years has led some executives to perceive it as a magic pill, whereas others simply dismiss it as "soft." The truth is, it's neither.

---

28 Karcher, Philipp. Forrester Research CIO Blog. http://blogs.forrester.com/philipp_karcher/14-05-05-winners_of_the_2014_groundswell_awards_business_to_employee_division

Yes, social media is game-changing technology. But as for any tool, it takes the right people and the right processes to make it work. And for social to work *really* well, it requires a fundamental shift in business mindset to a culture of collaboration and caring that supersedes functional group or role in the company. Business leaders are sensing the inevitability of social, but many fear the death of familiarity. They want to innovate but are concerned about the potential for failure in such public venues. They want to empower customers and staff but struggle to retain control of "the message."

It's hard to go from being a centralized organization that's powered by hierarchies and traditional business processes to a dispersed community that's powered by passion, fluidity, and collaboration.

No, building a social business is not easy. But remember, it is demonstrating your good intentions, being human—and even making mistakes—that gives relationships their resilience. And though these relationships might take time and focused efforts to blossom, forging robust relationships with customers will sustain community over the long term and bolster your company's capability to endure the ups and downs the market inevitably deals any organization.

2

The Reinvention of a Social-by-Design Business

Cory Edwards, Head of Social Business Center of Excellence, Adobe

Witnessing the Power of Social Taking an Entire Industry by Storm

Social media's explosion into mainstream culture during the past decade has transformed the world as we know it. Companies are rethinking business strategies, scrambling to adapt and survive in a new era in which social, culture, and technology intersect. Over the years, the path leading to a social-by-design business hasn't always been clear. And the journey, albeit fascinating, has been marked by both extraordinary success and magnanimous failure.

Today, when we think of what it means to be a social-by-design business, what do we envision? To me, it's about social being integrated or woven into operations so that every aspect of business harnesses the power of real-time social technologies to enhance the business. The modern social-by-design organization does more than occasionally post comments or engage in conversation; it combines the "doing" of social media with strong internal social operations. Yet, despite its early contribution, the significance of social and its import to business wasn't easily recognized, and the voyage began without so much as an "adieu."

However, failure equals learning and I've had my share of both. In fact, one of my first experiences integrating social into business didn't go quite as planned. At the time, I was working for Symantec, involved in the coordination of our annual Vision Conference. As is the case with most events of this size, scores of sponsors advertising on the conference floor leave many visitors overwhelmed, unsure of which booths to visit, or what is happening at any given time. In an effort to remedy what I like to call "classic conference hall conundrum," my team and I put together what we were sure was the perfect social solution for making the event easier to navigate.

Twitter, although relatively nascent at the time, was gaining popularity, and we thought it would be a great idea to give our partners a unique conference Twitter account for providing real-time information to visitors entering the show floor. The idea was to have the partners tweet what was happening at their booths to inform attendees about events on the show floor. To make it more helpful, we created a mash-up that combined the Twitter data with a map of the show floor on 60-inch TV screens that were hung at the entrances to the expo floor. Each time the sponsor tweeted using our conference hash tag, it would show up onscreen with the location of the booth. Attendees simply needed to look over the screens as they entered to learn about a giveaway, a demo, or where the best tchotchkes were. Real-time data would fill the screens. It seemed like a great idea and perhaps one that would work successfully today. The reality, however, was much different. Twitter was too new and few of our sponsors had any idea how to use it. Over a 3-day period, we amassed a dismal 150 tweets or so—it was a failure—despite how innovative the idea might have been at the time.

For me, years of trial and error defined by both success and a few failures along the way have culminated in a deeper understanding of what it means to be a social-by-design business. Social is after all, understood best through a collective lens, and it is through these varied, pioneering experiences that business and the larger world around us benefits.

My "ah-ha" moment with social—when I first recognized that there was real opportunity in the collective—occurred in the mid-2000s, prior to the Twitter screen mash-up debacle. While supporting Symantec as a PR manager on the agency side, I saw firsthand the power of social as I watched it transform an industry right before my eyes.

The Birth of the Symantec Security Response Blog

The Symantec Security Response group had long been known for providing accurate, detailed, and timely information on the latest virus or worm outbreaks. These virus hunters had tremendous insight on account of millions of customers feeding security information back to Symantec. Our team was inundated with requests from journalists and national news outlets for commentary on the flood of online threats that were infiltrating the digital landscape. Journalists wanted near real-time updates on the most aggressive threats, often calling every hour of the workday for new information.

I remember thinking, we are in an information-driven world, yet with new viruses showing up every day, how are we ever going to keep up with the demand for updates? It was around this time that we started hearing buzz about a new web platform called a "weblog." As we started to think about the potential application for Symantec and the challenges with keeping pace, we decided it might be worthwhile to start a blog as a way to disseminate information quickly and in real time. Authored by the Security Response team, the content reflected updates as they happened, and the team kept reverse chronological order of relevant changes and variants it was monitoring. When the blog was up and running, we told the news outlets that in addition to holding phone conversations, they could get the latest information directly from this new blog.

That was the genesis of the Symantec Security Response blog. Since its launch, thousands of news stories referenced the information the team provided. Eventually, we moved on to podcasts and other social networking platforms, but this was a defining moment and my first actual firsthand glimpse into the power that could be harnessed from these kinds of technologies.

From "Black Sheep" to "Golden Child"—The Social Journey

Although there were a few success stories in the early days of social media for business, there weren't many senior executives who were convinced it was anything more than a passing fad. In fact, more than a few prominent executives were not only "nonbelievers," but also adamantly against legitimizing it by giving it any kind of relevance at all. It was too "risky," too much of a "gamble," and as a result, not something many companies were willing to invest in.

Wait Just a Minute, There's Real Opportunity Here

A lack of understanding wasn't going to stop employees from having a voice, and everyone from frontline workers to management teams were starting to use social platforms as best they knew how. It was a sounding board to talk about their families, their interests, and by default, their companies. Like it or not, social media was having an impact on business, and it was becoming clear that it was not simply a game for college kids.

As employees reached out and started having conversations with customers, some companies immediately began to see the usefulness in connecting, engaging, and developing relationships. For other early adopters, interest in social media might have been due to strong executive support or internal agents leading change. Nevertheless, over time, more and more companies recognized the opportunity in social media and it took on a new reputation, moving away from ostracized "black sheep" to admired "golden child." Practically overnight, traditional marketing or PR strategies took a back seat to trying new customer engagement programs that were piloted using social media.

Finding a Home

For a long time, even as businesses were starting to recognize social as relevant, it was a sort of bolt-on strategy to existing marketing and PR work. For years, in fact, companies struggled to integrate social into a larger organizational plan, even if it were limited to marketing and PR. The problem was that the possibilities with social seemed to intersect so many different parts of the business. From the traditional PR and marketing teams to talent acquisition to support, everyone was exploring it, but no one knew for sure where it should fit.

Make no mistake, there were plenty of voices in the industry pontificating where social should live and who should "own" it and whether it should be independent or an add-on to an already established department. Some felt that the PR or marketing team should own social, convinced there were no new real skill sets needed, simply an adaptation to changes in process. Others disagreed. And although online communities and forums existed well before the blog was introduced, these early applications lacked the visibility marketers wanted and as a result were typically relegated to support.

More Challenges: Budgeting, Time, and ROI

Fast-forward a few years, and the social journey was fraught with even more challenges. Budgeting was an issue because it was difficult early on to show the real business value to be gained from investing in social media. Even more relevant than money was time and head count. Establishing a Facebook or a Twitter account wasn't expensive, but it was time-consuming if done right and nearly impossible to show the kind of bottom-line return that many were hoping for. The value of social was intuitive and its worth could be seen as customers appreciated it. However, with no hard ROI and no number you could cite back to say, "We made X because we invested Y," social media was still largely deprioritized when push came to shove in budget discussions.

As part of the Symantec Corporate Communications team, my main focus was PR, but I was always looking for ways to integrate social into the bigger picture. I pushed hard and was passionate about social becoming larger than it was. Fortunately, the vice president of Corporate Communications was a believer in the direction social technologies were headed. Like me, she believed it was positioned to become a difference maker and in 2007, gave me the okay to pursue social as a full-time initiative. At that point, I became the first social media strategist employed by Symantec.

Building a Social Media Infrastructure

Debunking the "if-you-build-it-they-will-come" mentality. Despite recognizing the value of social, businesses around the world were becoming a bit disenfranchised, particularly small businesses because they didn't know how to "do" social right. The "build it, they will come" approach clearly was not enough. It wasn't sufficient to simply create profiles to establish a presence on the networks and then post company updates and engage in marketing campaigns. Doing social right meant forging a parallel path between social infrastructure and social campaigns. In other words, companies needed to be present in the forums and on networks, communicating and posting, but they also needed to learn how to integrate social as a business operation model.

Weaving social into the business. For many of us, it was clear that social media was not just a way to waste time with friends but a real opportunity for businesses. But we needed to think about how social could be woven into the fabric of the company. How did it fit into not only marketing and PR, but also IT and product innovation? More broadly, how were we going to manage and govern all the different ways that social can be used when so many different teams across the company were beginning to see value and wanting to do it themselves?

Adobe's Social Media Center of Excellence

Last year, I was named head of Adobe's Social Media Center of Excellence. With nearly 20 million fans and followers, and 63,000 mentions each day, the Adobe brand is highly integrated in social media. Currently, we have a greater percentage of employees on Twitter than any other technology brand, and we've been highly successful at integrating social into our way of doing business. In fact, our efforts recently led to Adobe being named the "Most Social Technology Brand" in the Socia-Look Leaderboard, which evaluates social advocacy levels of employees at 50 technology companies.

The key to our success lies in our approach: how we manage social media operations (see Figure 2.1). The early masterminds at Adobe were led by the visionary ideas of Maria Poveromo, now senior director over public relations, analyst relations, customer reference work, and social media. Maria architected a social structure within Adobe that focused on integrating social into the framework of the overall business. She recognized early that social media managers needed to "do" social on the web, but doing it right necessitated a solid back-end operations role as well.

In much the same way sales or marketing teams frequently have a corresponding sales ops or marketing ops team, we've structured our CoE as a functional operations group. The blueprint for success with this program relies on our four foundational pillars: governance, enablement, measurement, and innovation.

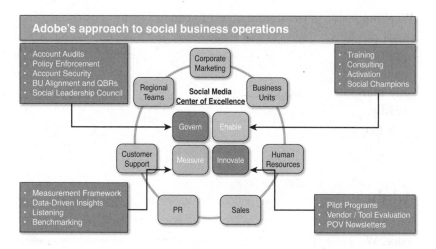

Figure 2.1 Adobe's approach to managing its social business operations

Governance

Our governance function was created with an eye toward protecting the corporate brand. To that end, our social governance lead establishes and maintains the appropriate policies and processes that are needed to ensure our branded accounts are protected. Regular audits take place with each one of our many hundred Adobe-branded social networking accounts.

Governance also includes creating standards for how we want our accounts branded. Everything from social handle names to colors, logos, images, even the appropriate voice are considered. Recently, we've undertaken an effort to enhance the security of our social networking accounts. As is the case in many organizations, social networking accounts are often created as a grassroots effort by various employees who simply use their work or even personal e-mail address as the username for login or account recovery. Unfortunately, if the account is breached or the employee decides to leave the company, access can be challenging. As a solution, we've migrated our branded accounts to specific Adobe e-mail addresses created for the social account—addresses that act as distribution lists, which we control. This makes managing our social accounts simpler and more secure.

Enablement

Just how important are employees in the world of social? According to the 2014 Edelman Trust Barometer, the average employee is far more trusted than a company's CEO. Enablement at Adobe is, of course, about enabling more than the average employee, but we increasingly believe our broad employee base is key. Part of our enablement program involves providing consulting to teams within the company who are looking for help building or executing against a set of social objectives.

For much of my career, I've worked tirelessly to convince executives of the importance of being socially active themselves. I still believe this, but I also think companies can find success in programs that focus on empowering and enabling the broad employee base—even as they might be hesitant to use social media for fear of retribution for saying or doing the wrong thing.

More enterprising employees have taken a look at the water and jumped in—headfirst. For example, one of our product evangelists decided early on that having social media accounts could be helpful for her work with customers. Not only has she amassed a large following, but also her individual efforts have generated more direct revenue than our branded social accounts! This is one of the reasons why one of our primary objectives is to educate our global Adobe workforce on social media with a focus on customer-facing employees.

Training: The Adobe Social Shift Training program is an integral part of Enablement and is organized into three parts: three gears if you will, using the racecar metaphor that we employ for this program. The three gears aim to take our employees from a state of awareness to empowerment and ultimately, social media excellence.

- **First Gear:** First gear is our social foundation training, which informs employees about Adobe's social media programs and the role they can choose to play individually. We share our corporate social objectives and how social media is used across the different functional teams. Training is in-depth and hands-on but focused primarily around Adobe's guiding principles for social media: Authentic, Involved, Responsible, and Respectful. For each principle, we discuss what it means using examples to illustrate right from wrong. Then we have employees participate in a class activity where each member sits in the "driver's seat" to evaluate a scenario and determine how best to proceed based on the principles we've discussed. We expect any employee in the company, who plans on using their personal accounts to discuss their work at Adobe or Adobe's products, to attend.

- **Second Gear:** Second gear is our strategy course and is a more advanced training for anyone who might use social media as part of their professional life—regardless of whether they're social media managers. Many customer-facing positions at Adobe are targeted for this training including product managers, marketers, corporate communicators, customer support personnel, and even sales reps. This second course teaches the art of both defining a strategy and then executing against it. We dive deep into content, listening, rules of engagement, and even targeting.

- **Third Gear:** Third gear in Social Shift is actually a series of courses that we refer to as our Social-by-Objective modules. Employees who've shifted through first and second gear can choose to attend courses that are relevant to their specific functional roles at the company. The classes teach how to do social for achieving specific business objectives: customer support, raising product awareness, lead generation, talent acquisition, event marketing, and more.

Although our training has been well received and attended within Adobe, our feeling is that training is only as good as the path it paves to actual involvement. Done right, social media training programs are interwoven with a robust employee activation initiative that takes trained employees, builds on their social literacy, and then empowers them to act within specific social programs and initiatives. This is where we are now focusing our efforts. Our goal is to create voluntary champion groups for employees to join after being trained that will have specific social tasks, such as identifying customers in need or perhaps something as simple as amplifying Adobe news.

Measurement

Although centralizing governance and enablement might seem logical, *measurement* as the next part of our CoE might seem puzzling. But keep in mind that measurement of social efforts is the responsibility of all involved. Our CoE has created social media measurement standards, which are used by the organization but also to teach groups how to get the information they need for their own reporting. Our measurement team is expected to align closely with other measurement groups within the company, like our much larger marketing insights organization, for instance. By working closely with the individual social media strategists who are actually doing social media on behalf of the business units, our measurement team can identify appropriate measures to help highlight both successes and failures of our efforts. Ultimately, we want insights that can help improve our approach.

Determining the right metric depends in large part on what the objective or campaign is that a particular group is pursuing. For example, if the key objective is engagement with customers, the team will identify the appropriate engagement metrics that can show how our teams are doing relative to our past efforts and perhaps relative to competitors. Is our content strong enough to elicit high engagement levels, or does it need to be improved?

One set of metrics that we've increasingly seen interest in is the impact social media has on sales and leads and how effective it is at driving traffic back to our website. Our CoE measurement team provides the tools and know-how for social media teams that support business units to analyze this data. Each week, month, and quarter we help them generate reports that show how much social media is driving new subscriptions or leads, both directly (measured through last click attribution) and indirectly (measured by social media as part of the purchase path that helped to assist in the sale).

Among the more intriguing findings we've seen during the past year at Adobe is that we are twice as likely to see a prospect convert to a sale if some interaction through social media appears in the purchase path—or the life of the website cookie. The corollary, of course, then is that customers who do not have some touch point with social media are one-half as likely to convert than if they did.

Our measurement team has worked closely with the experts at Altimeter to try and structure our measurement and insights efforts in alignment with Altimeter's Social Data Maturity Model.

Innovation

We have a specific pillar of our CoE focused on innovation to ensure we are continually looking for strategies to disrupt traditional business processes in positive ways. Doing this right involves having an established framework for systematically identifying needs within the business that social can perhaps address.

This is tricky—particularly when you consider part of our mission within Innovation is to identify new technologies that can help us. When we're not disciplined, we find ourselves evaluating new technologies from vendors simply because of the "cool" factor and not because there is some specific business need we are trying to address. That approach can be akin to the tail wagging the dog. And it has forced us to focus first on the business and the challenges we face.

Part of the focus in the Innovation pillar is on maintaining close working ties with the most relevant social networking vendors. Our partners at Twitter, Facebook, LinkedIn, and Google, among others, are extensions of this Innovation pillar helping us to look for new opportunities. The result is that we are on the shortlist of corporations that these social networks contact to pilot new functionality.

Together, these four foundational elements of governance, enablement, measurement, and innovation comprise what I believe to be a great blueprint for organizing a social business operation. They are, in many ways, a cornerstone for reinventing a social-by-design business.

Social-by-Design Case Study: The American Red Cross

Although we're making great strides in our own efforts, I think it's helpful to see how another organization has not just reinvented its own approach to social, but also frankly revolutionized an industry by thinking in a social-by-design manner.

At the end of 2011, while working at Dell, we began to talk with The American Red Cross about building the organization a social media command center. We had a command center at Dell, which helped us listen to conversations about our brand and industry online. The

American Red Cross envisioned much more than a mere brand-monitoring center. It wanted to integrate social monitoring into its Disaster Operations Center and its approach to helping people impacted by disasters.

Typically, when disaster strikes, the American Red Cross quickly staffs its Disaster Operation Center in Washington DC. The facility is amazing and the response team is equipped to handle a high-level, coordinated response. However, it envisioned a way to enhance disaster response with a *Digital* Operations Center—a social media command center built within its primary disaster operations center. The American Red Cross believed this would allow it to shorten its response to people who were in need during and shortly after disasters.

The center would give it the capability to track, in real time, what people on the ground were saying about the disaster and how they were impacted. During a tornado, hurricane, or other natural disaster, it's not uncommon for power loss to be widespread. With no electricity or landline telephone service, it can be difficult to disseminate information. Yet despite destruction, the one thing that often works is a cell phone, and people turn to Twitter or Facebook to reach out for help.

The American Red Cross recognized that this information was critical in times of crisis and that by organizing the data, it could uncover trends allowing it to more effectively determine where it needed to provide aid and comfort. As a relief organization, the American Red Cross made social media an active part of business operations and changed the disaster response industry in the process. In March 2012, we jointly announced the launch of its completed Digital Operations Center that it has used during disaster situations since.

For organizations worldwide, social is much more than a marketing tool. The experience with the American Red Cross taught me that social technologies could be integrated into business to transform it, and that a social-by-design business is a positive development on a much larger scale.

Conclusion

The concept of a social-by-design business isn't radical or avant-garde but a real opportunity for business to make a real contribution. It's not about exploring social marketing by running Facebook and Twitter accounts to push information. Rather, it is a conscious decision made by business to harness the power of real-time social technologies to enhance the business. Companies that have been successful at combining the "doing" of social with strong internal operations that can create a parallel path for social infrastructure and social campaigns in a way that brings success. They use social networks as tactical channels as they build social plans and strategy to match business goals.

What is the next frontier for social? Perhaps as businesses start to experiment with combining social capabilities with customer relationship management strategies, social media will evolve even more. As doors open for brands to get closer to their customers, recognizing and understanding the motivations behind their decisions can lead only to improved products, better service, and enhanced relationships.

At Adobe, our approach to social business operations is based on the four core pillars of our Center of Excellence. It's a methodology that works well for us as we attempt to harness the power of social, weave it into the fabric of our business, and empower our people to use it effectively.

3

Don't Be Creepy: The Right Way to Use Social to Listen to Your Customers and Engage Your Organization

Sara Del Grande, Senior Manager, Customer Interaction
Network, Cisco

"What do we know about social media? Can social media tell us about customer sentiment toward Services? Could we replace customer satisfaction (surveys) with customer sentiment in social media as a KPI?"

We were in the midst of our annual customer satisfaction target setting process when the SVP of Technical Services issued this challenge. Three-plus years, a few bumps, and numerous iterations and expansions later, we have a robust Social Sentiment program in place that drives insight and action for the Cisco Services organization. We have yet to retire customer satisfaction as a Key Performance Indicator (KPI), but more on that later.

When we first embarked on this journey, I had a team of experts in survey design, deployment, and analysis, but knew little to nothing about social media. I had no idea what a hashtag was or did, and I didn't even have a Twitter account (although that was quickly remedied). So we started by reaching out to the team that was already engaged in listening to customers in social media: marketing. It turns out our Services Marketing team had recently acquired software for monitoring social media buzz around Cisco. Marketing was interested in what customers were saying about the Services *brand* while we wanted to hear what was being said about Services *experiences*. We piggy-backed on Marketing's instance and started to build the profiles that would identify the conversations we wanted to monitor. This led to our first lesson.

Lesson 1: Do your homework. Pick the right tool for the job.

We learned this lesson the hard way. As we struggled to get past the echo chamber created by the content that Cisco was posting in social media, we discovered some key limitations in the tool we were using. We needed to exclude Cisco's voice to focus on the voice of the customer. We also needed to exclude job postings and other irrelevant content that consistently came from the same sources. We needed a better way to select and filter the channels and sources where we were listening. Our social listening software couldn't support these needs, and the engagement model with the software provider prevented what little self-administration was available. Although that model worked for clients who didn't want to "look under the hood" and fully own the quality of content search results, it didn't work for us. We needed a different tool.

Corporate marketing was also listening to customers. It was using the market-leading social media measurement tool. We made a decision to scrap our current work, cut our losses, and switch platforms. The difference was immediate. In short order, we had created the profiles to both find the right content and exclude the wrong content. But these initial experiences were far from a waste of time. As we slogged through thousands of comments and conversations daily, we learned another valuable lesson.

Lesson 2: Relevant conversations happen everywhere. Cast a wide net.

Initial skeptics of our program were sure that Enterprise customers were not talking about their support experiences online—social media was a place for consumers to gripe and Millennials to connect. Surprisingly, not only did we find relevant conversations around Cisco Services, but we also sometimes found them in unexpected places. Certainly we had a wealth of customer sentiment to mine from our Cisco-sponsored Twitter accounts, online communities, and Facebook pages, but we also found content on competitor pages, support forums, and blogs. We even discovered a conversation on the value of Cisco support contracts buried in a car collectors' forum.

We started our foray into social media hoping to find answers to specific questions. When we could not find these answers, we realized a fundamental disconnect between what we thought was important and what our customers were discussing.

Lesson 3: Listen for what is said; it's often not what you thought you would hear.

One amusing example of this disconnect happened when we tried to find content in social media related to language and accents. A few recent survey comments had made reference to dissatisfaction with communication and alluded to issues with the accents of engineers. We embarked on an effort to see whether we could corroborate via social media that accent was the communication issue. We found nothing on the topic of accents or communication. Instead, we found a wellspring of sentiment complaining about a recent Cisco ad campaign featuring Ellen Page—pretty big disconnect!

The unsolicited nature of social media is both a blessing and a curse in the realm of customer listening. Because you are not driving the conversation as you do with a survey, customers are free to take the conversation in the direction that is most meaningful and impactful to them. What you want to listen for might not be what people are speaking about.

Finding what you want to hear is not within your control. This means that social provides excellent opportunities for identifying previously unknown or emerging customer pain points, but it can also lead to some embarrassing experiences (and a fear of real-time demos!) before you learn how to filter certain words, phrases, and content.

Early in our program development, one of the members of my Social Sentiment team ran into my office. "I have a serious problem! I've been tuning our Social Sentiment results and accidentally clicked on a porn link. Am I going to get fired for accessing porn at work?"

The type and amount of finesse required in social filtering and tuning is not dissimilar to text analytics. For brands with well-defined products, keywords might not be as much of a hurdle versus our need to define all the various ways customers could be discussing their software licensing or support entitlement experiences. It's important to keep in mind the groundwork required is extensive but well worth the effort, and no tool works out-of-the-box for all companies. Now before you start to worry, I did not fire that team member.

With the right tooling and tuning in place, we thought again about how we might replace customer satisfaction with customer sentiment.

At this point, it is important to note that Cisco has a strong customer satisfaction culture supported by an annual customer survey that influences the bonus calculation for all Cisco employees. If customer sentiment were to replace customer satisfaction as a KPI for Cisco, it would need to be something that we could accurately and consistently measure and trend over time to identify issues and monitor improvements. We developed a customer sentiment score modeled after a political approval rating. Month-to-month we tallied the number of positive, negative, and neutral comments posted in social media regarding Cisco Services. Our Customer Sentiment Tonality Score added all positive and negative comments and divided by the number of positive comments:

Tonality = (Positive + Negative) / Positive)

It took some time for my team of survey experts to fully grasp the fundamental ways in which social media was different from surveys. Applying survey logic to the world of social media is a recipe for failure. This is true not just in how you mine the source, but also in how you measure and report the output.

Because you are not controlling the sample as you would with a survey, wide shifts in your population size and compilation make it nearly impossible to understand the statistical relevance of changes. Did the Net Positive Tonality Score change this month in response to negative reception of a newly released self-service tool, or does the change merely reflect the opinion of a differently composed sample? Does the score reflect the opinions of your core customers, or is it primarily composed of comments from Internet trolls?

To replace customer satisfaction with customer sentiment, we would need to set a target and identify actions that would influence and drive the score. The uncontrolled nature of the customer sentiment sample makes this unrealistic. Rather than focus on what we couldn't learn from our Customer Sentiment Tonality Score, we shifted to focus on how we could leverage this data. With a few months of data in hand, we could see a relatively stable trend. When our sentiment score rose or dropped significantly from the normal trend, we could review the positive and negative comments for that time period to identify the probable cause of the change in sentiment. Feeding this insight back into the organization, we could learn from our mistakes, thereby influencing an improved customer experience.

In one example, there was a question of why we were seeing a drop in conversations for software licensing. Were customers not discussing this as much because they were happier with the experience due to recent improvements, or was it something else? Some research into the positive comments overlaid with themes provided an interesting answer. When we shared improvements and plans for the future with our customers, positive discussions spiked in response but quickly fell off while negative comments continued (see Figure 3.1). Without a rise in positive comments, the score was misleading. The recommendation back was "More communication, more often."

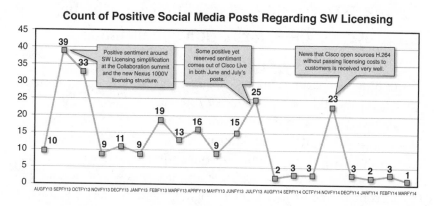

Figure 3.1 Analysis of social media trends regarding software-licensing comments

Lesson 4: Don't just look at yourself; unlike competitors' customer survey data, customer sentiment is public domain.

We found that we could also calculate a Customer Sentiment Tonality Score for many of our key competitors by monitoring and measuring customer conversations on their competitor support experiences. Finding a new source of competitive comparison was a welcome surprise.

While monitoring social media sentiment around our service offerings versus our competitors, we encountered many forum threads where customers were comparing vendors and asking the community's advice before purchasing. Often, the community would recommend one vendor over another for various reasons, but one close competitor was repeatedly touted for its warranty program as being more than enough (versus purchasing support from Cisco), effectively comparing apples to oranges. In recent months, however, that same competitor has changed some key resources from being free (under warranty) to requiring a contract. We have observed the sentiment tide turning and what appeared to be an advantage, effectively lost. Sharing this insight with our stakeholders gave them a view into the market landscape from the customer's perspective—a perspective they had previously never had.

Lesson 5: Don't hide your light under a bushel. More eyes on the information equals more opportunity for action.

In addition to reporting our new customer sentiment score, we started a practice of monthly Social Sentiment readouts. In this monthly forum, we shared the Tonality Score trend, the competitive comparisons, as well as a focus on the common themes. We invited a broad audience of representatives from various functions within Cisco Services to our readouts and saw this audience grow organically as people found value in the content and invited their colleagues to join the next call. Teams discovered customer feedback related to the processes they supported and engaged us in efforts to dig deeper into specific topics. Special analysis and reports were born.

One example of how customer feedback in social media provided valuable insight to stakeholders came through our partnership with the Learning@Cisco department and led to revenue protection for Cisco Services. The Learning organization had been relying on word of mouth and other tips to help identify websites where Cisco certification exam content was being compromised. Adding to the challenge, cheating websites continually moved around to avoid detection and legal action from Cisco. By leveraging our Social Sentiment profiles, we have created a mostly automated and sustainable approach to identify these sites and protect the integrity of Cisco certifications.

Monitoring and reporting Social Sentiment was contributing to a library of success stories where listening to the customer was driving improvements to customer experiences with Cisco. We couldn't help but wonder, how would customers respond if they knew how much we valued and leveraged their input? We saw an opportunity to close the customer feedback loop by sharing these successes directly with our customers. The "We're Listening" blog was born.

In the "We're Listening" blog series (http://blogs.cisco.com/tag/we-are-listening/), we invite executives across Cisco as guest bloggers to summarize what they have heard from customers and what improvements they are implementing in response. Initially, we worried that customers might be unsatisfied with the improvements creating the potential for a negative feeding frenzy (where one comment spurs more in response), yet we decided to honor the spontaneous nature of social media interaction by not inserting a moderator to govern the comment process. Our decision was put to the test when one confrontational blogger responded to a post by sharing his opinion along with the personal cell phone number of our sponsoring executive. But while we waited for the cell phone to ring, we instead saw customers ignore the bait and instead thank us for our honesty and transparency. To date, the "We're Listening" blog series has 19 posts and more than 4,800 visits as well as being shared via Twitter and Facebook hundreds of times.

While we were getting great traction through our monthly readouts and reports, we knew there were many more people who could benefit from exposure to the customer conversations in social media. As part of our organizational vision, we wanted to integrate the voice of the customer

(VOC) into Services. By leveraging Cisco technology, we found a way to make this VOC accessible, interactive, and top of mind.

Introducing the Cisco Digital Signage Kiosk

If you've attended a CiscoLive event, you've probably seen Cisco Digital Signage or a kiosk in action (see Figure 3.2). The kiosk is a device standing a little more than 6 feet tall and 3 feet wide that includes two touch-interactive screens where you can present any content available on a web page. Our Cisco Services Customer Barometer kiosk presents two dashboards of customer feedback. On the first, we have displayed a heat map of the world that pops up customer tweets related to Cisco Services as they happen in real time while color-coding the countries on the map to indicate where most conversations are happening. Using the touch-interactive features of the display, you can click countries to see a scrolling stream of recent customer comments. On the second screen, a dashboard displays the numeric survey scores combined with the results of text analytics of the customer comments from one of our customer satisfaction surveys.

Figure 3.2   Introducing the Cisco Services Customer Barometer

By placing the kiosk outside the elevator doors in the building where a majority of our Cisco Services employees work, we have put the voice of the customer front and center for every employee every day in the office. In this way, we are inspiring action to address customer feedback by making that feedback easily accessible and by providing a daily reminder that everything we do should be in service to our customers. In the next year, we will be expanding to provide wall-mounted digital signage displays in other locations on the Cisco campus. Improvements to visual representation of the data including new dashboards and more interactive features are also underway.

Behind the scenes, we continued to monitor social media and evolve the scope of our listening. The software that we leverage does an outstanding job of aggregating and searching content in real time. But the ever-changing nature of social media requires that we invest time in regular tuning of our profiles and search criteria. As we spent time reading and reviewing the available content in social media, a new lesson presented itself.

Lesson 6: Be open to redefining success around new value opportunities.

In the midst of reviewing social media, the Cisco Social Sentiment team observed a growing volume of complaints that surrounded network outages. This was not a scenario of a customer asking for help in social media. This was crowd-sourced network monitoring.

Our initial pitch to leverage social media as a proactive monitoring tool, however, was met with mixed reviews. The most common concern was something we called "the creepy factor." Wouldn't customers find it creepy if we reached out to them in the event of an outage that we discovered online? Wouldn't that feel like Big Brother? Wouldn't they just call us if they were experiencing a problem anyway? Undaunted, we proceeded into the void to create a profile tuned to identify outages without narrowing our focus to specific customers or even Cisco products. Maybe a specific example was necessary to illustrate the benefits of outage monitoring.

The Ah-ha Moment: A large airline company was struggling with reservation system issues following a merger. Our Social Sentiment team noted airline customer complaints on Twitter about flight delays and cancelations, being unable to access the reservation system, and so on, and notified a Cisco VP who was scheduled to visit the airline's executives later that day, unrelated. Equipped with foreknowledge that the company was having issues that day, the Cisco executive empathized and offered Cisco assistance in recovery even when our products were not involved. The account team and executive offered support and engaged the Cisco Services organization quickly and proactively to assist the airline in troubleshooting the outage, restoring the computer system, and enabling flights to resume.

We had the case study to demonstrate how monitoring social media for customer outages could enable proactive support. And interestingly, no one described our assistance in this event as creepy. We moved forward quickly to develop a pilot for using social monitoring to connect our services and sales organizations to better enable customer success.

Lesson 7: Don't fear version 0. Iterate, iterate, iterate.

I recently saw a tweet that resonated with our beliefs, "Perfection is the death of invention." When designing our Social Monitoring program, we didn't wait to have our strategy and process perfectly defined. We launched fast and iterated often. Our initial foray leveraged our existing Social Sentiment team for monitoring, but we knew this would never scale. We documented guidelines to help identify which events were of interest (for example, we didn't need to engage if the issue was a power outage), built a special profile in our Social Media management tool, and engaged outsourced resources to begin monitoring. When potential situations were identified, we escalated to employee resources to notify the appropriate parties within Cisco to take action. The following is another example of social outage monitoring in action.

A major mobile phone provider experienced a service outage for legacy e-mail and messaging services within several provinces. Social media mentions began trending, and our teams were alerted. Cisco Services resources identified a possible related service request, and notified support teams of the customer business impact and external coverage, who in turn rallied escalation engineers and engaged existing escalation processes to focus on recovery.

With each event, we found ways to improve the program. We refined the process to pinpoint the resources that were in the best position to assist the customers experiencing an outage. We added executive notifications to provide visibility across the organization. And eventually, we grew the program to enable 24x7 monitoring and notifications.

It's a Friday morning, and telecommuters across many U.S. cities light up Twitter with complaints of an outage of their phone/Internet/cable service being down. A major telecommunications service provider's services are affected by a suspected denial of service (DOS) attack, and because it's not a Cisco product at the root, the customer has not raised a case with Cisco. A notification is raised, and Cisco support resources contact the account team who reach out to the customer and encourage them to leverage their Cisco High Touch Services to engage, help isolate the issue, and speed restoration, even though the root cause is not Cisco-related.

In the past 20 months since the program's inception, we have identified more than 200 customer outage situations with an opportunity for Cisco to proactively contact the customer to offer assistance thereby strengthening customer relationships and mitigating possible Cisco exposure.

Now that we have invested in the resources that we have in place for social outage monitoring 24x7, we are finding more ways to leverage that investment by monitoring for specific customers, around events (for example, World Cup and the launch of Healthcare.gov) and for disasters. Not directly related to Cisco Services, we found that social media was a great source of information for natural disasters. Cisco already had a team in place as part of its philanthropic focus that provided assistance in restoring core services for disasters (think restoration of communication services to support EMS). Social monitoring now supplements the many sources they use to identify events where Cisco will proactively offer assistance.

Because start-up costs are relatively low, it's easy to iterate quickly. Even the leading social media monitoring software suite has a low-cost step-in tier to get started. With the recent industry move toward software-as-a-service (SaaS) using cloud storage, no IT resources or implementation is required, making social media monitoring accessible to even the smallest of companies.

Has Customer Sentiment Replaced Customer Satisfaction?

Going back to that original SVP challenge: Did we replace customer satisfaction with customer sentiment? No, they complement each other. We continue to leverage surveys with statistically valid sampling to provide trends and highlight improvement over time. Surveys continue to help us identify the main themes, but by leveraging social media, we can supplement that "big story" with the "small story."

Social media can play a powerful role when combined with listening data from different sources. We compare themes from surveys, social, and even anecdotal information from our customer-facing teams, allowing us to triangulate on the most important customer issues. The key benefit that social content brings in this scenario is the unfiltered voice. Surveys and personal interaction can each introduce an element of bias as customers conform to the structure of the conversation or strive to be polite. Customer sentiment and tone is at its truest when provided freely in social media.

Our program costs include a project team (we started with one program manager and one business analyst and eventually expanded to include a second business analyst), software licensing, and outsourced resources to support our monitoring programs.

In return, we reap the following business and customer benefits:

- Increased customer satisfaction and loyalty by driving action to address customer pain points

- Fifty percent faster case resolution when we have identified and corrected an outage-related case set to the wrong priority

- Revenue protection in the millions by proactively engaging in outage events to avoid critical (potentially revenue impacting) situations

We use the power of the emotion and unsolicited voice in social media to mobilize action, and you can do this too if you keep these lessons in mind:

Lesson 1: Do your homework. Pick the right tool for the job.

Lesson 2: Relevant conversations happen everywhere. Cast a wide net.

Lesson 3: Listen for what is said; it's often not what you thought you would hear.

Lesson 4: Don't just look at yourself; unlike competitors' customer survey data, customer sentiment is public domain.

Lesson 5: Don't hide your light under a bushel. More eyes on the information equals more opportunity for action.

Lesson 6: Be open to redefining success around new value opportunities.

Lesson 7: Don't fear version 0. Iterate, iterate, iterate.

Oh, and one last thought:

Lesson 8: Trust your instincts. Offering help is never creepy.

4

Trailblazing a Successful Path to Enterprise Social Business Transformation at Unisys

Gloria Burke, Chief Knowledge Officer and Global Portfolio Leader, Unisys

In June 2010, Unisys launched its ambitious enterprise social business transformation initiative to enhance connection and collaboration among its 23,000+ global employees, clients, and business partners and to increase the company's market agility.

Just 18 months later, the company had achieved an adoption rate of 91 percent of its targeted 16,000 employee audience, whereas 78 percent of all global employees were using the enterprise social network; and 100 percent of senior leadership had active company social network profiles and were leveraging blogs and newsfeeds to better engage with employees. Today, the company continues to expand its use of social business tools by integrating them into key business processes internally, as well as extending social capabilities within its extranet environment.

Unisys is now bringing its experience and cutting-edge enterprise social business transformation solution to clients around the world to help them improve operational efficiency, increase employee effectiveness, drive innovation, and gain competitive advantage.

Why Unisys?

I already had what I considered to be the ideal job when Unisys came calling in 2009. As the global knowledge and collaboration manager for a prominent international management consultancy, I had the privilege of bringing the emerging, game-changing miracle of social collaboration to internal colleagues as well as Fortune 500 companies externally.

Much of my consulting work had consisted of persuading senior management teams that an enterprise social business platform was essential to their companies' future competitiveness. Unless management clearly understood that, our efforts to harness the maximum value from social technologies across the company would not take root; senior leadership alignment and stakeholder engagement were key to a successful implementation. But five years ago, this was not an article of faith in the C suite, and many top executives were inclined to be skeptical.

So when Unisys approached me with the opportunity to develop its enterprise social business transformation strategy and governance model, I was surprised and gratified to realize that the impetus was coming from the top—from Unisys CEO Ed Coleman. And he wasn't looking to simply check a box or test the concept or create a perfunctory social business practice for the bragging rights. He was committed to transforming the company's way of doing business. He had a vision of how social business would forever change how we connect, collaborate, and innovate.

Joining Unisys also provided the opportunity to work with a highly respected team of senior IT professionals—Chief Information Officer Suresh Mathews, Chief Technology Officer Fred Dillman, IT Chief Technology Officer Chris Odom, and VP of IT Applications Upinder Phanda. They, too, were visionaries and viewed social technologies as a disruptive trend—one that they wanted to harness and fully exploit in order to keep Unisys on the cutting edge in delivering new and differentiating technology capabilities to its clients. They had assembled a talented team of IT, knowledge, and collaboration specialists jointly led by IT director John Knab and CTO directors Lee Beyer and Rajiv Prasad, who had built a strong foundational infrastructure to support a social business platform. In addition, Lee Beyer and knowledge and collaboration specialist Susan McCabe had secured a patent for their successful approach to knowledge management processes and practices, a critical cornerstone of the platform. Together, we would form the core Enterprise Social Business Transformation leadership team that ultimately transformed the future of work at Unisys.

No further coaxing needed. I was on board.

The Mission: On the Enterprise Social Business Train, We Should Be the Engine

Describing the mission ahead, Ed shared that he viewed the disruption of social technologies as a "train fast leaving the station." Our mission as a cutting-edge technology company was not to simply have a seat on that train, but to be in the front car, blazing the trail.

In other words, he wasn't interested in just leveraging basic elements of a social business platform such as social networks, newsfeeds, and blogs. He wanted to fully exploit the use of social technologies and embed it into our key business processes and make it an intrinsic and integral part of our culture to maximize its value across the business enterprise. He wanted us to build a cutting-edge enterprise social business platform that from the moment it was up and running would streamline operational effectiveness, increase connection and collaboration, drive innovation, and define us as a thought leader in this new, exciting, and disruptive technology trend.

Beyond that, Ed wanted us to leverage our expertise in delivering these new, game-changing capabilities to our clients, helping them to leapfrog their own social business learning curve so that they could begin reaping its rewards in a more expedient and cost-effective manner,

It was breathtakingly ambitious for a CEO in 2009 to have such a clear vision of what social business should do for the enterprise. Over the next months and to this day, Ed's image of the fast-moving social business "train," proceeding on its firmly laid rails, waiting for no one and brooking no obstacles, serves as a powerful vision to me, as well as for all Unisys employees.

All Aboard

Before embarking on our journey, we conducted a rapid but thorough assessment of the company's social business "readiness." First came interviews with the entire senior leadership team to determine their views on how social technologies could add value for the company. Simultaneously we performed an external benchmarking to understand market trends, available technology, and best practices. Then we quickly dove into an area that we knew would make or break our efforts: engaging cross-organization "stakeholders" to help us identify common issues and pain points so that we could address and remove any potential barriers to change. It is my firm belief that people support what they help to build and, once engaged, have an ongoing stake in its success. Together, we would form the strategy and implementation roadmap that would forever change the future of work at Unisys.

On Our Challenges

Let's be honest. It's hard becoming your own client—to peel back all the layers of the onion to reveal the core, openly and frankly diagnose your challenges, and then take the necessary steps to bridge them. But, that's what we did. What did our initial assessment unveil? We found our own version of what I think most large companies would find: a lot of value in knowledge both in explicit and implicit forms, uncaptured and dissipating—but representing huge potential if we could harness and master it. They included the following areas.

Difficulty Identifying and Connecting with Subject Matter Experts

One of the top challenges we encountered was the difficulty employees were having in the ability to identify and connect with subject matter experts at the time of need. We knew we *had* experts, in fact many. But if you were a salesperson trying to close a deal in Portugal, and your prospect had one final question about cloud computing and that wasn't your area of expertise, it might take you literally days to get the right answer. The answer would be impressive when you got it, but that's not good in enough in today's 24/7 world. Talent that you can't tap when you need it is talent (and expense) squandered. A delayed response does not meet the level of customer service that clients now demand.

Inefficiencies in New Hire Onboarding and New Role Assimilation

We also saw that shortcoming of connecting employees with subject matter experts magnified in our new hire onboarding. We were attracting some great new talent, brilliant in their fields with a lot to offer the whole company. But without an easy way to introduce them and give people access to them, it sometimes felt like we were squandering what we were going to such pains to accumulate. It was frustrating for the new talent, too, who wanted a more seamless way to build a company presence, connect with colleagues, and to contribute as soon as they got here. We encountered similar issues when an employee was transitioning roles within the company.

Lack of a Common Collaborative Platform

When you're a company filled with ambitious technologists, engineers, and thought leaders—people for whom collaboration is second nature—and you don't offer them a way to easily connect and collaborate, they will find a way to do so outside the company. In fact, we found just that. Approximately 1,800 employees had created and joined a Unisys community hosted by a third-party vendor outside the company's firewall. That obviously created some risk for the company and certainly didn't do anything to socialize our intellectual property internally.

Knowledge Silos

We were becoming fiefdoms of expertise; knowledge tended to be siloed to the group where it was born. A client in one vertical market might never get the advantage of great work we had done for a client in another vertical. We might be world class in one country but just fledgling in another. Great work done in one business unit would have to be re-created from scratch in another unit. Reinventing the wheel was causing a big loss of agility, creativity, and valuable resources. The unevenness wasn't good for morale, client service, or revenue growth.

In a noncollaborative environment, you know what happens: "Knowledge is power," so it gets hoarded. Knowledgeable people keep it close to the vest instead of sharing it transparently because that is what gets rewarded. That mindset was precisely the opposite of what we needed from our best people.

Disconnect Between Ideation and Innovation

Innovation was also impacted. Our employees generate great ideas, but they were shared in an insular manner. The means to transparently share or crowd source thoughts and ideas across organizations and geographies did not exist. The channel was missing to bring these ideas onto the innovation track. The innovation team had to proactively "scout" ideas rather than allowing ideas to bubble up inside an innovation incubator.

Disparate Levels of Social Media Savvy

Finally, we discovered, to no surprise, that due to our workforce spanning multiple generations and varying levels of social savvy, we would have to do some level-setting about the value of social technologies and their practical use in business. At first that might look like a daunting challenge, but from years of experience in leading change initiatives, I've found that people adapt, usually with alacrity, when *and only when,* it serves their needs or interests. The least tech-savvy people climb the learning curve fast when you help make the value apparent. The most tech-savvy people will assiduously ignore the sexiest applications if they don't see the purpose.

Our challenges were not unique to a large, global company, but we knew them to be persistent, and resistant to new directives, cajoling, or grass roots evangelism. We knew we needed to offer a better and intrinsic way of working if we hoped to change the culture of the company. The change would have to be people-centric and focused on delivering tangible value to each employee in his particular role. We had to face the hard fact that people inherently do not embrace change unless you address one fundamental question upfront, "What's in it for me?" We knew that embracing this new enterprise social business model would deliver value to the company. However, the key to unlocking that value was firmly embedded in our company culture and people.

On Vision and Strategy

We set out to develop a vision and strategy that would enable us to fully exploit social technologies across the enterprise. We knew that to maximize value, we would need to create a strategy and approach that were holistic in nature. If our strategy had been myopic, let's say to "Deploy a collaborative platform within the intranet environment" and we did not think about how to scale it out to our extranet environment to facilitate better collaboration among clients, business partners, vendors, and others, then meeting our overall objective to improve connection and collaboration would have fallen short. I wouldn't be writing this chapter.

Creating this type of vision and strategy meant that we needed to take a step back and understand the unique needs and requirements of all parts of the business before evaluating social technology solutions. We intentionally put strategy ahead of technology. This was key to our success.

We enabled a cross-organization Stakeholder Council and engaged it in a workshop to identify and prioritize business issues and map specific requirements. Armed with this critical information, we then evaluated and selected the right social technology solutions to meet our specific needs and build a compelling business case for change.

It can't be said too often: You have to be explicit at the start about what you hope to accomplish. Your strategy should begin with an end-state vision that can be clearly articulated to leadership, stakeholders, and employees. You can't build a roadmap if you don't know where you are going. The vision should illustrate the ways in which social business will change the way your company does business and the value it will provide. Most importantly, you must socialize the vision and values in a way that will resonate with each stakeholder audience, whether it be leadership, organization stakeholders, or role-based employee groups. At the end of the day, everyone wants to know "What's in this for me?"

With a clearly defined vision, specific objectives and goals and a business case for change in hand, we spent six months developing a comprehensive transformation strategy and approach. We broke our strategy down into five key focus areas: technology, culture/people, process, governance, and economics (value/ROI):

- **Technology**: The technology, systems, processes, and protocols that provide the foundational and social business platforms for enabling the sharing of knowledge and information, including security and mobility access and privacy issues.

- **Culture/People**: The company's philosophy, approach, and behavioral patterns around knowledge sharing and collaboration and its capability to engrain these into its culture and to adapt as business circumstances change and practical business use of social technologies evolve.

- **Process**: The frameworks, approaches, methodologies, processes, and practices for leveraging and integrating social technologies into business workflows.

- **Governance**: The model for corporate oversight and leadership that governs the enterprise social business environment and the policies, guidelines, standards and practices that guide and manage its proper use. This model defines the rules of engagement and the role of players internal and external to the organization. It ensures compliance, upholds the integrity of the social business environment, and mitigates the company's risk.

- **Economics (value/ROI)**: The ability to obtain adequate funding and people resources to implement the knowledge sharing and collaboration and culture change initiatives, manage budget and external impacts that influence how resources are allocated and managed, and leverage metrics and measurements to track progress and validate value and ROI to the company.

Strategy should not be confused with tactical problem solving. Strategy requires that you understand the effects and impact of a projected solution across the enterprise. What works in one organization might not be practical for another. What can be easily implemented in one geographic area might have technical issues in another. Without an end-to-end view of where and how social technologies should be deployed across the enterprise, there are two outcomes. You waste time and resources deploying tactical point solutions that will not scale. And you fail to reach critical adoption mass to deliver the desired value.

Our end-to-end approach focused on addressing the needs of our entire business across eight key focus areas: Connection and Communications, Social Collaboration, Knowledge Management, Culture and Employee Engagement, Technology Infrastructure and Application Modernization, Ideation/Innovation, Business Process Integration, and Social Data Analytics.

We divided our transformational journey into five key phases:

- Setting the Foundation
- Building the Collaborative Ecosystem

- Institutionalizing Social Behaviors

- Integrating Social Technologies with Business Processes

- Optimizing Effectiveness and Value

On Choosing the Right Technology Components

Like any other cultural change supported by a technology platform, there's the perennial temptation to pick the popular social engine platform and then retrofit it to the various business requirements within the enterprise as it is implemented. When I hear of a company following that sequence, I foresee a doomed transformation along with a huge amount of employee frustration resulting in low adoption, unnecessary cost, and value left on the table.

When architecting the enterprise social business platform and selecting vendors, there is no one "best" technology platform or solution. The right choice for your company depends entirely on your company's business needs and the strategy you have carefully rationalized and chosen. No matter how many technology analysts recommend a particular platform or vendor solution, nor even whether that same platform or solution is working great for your competitor, evaluating vendors and choosing your technology platform are subordinate to your unique strategy and business needs.

But here's the good news about sorting through the plethora of technology options: When you have your strategy nailed down, the technology almost chooses itself. Strategy makes clear which platforms will or won't work.

When I arrived at Unisys, the company was in the process of migrating its SharePoint-based intranet platform from SP2007 to SP2010 and was planning to implement Enterprise Search. This provided a great foundation on which to build a social business ecosystem and facilitated the selection of a social engine that could be integrated without a high level of customization.

This was an important factor in our decision to select Sitrion (formerly NewsGator) because it was specifically engineered for integration with a SharePoint environment and required little customization. Learning from past migration efforts, we wanted to limit customized coding and ad hoc designs within our new SharePoint 2010 environment. Leveraging Sitrion out-of-the-box, in addition to its enhanced capabilities within employee profiles and communities, made it all the more appealing.

On Knowledge Management

Sharing knowledge in a socially enabled environment brings a new dimension to foundational knowledge management. How you organize, classify, and tag this medium of knowledge and information is every bit as important as the metadata and taxonomy standards that you apply for explicit content. The greatest value from knowledge comes from its capture, repurpose, and reuse. The ability to transfer critical knowledge from exiting employees, either from voluntary reduction or retirement, is a now a pressing issue for most businesses, especially those with narrowing labor pools such as engineering and manufacturing. The capture and repurposing of knowledge also helps to eliminate redundant work, increasing operational efficiency and market agility.

At Unisys, to ready our knowledge base for the influx of this new content, we took time to review our knowledge management structure, content, practices, and governance model. We launched a content clean-up exercise in concert with our SharePoint migration. All organizations and site owners were required to review and tag all knowledge content before they could migrate to the new SP2010 platform. And there were no exceptions. I'll admit that our hard-liner stance probably resulted in our team photos being used as dartboard covers across the enterprise, but the result was worth it. We retired more than 57 percent of nonrelevant content from our environment and enabled a new archiving system and review process to prevent future knowledge and information landfills.

We also realized that you cannot rely on end users to classify and tag content as they are sharing it. Some are diligent in classifying and tagging explicit content when they are creating it or uploading it to a library but forget to use hashtags when sharing tacit knowledge in a blog or newsfeed post. To bridge the gap, we recommend leveraging an auto-classification and tagging tool.

Our content clean-up initiative coupled with good knowledge management policies, practices, and governance enabled us to streamline access to knowledge and information across the enterprise. Search effectiveness and end-user satisfaction were greatly improved.

On Transforming Our Culture

The success of any enterprise social business platform is dependent on people and their willingness to adopt new behaviors and engrain them in their everyday work. Social technologies are just enablers.

It bears repeating: If leveraging your social business tools becomes an extra thing that employees have to do—if it adds a layer to their work—it's pointless, and it will fail. You can't claim social business transformation success until its use becomes firmly embedded in the way your employees routinely do their jobs.

If employees are not blogging about exciting developments, using social tools to discover and connect with internal experts, and sharing and learning through daily emersion in community environments, then it's not actually working yet. If blogs are going unremarked and uncommented on, or if employees aren't leveraging the social network and newsfeed to transparently share and learn from one another, then you're only partway there. And if employees can't connect to your social network 24/7 from any device—well, you have an even longer way to go than you envisioned.

It has to be a seamless and intrinsic way of working before you can claim victory. Only through adoption and sustained use can a business fully tap the enterprise social "network effect" that drives so much value.

Employees should feel empowered to share what they know. This was stressed in a quote delivered by Unisys CEO Ed Coleman during an employee town hall meeting. He said, "The key to fueling the success of social collaboration at Unisys is for our employees to 'be curious' and 'feel empowered' to openly and transparently share." When social business is clicking, you see it in employee behaviors. They write blogs about their experiences; they share valuable insights and information through newsfeed posts; and they engage in communities to evolve their own expertise and contribute to the learning process for others. But these behaviors don't materialize without close attention, at every stage of your implementation, to four core culture change components.

Awareness and Communications

Building an awareness and communications campaign is essential to the success of your transformation. Your campaign should clearly communicate the change that is taking place, when it is taking place, how the change will affect the business, and more importantly, how the change will affect the end user, and detail what actions are required to embrace the change—again from the end user perspective.

Awareness and communications elements should take advantage of all the forms of communication available; people absorb information in different ways. Consider leveraging e-mail, intranet-featured news stories, visual media such as posters and e-cards, community announcements, newsfeed postings, videos, and employee testimonials. Customize communications based on organizations, geographies, and personas.

Education and Training

Social technologies are designed to be intuitive. Nonetheless, for employees who have not embraced social technologies in their personal lives, applying it within the business enterprise can be daunting. This learning curve requires a large training component, but nobody sits down and learns it all at once. And when people do sit down to learn, they need to learn at their level—tech-savvy, business-savvy, or no savvy at all—and focus on the element or elements that matter to them at that particular time.

At Unisys, our workforce demographic ranges from millennials to baby boomers, with disparate levels of social savvy, so we made our training "customizable" to an individual's needs at the time they were learning. We indexed our social business video-based training module and made it easy for users to simply point-and-click one small element of the video at a time, typically about two minutes long.

You want to update your profile photo? Here's how. Add a skill to your profile? Write a blog? Crowd source an answer to a question in the newsfeed? Find an expert? And so on. Again, our philosophy is when employees *want* to learn, they *will* learn. So make training a tap-on-demand resource.

Value Case Socialization by Role/Personas

The quickest way to drive adoption and use is to socialize its value in a way that resonates with each of your employees. At Unisys, our approach was to illustrate the value and practical use cases for our new social tools and capabilities on a role-by-role basis so that our employees could see tangible value in their everyday work.

We conducted value-case development workshops where a cross-section of global employees within a specific role worked together to identify key benefit areas in which social tools could add value in their particular role. Employees then used the tools as part of their daily work practices and captured value case scenarios that could be shared with role-based peers. This proved to be a successful approach, because we learned that nothing sells the use of a new technology more than a peer colleague sharing that it worked for him or her.

Remember, at the end of the day, you must be prepared to answer the burning question in the minds of end users adopters: "If I change my behavior to use this new technology, what's in it for me?" Modernizing your technology platform is the easy part of social business transformation. Transforming company culture by influencing employee behaviors requires you to delve deeply and with an open mind into their habits, motivations, and needs. People drive the success of any social business implementation, so keep them top of mind.

Incentives and Gamification

It's hard to find a social business case study without some discussion about leveraging gamification to incent desired employee behaviors or to foster learning. And Unisys is no exception, other than to note that we were selective in the timing of its deployment. We leveraged gamification at the onset of our implementation in the form of adoption leaderboards by organization, geography, and role. We also created a virtual "knowledge scavenger hunt" activity for regional and organizational "all hands" meetings that required employees to break out into small competitive groups and use social tools to find specific pieces of knowledge and information. This gamified approach facilitated learning and provided employees with hands-on experience in using the tools. We enabled star icons in search results to more easily identify subject matter experts but reserved the introduction of more elaborate curated and earned badging within employee profiles, such as patent holders, top sales executives, and thought leaders for when our adoption reached a tipping point.

The motivation that comes from incenting, recognizing, and validating positive behaviors provided the necessary fuel to energize our social business initiative at a critical point in the change management cycle, when initiatives are most likely to wane or fail.

On Creating Evangelists

No matter how long you do this, one thing never gets old. Those moments when newcomers to social business discover how social business tools and processes serve them—whether it's to make their jobs easier, or more efficient, or help them in their careers, or to serve their clients better—are both exciting and rewarding.

Nowhere was this more evident than in our Knowledge and Collaboration Stakeholders Council. Bringing together representatives of every business unit and services organization in the company—back to front—provided my team with the opportunity to facilitate members to those exciting discoveries. It would have been impossible for us to provide all the answers going in to our transformational journey, and even if we did, we felt that self-discovery was essential to learning. It has to be realized through hands-on application and use.

The importance of that "ah-ha" moment when someone "gets it" cannot be overstated. In that moment, the value of social technologies clicks and stakeholders become champions and evangelists. Defining the value could not just be received wisdom from us.

Whether the stakeholders arrived to our first meeting resistant, skeptical, passive, or outright curious, our job was to provide the leadership, ask the probing questions, and provide the necessary education about the tools. We might even propose potential scenarios that we saw working at other companies. But at the end of the day, it was up to the stakeholders themselves to discover how social business could be of value to them and to their respective organizations.

It is always a privilege to be present when, for example, a recruiter would realize, "Just imagine how much easier it will be for us to understand the job specs for a position in a new field! I can go straight to the expert to get my technical questions answered."

Or an engineer will realize, "This is really going to propel my career! Instead of just being the resident expert in this small unit, I can contribute across the company and be recognized in different portfolios and verticals and countries for the expertise I have in this area."

Or a marketing team will recognize how seamlessly, accurately, and speedily they can educate various internal groups on the go-to-market strategy and messages for a new product.

Or a salesperson gaining a new level of confidence about broaching key topics to clients because they know they can quickly tap into expert colleagues if the client expresses interest beyond the salesperson's own expertise.

When exciting moments like that happen, each stakeholder group builds up its store of use case scenarios for leveraging social business. They begin making social business an intrinsic part of the way they work, embedding social business into standard workflows. What you have just created are impassioned evangelists for your initiative. They become agents of change.

On Tipping Points

Throughout the process, we were plowing a lot of new ground, and moving rapidly, so it wasn't always clear that success was in the offing. But I remember at least two powerful moments in which we definitely saw a bright light at the other end.

One involved our sales organization and the capability to quickly find and tap subject matter experts. It was shortly after we had extended our social business platform to employees via tablets and smartphones. We received feedback from a salesperson about a recent meeting with a big client who unexpectedly asked him a question that the salesperson was unable to answer. Using his iPad, the salesman quickly did a search for Unisys solution subject matter experts, found our leading expert *and* saw that the expert was online. Using our Unified Communications solution, he quickly input his client's question, and on the spot, got the answer, and gave it to the client. "I looked like a rock star!" he exulted.

So there we had our sales evangelist. And do you know who salespeople trust most? Other salespeople. We immediately got a huge uptick in salespeople engaging with the social business tools. How do we put a value on it? I guess I could add up the value of a salesperson's time, taking a day or two to find that same answer, after a plaintive mass posting, "Does anybody know...?" But how do you calculate the value of a surprised and impressed client? How much is true marketplace agility worth?

The other major inflection point involved blog posts and the initial use and traction on our microblog newsfeed. We needed people to be proactive in blogging about matters in which they had insights. We needed them to be willing to put themselves "out there" and open and transparently share those insights. That's no small behavioral change to embed if that hasn't been part of your culture. For dialogs to happen, you have to be willing to invite disagreement, contradiction, and new insights from different perspectives.

But at first we encountered some timidity. Only established thought leaders were posting. So I posted a blog about some aspect of social business that federated to the company's global newsfeed where all employees could view it. Who was the first person to respond? Our CEO, Ed Coleman. And he didn't just chime in with platitudes, but he wrote to provoke a response, and not just from me. He raised questions— politely, but he made his point—actually, three points. One, the CEO follows blogs assiduously. Two, the point is to start conversations, not just issue facts. And, three, curiosity is good; if you have questions, ask away!

Again, our CEO modeled himself with the behavior he wanted to see from the entire company, and this immediately spawned imitators like no amount of preaching would have done.

In fact, here's how Ed puts it firmly but cheerfully in a video all employees see when they are introduced to our social business tools: "I check my (social microblog) newsfeed throughout the day, I read our blogs as soon as they hit, and I follow my colleagues." If he does all that (and he does), how could it be too much trouble or too little value for other employees to follow his lead?

On Using the Tool to Prove the Tool

From the start, we knew that we, the Unisys internal Knowledge and Collaboration team, had to be our own guinea pigs. We had to make our own social business activity work remotely. As chief knowledge officer, I led the initiative remotely except for commuting to Unisys headquarters to engage with senior management and core team members during the initial strategy development phase of the initiative.

Our global program director was in Pennsylvania, our program manager was outside of London in the United Kingdom, our project managers were spread across the United States, and some of our developers were in India. We sampled everything first, which made it easy for us to be highly critical of the platform because we had to use it to do our work! If it were clunky for us, or non-intuitive, we knew it wouldn't work for the rest of the company. It also provided us with our own challenges in changing established behaviors—leveraging a collaborative community, rather than a static team room, to organize and run the initiative, sharing information transparently via the newsfeed rather than e-mail, and creating blog posts to share insights, experiences, and project updates rather than typical weekly reports.

A great proof point came during our initial My Site Profile adoption campaign. Knowing that photos would be an important element within the profile, we set standards to ensure appropriateness to the business. However, not all employees had a business headshot or means to engage a professional photographer. So we quickly set up a day in each geographical office where employees could come in and have a professional photo taken. We were on a tight budget, so when we set out to hire photographers, we decided to let our social network newsfeed do the work for us. We posted a query with the hashtag (#photographer), as well as the geography, and asked for employees who had photography experience and equipment—even if as a hobby—to step forward if they were willing to help. Within several hours, we found several photographers within our employee base who were delighted to do this. In fact, in the United Kingdom, it turned out that one of our employees was formerly the official photographer for the Royal Air Force. Needless to say, you should see the impressive photos of our UK contingent!

On Building the Collaborative Social Networking Platform

Fundamentally, the implementation of social technologies requires a platform that we provide employees with a positive environment that enables them to more seamlessly and transparently share what they know and to access the information, skills, and tools necessary to more effectively perform their jobs.

Key components of a well-orchestrated collaborative platform include rich employee profiles displaying skill sets and areas of expertise and an enterprise-wide news and activity feeds; integrated unified communications capabilities to enable employees to easily identify and connect with subject matter experts; a centralized blog, newsfeed, and wiki capabilities to facilitate knowledge transfer; a social and mobile-enabled intranet to eliminate knowledge silos across organizations and geographies; optimized search capabilities and effective enterprise content management streamline access to knowledge; information and expertise at the time of need; and a strategic communities model that provides an ecosystem to foster collaboration, evolve skill sets and expertise, and facilitate the sharing and crowdsourcing of ideas that can be channeled into new and refined innovations. All of these contribute to revenue growth.

Employee Profiles

At Unisys, My Site profiles are a foundational element of our collaborative platform. These profiles enable employees to create a company presence, introduce themselves to the company, build a valuable network of colleagues, and have helped us to overcome our difficulty in finding subject matter experts by making profiles accessible to all employees and searchable by key words. Profiles not only provide basic contact information, presence, expertise, and skills, but they also enable employees to make a virtual connection by understanding colleagues' roles and responsibilities within the company, learn about their interests and former projects, and view their photos before connecting at a physical meeting.

Employees can also add free-form topics to the "Ask Me About" section of their profile. These topics integrate with search to connect questions posted by employees with a topic hashtag and direct it to colleagues who have the respective topic tag in their profile. If you have a question about "cyber security," you can post a question in the newsfeed using the hashtag "cybersecurity" and your question will be directed to experienced cyber security professionals. Long gone are the days of the "does anyone know…?" e-mail. If you want to connect directly with a cloud expert, you just search #cloud and immediately discover who the cloud experts are within the company.

Unified Communications and Real-Time Presence Indicators

Employee names throughout the intranet environment are hyperlinked to profiles, so employees can easily click and see colleagues' basic information such as their organization, where they are located, and what they do in the company. And because we integrated our employee profiles with real-time presence indicators (via Microsoft Lync), it is immediately apparent whether the person is online and available to connect directly via instant message or voice.

Blogs, Micro-Blogs, and Newsfeeds

All employees have the ability to create and share blogs that are automatically federated to the company's global newsfeed, which enables the transparent sharing of knowledge across organizations and geographies and foster serendipitous learning. The global newsfeed forms the backbone of the new communications network within Unisys and communities serve as network hubs. Employees are encouraged to develop a personalized social network by following company thought leaders and colleagues who can influence their work and facilitate ideation and collaboration.

Balancing Social Network Engagement and Information Overload

Employees are also encouraged to join communities of practice to help evolve their expertise and skill sets and to share what they know to help the growth of others (see Figure 4.1). To avoid information overload, employees are empowered to manage newsfeed consumption and community memberships. All employees are hard-aligned to their respective organizations and home office. This provides the company with the necessary vehicle to push targeted communications, while allowing employees to customize newsfeed views and manage their participation across various communities that bring value to them in their particular role.

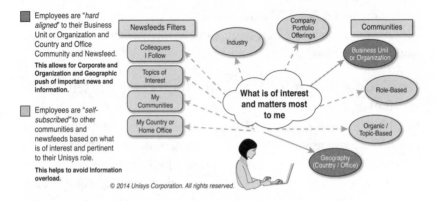

Figure 4.1 On communities as the hub of social collaboration

Ask any knowledge and collaboration strategist what the driving force is behind successful enterprise collaboration and he or she will undoubtedly say "communities." I'll venture further to say that it is company-sponsored, strategic communities that make social collaboration most successful and valuable to the business enterprise. This is not to say that organic communities do not play an important role in social collaboration. They do. But strategic communities strengthen knowledge transfer, evolve expertise and skill sets, and foster ideation that lead to innovations in areas that matter most to the business. Unlike organic, informal communities, strategic communities require an infrastructure that closely integrates company subject matter expertise, authoritative knowledge content, education and training, as well as external market data to be truly effective.

However, creating a model for strategic communities might require significant investment of time and resources. First and foremost, it requires planning. Positioning strategic communities to support a company's market areas of strength, target industries, and key employee roles, and aligning them to business objectives and goals is essential. The Unisys model shown in Figure 4.2 places emphasis on strategic communities of excellence, which have the greatest impact on employee learning and innovation.

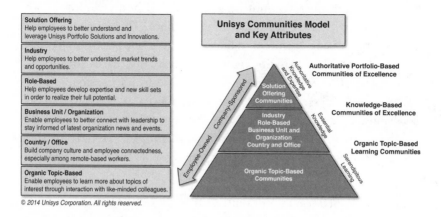

Figure 4.2   Unisys communities model

Second, developing a framework for enablement and evolution is critical to sustaining a successful community environment. Effective frameworks include a project plan, a communication plan for socializing the purpose of the community to attract and retain members, and a culture transformation plan to help employees understand the value of community participation.

Third, communities must be well managed. I like to use an analogy created by my former Booz Allen colleague, Walton Smith, who likened communities to gardens, each requiring a gardener to "seed, feed, weed, and harvest." Too often companies launch communities with a "build it and they will come" mindset. Employees might come, but will they stay and engage?

To sustain and attract new members, communities must provide ongoing value. Community managers play a pivotal role in keeping communities viable and helping them grow. They engage subject matter experts who can provide the right answers to questions at the right time and transfer knowledge and best practices to help community members evolve their skill sets. They seed content and motivate members to share and engage with each other through newsfeeds and community webinars. They promote the exchange of ideas and harvest and repurpose valuable knowledge. They also capture metrics to measure community growth and effectiveness.

Finally, communities cannot be successful without employees who are enthusiastic, engaged, and willing to share. This is where culture transformation comes into play. Successful strategic communities have clearly defined key benefits areas and related use cases to illustrate how community involvement delivers value to its members as well as to the business. Nothing drives behavior change more than a colleague's positive experience with a new tool, a process, or community involvement. Savvy community managers capture and repurpose these success stories to drive membership, increase adoption, and validate business value.

Bottom line: Strategic communities that are well planned, properly enabled, and effectively managed can significantly impact the success of social collaboration within the business enterprise. Take a look within your own organization and assess how strategic communities can play a role in the success of your social collaboration efforts.

On Measuring Success

If you subscribe to the premise that social technologies deliver the greatest value to business only when they become embedded in key processes and employee behaviors, then measuring employee adoption, effectiveness, and derived value is critical to achieving this success. A primary component of maximizing your return on investment lies in capturing adoption metrics as well as social data analytics to assess effectiveness and value to the business. Social technologies generate immense amounts of mission-critical data. Social data analytics provides the platform and capabilities to leverage this information to improve business performance, proactively in real time.

Metrics Matter. Actually, They Matter a Great Deal

The potential for leveraging your social data to drive business performance is immense. For enterprises struggling with low social adoption rates, social data analytics can help you target the highest potential opportunities for improvement. If increasing the contribution of your SMEs to your enterprise is the goal, social data analytics provides the means to understand how your SMEs are connected and collaborating. If driving critical business insights is the objective, social data analytics allows you to identify and understand emerging trends and discussion topics.

A structured metrics and measurement model and approach is required to effectively develop and deploy social data analytics capabilities. There must be an explicit linkage between the developed analytics and the identified and documented business needs. In addition, effective governance and processes must be developed in order to leverage the capabilities and capture the business value. The reward is clear: Organizations that harness social data analytics to maximize the return on their social technology investments will be best positioned to succeed.

At Unisys, our initial step in developing metrics and an analytics model was to create a measurement framework and timeline for tracking adoption progress over an 18-month period. We created a baseline using the Rogers Adoption Innovation Curve and measured our progress against its five established adoption point percentages shown in the legend in Figure 4.3: Innovators, Early Adopters, Early Majority, Late Majority, and Laggards.

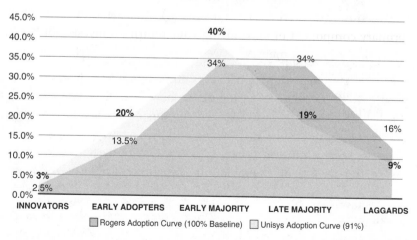

Figure 4.3   Adoption point percentages

We defined adoption as an employee having created his or her profile and completing all tasks such as uploading a photo, creating biographical description, adding expertise topics and interests and importing skill sets, as well as enabling his or her blog site page.

Within only 18 months of launching our social business platform, we achieved a 91 percent adoption rate of our targeted employee audience of 16,000, 78 percent adoption of all global employees, and 100 percent adoption by the company's executive leadership. This is indeed remarkable given that among all companies that have made the transition to an enterprise social business platform, only 17 percent have achieved and sustained an adoption rate of more than 75 percent, with most hovering around the 30 percent to 35 percent mark. For us to achieve this success, we had to answer the question that underlies every single change management initiative: If I change my behavior to adopt the use of this new technology, "What's the value in it for me?"

Value and Effectiveness

We had to find the early signs of change, encourage them, and build on them. It wasn't long before we started hearing people say, "Share it in the Newsfeed—I'll grab it there." Or, "Post it in the Community so everybody has access to it." A tipping point came when the casual exchanges in the newsfeed from employees dipping a toe in the social stream such as "Happy birthday!" or "Congratulations on your certification!" were overshadowed by deeper, more meaningful knowledge exchanges to advance learning.

We started to see a shift and uptick in mentoring activities. Some senior executives started sharing experiences or thought leadership on a topic—putting it all out there in a blog or the newsfeed obviously enjoying the opportunity to mentor one to many, instead of just answering a question for a single junior employee and then answering it again and again, without gaining traction or standing. Obviously, both sides of the mentorship were seeing the value and constantly engaging more deeply, widely, and thoroughly.

In communities, we began to measure activities of members to gauge community maturity and growth as well as the effectiveness and value being delivered to members and to the business. Henry David Thoreau remarked, "It is not enough to be busy. So are the ants. The question is: What are we busy about?" This analogy can be applied to communities within the social business environment. It's not that employees are busy sharing knowledge or information in the newsfeeds, blogs, or libraries, or presenting or attending webinars. It is how that content is consumed or leveraged to bring about operational efficiency, evolve learning and expertise, or drive innovation that matters. What is the end state value that is delivered to the community member as well as to the business?

How Employees Describe Value

Other success measures were less quantifiable but equally observable. When we ask people what they like best about their new social business tools, we hear a lot about *seamlessness*. "It's how I do business now." The capabilities of our new social tool offers employees pro-active guidance. It suggests colleagues for employees to add to their network based on their shared interests. It suggests communities for them to join based on role. It tells them about like-minded people to advance learning and for honing their skill sets.

They also talk about *speed* to access knowledge and information, especially if they are new employees accustomed to spending days trying to get questions answered from internal experts.

We also hear about a new culture of *sharing*. Our social business model doesn't reward information hoarding. It rewards transparency, mentoring, and sharing. In our HR model, managers can now set annual performance objectives for sharing and collaboration. We have introduced gamification and badging to incent and recognize positive social behaviors and more easily identify subject matter experts and thought leaders.

On Governance

One of the biggest pushbacks I hear from the C-Suite when someone mentions adoption of a social business platform is risk. Risk can be safely mitigated by establishing and *socializing* explicit social media policies, guidelines, and rules of engagement. I stress the importance of socialization because policies and guidelines do nothing to mitigate risk if employees do not read or understand them.

At Unisys, we made social media a shared responsibility among our leadership as well as all employees. Although we have formal policies and guidelines for the internal and external use of social media, we distilled the key tenets of our social media policy into a three-minute video titled, "How We Connect." The video features our own employees sharing the rules of engagement: Be Respectful—Maintain Confidentiality, Protect Privacy, and Ensure Accuracy.

The video has been incorporated into our enterprise social business training module within new hire orientation, and it is part of our annual social media awareness campaign. Providing a practical working knowledge of social media policy and rules of engagement is extremely important, especially to millennials who are accustomed to transparently sharing just about everything in their lives through social media. They will abide by the rules if they know what they are, but don't expect them to sit down and read a 10-page policy document. They are multitaskers, and video is their preferred means of consuming information and learning, followed by microblogs and blog posts. Make it easy for them to tailor their behaviors to your policies and guidelines.

We also enabled a Social Media Advanced Guard committee to provide governance and to ensure the integrity and sustainability of our enterprise social business environment. We perform an annual social media audit to review activities and processes to assess future risks. In addition, we have leveraged software to catch inappropriate language or sensitive topics being discussed, and we have a process to randomly scan profiles for inappropriate images or content.

Since our transformation journey began, we have not had to take any corrective actions other than to ask a handful of employees to replace the images of their "hot cars" or photos with family or pets in their profile with a more appropriate business image. Certainly it helps to have a senior leadership team actively visible in your social newsfeed and communities. You can't absolutely prevent an employee from posting something they shouldn't. But the fact that the social business platform is so transparent and self-policing makes employees think twice about what and how they share.

Bottom line: Establish policies, guidelines, and rules of engagement. Socialize them well. Put governance and processes in place to proactively monitor your social business environment, and have an actionable plan to take corrective action when and if it is needed. Make social media a shared responsibility and trust your employees to rise to the standards you set.

On the Economics

We are realizing benefits from our enterprise social business platform in many ways: streamlined access to knowledge, expertise, and information; enhanced communications and collaboration among employees, business partners, and clients; increased operational efficiency; more transparency and fluidity of ideas that lead to new and refined innovations; heightened customer service; and increased market agility. However, for most of these benefit areas, it is hard to assign a hard dollar value. We could throw a lot of numbers around, but there's one specific element of our social platform that stands out: our deployment of Unified Communications (UC).

We knew we wanted our enterprise social business technology solution to include real-time presence and seamless connection and communications capabilities. It wouldn't be enough to just identify the expert who could answer your question. Your next question would be, "Is that person online and available to connect with me?" You want to post or ask a question, get answers immediately, and have the ability to bring others into the conversation and even share materials relevant to the conversation visually—all in real time.

To achieve that, we needed to modernize our telecommunications platform and integrate this new communications technology with our social business engine. So we replaced our existing aging infrastructure system—including more than 17 PBX systems—with our Ensemble Unified Communications solution based on Microsoft Lync. We integrated it with our SharePoint platform and Sitrion social engine so that presence indicators appear adjacent to employee names throughout the intranet environment and mobile platforms, making it seamless for employees to identify, connect, communicate, and collaborate in real time.

The results are impressive. We are achieving annualized savings of more than $5.2 million in overall operating expenses related to communications. We were able to do this through the centralization of our voice circuits at more than 170 locations to a few key locations. In addition, within a few short months of deployment, we moved all 23,000 employees to our Ensemble UC solution from expensive third-party hosted audio and web conferencing services. Through the enablement of this technology, we were also able to drive savings through reduced travel.

In addition to these financial achievements, Ensemble UC has also greatly improved customer engagement through federation to our customers' UC platforms, extending the presence information and communication capabilities outside of the organization. Employee productivity and satisfaction have also been improved helping them achieve efficient communications and enabling a single application for all communication needs.

On What We'd Do Differently

In retrospect, there's only one thing we would do differently today, if we had a do-over, and here I'm going to depart from what most practitioners in my field recommend. It's the matter of test pilots. Most would recommend avoiding a mass deployment initiative in favor of a series of small pilots that could eventually be scaled up. Try it in a small, controlled environment, work out the bugs, perfect it, move to another area, roll out another pilot, and so on. But just like you can't be a little bit pregnant, you can't actually test and gauge the full value of enterprise social business in small pilots within siloed organizations.

We did do one pilot—in our Program and Project Managers unit—and I won't say we didn't learn some things, but if your goal is *enterprise* social business, a pilot almost contradicts it. A key aspect is to have all parties involved to be reaching far across the company, breaking down geographic, organization, and role barriers, enabling collaboration broadly with areas and people you don't know—not just with others whom you know perfectly well. It works only when everybody is in it.

Test pilots also create temporary "in groups" and risk alienating the "out groups." You run the risk of driving the out groups to seek their own social business solution, and it can be hard to reel them back in.

Ultimately, you have to trust your strategy and approach. If you spend the time upfront developing a comprehensive transformation plan that includes the five foundational building blocks, addresses the critical needs of the business, engages leadership and stakeholders, and influences the culture of the company, you will succeed. Dive in to the deep end of the pool. Wading in from the shallow end just postpones the inevitable.

Conclusion

What I know for sure is that the journey of enterprise social business transformation is one that will continue to present new challenges and paths to trail blaze as technologies evolve and end users discover new ways in which to exploit them. So, I will share the belief that enterprise social business transformation, like life itself, is as much about the journey as it is about the destination. Granted, we all have an end state vision of what the culmination of our lives will be, or in this case, what the success of our businesses should be. But the true value lies not only in the end state, but also in the discoveries, the lessons learned, the sharing of ourselves and what we know, and the exchange of ideas that lead to innovation, which ultimately shape and define who we are as individuals and what our companies are.

John Donne said, "No man is an island." What was true in his time is even truer in our hyperconnected, diverse world. Success takes leadership alignment, a talented and dedicated team of IT professionals, cross organization stakeholders who are willing to collaborate, and employees who are both curious and eager to transparently share what they know and to openly learn from one another to make this all work. Above all it takes patience and perseverance. Enterprise social business transformation is, after all, a journey.

Social technologies are not a passing fad. They are the enablers of a game-changing shift in the execution of business, economic growth, and social responsibility. It's not a matter of if your company should get on the social business train. It's a matter of when. And "when" defines competitive advantage and the future growth and success of your business.

5

360° Social—A Case Study in the "Socialization" of an Organization: Merging Social Media with Social Events

Shar Govindan, Director, Social Learning, Bentley Systems, Inc.

Isn't it interesting that for centuries, when people referred to the term *social,* most thought of in-person gatherings, and today most think of the term social as online media? The rather geometric title for this chapter is to underscore that "360 degrees of social" are continuous combinations of face-to-face meetings and online interactions.

A Personal Transition from Business Technical to Business Social

For nearly a decade, I served in a support and training role, contributing to our company's mission of sustaining infrastructure. I taught engineers and modelers around the Americas, Europe, and Asia (from Kingston, Jamaica in English to Guiyang, China with a translator) on how to design, analyze, and improve their water networks. This was a fulfilling role, and I continue to be proud of the enormous social impact that our company continues to make around the world through our software users.

As a hobby, I was a voluntary moderator for TalkCity.com in the early 1990s and have built hundreds of other nonprofit web communities since then. I was given an opportunity to contribute to the book titled *Social BOOM!* by Jeffrey Gitomer, a *NY Times* best-selling author. *Social BOOM!* became an instant hit on Amazon.com and retained #1 ranking in 2011 under multiple categories. This publicized my passion for community building and created the opportunity for my transition to a new role within our company.

The "Aha" Moment

I interviewed with George Church, a senior vice president at our company, during the Technology Services World Conference in Las Vegas. One of the first questions George asked me was, "Who do you think should own social media within a company?" I was quick to reply, "marketing." George smiled and asked, "Are you sure it isn't everybody?" and then his point hit me, and it hit me hard. George was absolutely right. True social media success could be achieved only when everyone in an organization was actively engaged in building relationships, both online and offline, internally with colleagues and externally with its software users and prospects. I agreed with him wholeheartedly and my expanded social learning role began in January 2012.

The Transformation Begins...

Our company won *The Innovation Award of the Year* from the Computer Education Management Association (CEdMA) for social learning. Here's why.

Traditionally, training classes offered little to no interactions between the trainers and students before and/or after the class. Many of our trainers were well liked, had taught hundreds of people, published whitepapers and books, presented at conferences, won awards, and always received excellent feedback and testimonials from former students. The problem was that most of these trainers' credentials were unknown to potential students and their former students' social networks. Most of these trainer-student relationships were limited to e-mails, phone calls, and in-person meetings, and our trainers continued to help them post-training using these traditional one-on-one private channels. (This is the primary reason why GREAT work goes unnoticed many times!) I observed from working with trainers that they are seldom motivated primarily by monetary incentives—a major surprise to me. Our trainers genuinely loved to help others, and that drove their performance. They are intrinsically happy from inspiring someone to learn—how to do something new or work more efficiently. They are experts at helping our users unlearn and relearn.

Therefore, we wanted to magnify the "humble/helpful" trainers' popularity on social media by leveraging their followers and endorsements—in essence, we wanted to create a social butterfly effect. We wanted to increase the engagement levels and enable continuous, collaborative learning in a more public venue. We wanted to promote the trainers' "professional brands" and reputations online, on social media sites, and in search sites. One of the primary questions I ask my colleagues while assisting with their social reputation is, "What does someone see when they do an online search of your name and our company name together?"

As a first step, we had to train the trainers in social. We began by training our consultants and trainers during our company's Global Professional Services Leadership Meeting, which had a broader agenda. To deliver this comprehensive training on social media platforms, I teamed with other social savvy colleagues from our support and marketing departments. The format was designed to include 90 percent hands-on workshops and 10 percent lectures. Back then, everyone had heard of social media through videos and presentations, but many created their first social media accounts that day because of the hands-on workshop format.

Organizational Challenges and Management Support

During our workshop discussions, we observed a few challenges from our colleagues who were new to social media:

- They preferred to use e-mail.
- Social media was viewed as personal.
- Social media was viewed as marketing's job.
- There was apprehension to share content publicly.
- There was not enough perceived value.
- Forming this new "habit" for professional use was going to be hard.

- They were unsure how management would perceive them.

- They were unsure if/when they needed to ask permission.

Thanks to the outstanding support provided by our management, all these concerns are now gone. George instituted a three-word *Just Do Social* policy. People learn better when they "do"—this was evidenced by all the new social media accounts created that day and most improved their online social presence, including myself.

For instance, my colleague Peter Huftalen asked me, "You follow a lot of people on Twitter, but why don't you tweet more often?" I replied, "I am more of a listener of others' tweets, but I'll start tweeting more." A few thousand tweets later, I am glad Peter asked me that question.

For true social media success, it is important for individual managers to not only support the related initiatives and encourage their teams, but more importantly to display social behavior through their own actions. Our CEO, Greg Bentley, starred in a series of Vine videos, and this inspired a lot of our colleagues (see Figure 5.1).

Figure 5.1 Vine video of our CEO, Greg Bentley (Credit: Tyler Queen)

Millennials: Born with the Social DNA!

I continue to be humbled by our next-generation colleagues who tweet at magnitudes that are exponentially larger than most, as shown in Figure 5.2.

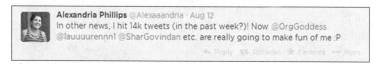

Figure 5.2   Tweet by Bentley colleague Alexandria Phillips on reaching 14,000 tweets (Credit: Alexandria Phillips)

There are several colleagues within any organization who are naturally social, but social media might not be part of their job description. It is critical to identify these colleagues and train them (on both what to do and what not to do), but it is more important to empower them and have them be the organization's social ambassadors. Figure 5.3 and Figure 5.4 show some examples from within our organization.

Figure 5.3   Tyler Queen championing our LEARN photo booth. Pictures taken at the booth were shared on social media and e-mailed to our users, so they might also share it themselves. (Photo credit: Shar Govindan)

Figure 5.4 Elevator selfie with our software users taken at the Bentley LEARNing Conference (Photo credit: Danielle Chmelewski)

The Be Social Award

In February 2012, we instituted the monthly Be Social award program with the purpose of recognizing trainers and consultants active on social media platforms. The idea behind this was to inspire through examples, each month, how other colleagues excelled on social media while having a similar work role and life. Studies have shown that humans are more inspired when they view a *leaderboard* of those they know personally, than record-level achievements by unknown people.

More than 50 colleagues have won the Be Social award to date, and each month we publish stories with photographs and screen shots on how the award-winner was outstanding in the application of social media to engage with our software users.

The concept behind the award has remained simple: Every month someone would nominate a colleague or I would analyze multiple social platforms using social listening tools and pick a deserving winner. The winner would get a printed book or eBook, usually a best seller on business social media.

Here's why many of our colleagues have won this award:

- Helping our users—answering forum or group questions

- Blogging original content

- Actively networking with colleagues, software users, and prospects

- Promoting courses created or delivered by them

- Leading discussions within niche communities (for example, LinkedIn Groups)

- Sharing industry-relevant articles regularly

- Building their personal brand

- Offering greater value than our competitors while helping our users

Colleagues continue to be recognized like clockwork every month, and I now call it the *Be Social Wall of Fame*. The positive impact and excitement transferred because of their social leadership to the rest of the team is immeasurable through any standard metric, and it continues to inspire more people every day.

Internal Enterprise Social Growth

By then, we were evaluating internal enterprise social collaboration tools to foster communication between our colleagues. One of the tools that we were evaluating went viral and several hundred colleagues joined this platform within a week. We soon got buy-in and interest from other departments and our CIO. We started to observe colleagues interacting with each other publicly in the All Company group like never before. Many posted informative articles and were helping other colleagues located across the world. (Some even used language translators to communicate.) Others would use it to praise and welcome new colleagues, share success stories, schedule events, and ask questions/create polls.

We have since formed groups for our trainers and consultants to discuss training content and project proposals, to share industry news, and more. Our training delivery group has one of the highest social interaction levels within our company. Trainers have used this group as a book club, to share inspirational quotes, professional videos, whitepapers, and ideas, and to ask thought-provoking questions that lead to group discussions. This internal platform has been an excellent way to increase social engagement between trainers.

Meet Us—Videos, Blogs, and More

We saw our conferences and events as great opportunities to promote our trainers on YouTube. Prior to the conference, we had our trainers create informal videos (versus too formal), introducing themselves and what users will learn from their sessions (see Figure 5.5).

Figure 5.5 Screenshots of Meet the Trainer videos on YouTube.com/Bentley systems channel

We requested that they develop a script using their own words and to record the video using their webcam. This simplistic approach helped us create several videos quickly. In 2013, these videos garnered a few hundred views on YouTube. However, with enough lead time in 2014, the next set of Meet the Trainer videos garnered several thousand views. We also requested that our trainers blog about their sessions by describing what someone would learn by attending them. In addition, trainers created forum posts where dialogues would start pre-event but would continue post-event.

Series of Efforts and Innovations

We wanted to scale our efforts globally, so we started training our consultants and trainers through OnDemand presentations on the value of social media and how they could leverage social media to connect with our users. These were typical voice-over presentations. This didn't create a huge impact, so we revamped our training series using colleagues who had a zeal for life and shot it outdoors (more on that later...).

We then implemented sharing abilities on our learning web portal by integrating the AddThis.com widget (see Figure 5.6). Our content was now shareable on more than 300+ social media platforms and have since been shared several thousand times. Interestingly, e-mail continues to be the most popular way of sharing. In my opinion, any sharing, including via e-mail, is social behavior.

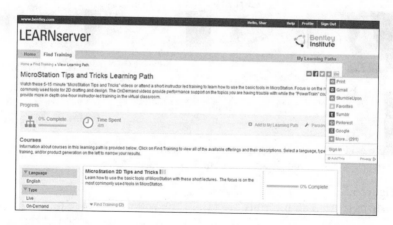

Figure 5.6 Social-sharing widget (upper right) enabled on Bentley LEARNserver

We then promoted our largest user conference by creating multiple YouTube videos and also organized a Twitter contest.

We set up a Be Social booth at the conference that showed people how to share on social networks and win prizes for tweeting something valuable. If the conference attendees weren't on Twitter already, we would help them sign up at the booth. This helped create an online buzz throughout the conference, and we had record-level social activities by both our colleagues and software users (see Figure 5.7).

The Twitter contest had the following steps:

1. Our conference attendees would register their Twitter handle with us at the Be Social booth.

2. They would follow our corporate Twitter account.

3. They would then tweet a picture or something they learned with our conference using the conference hashtag.

We then picked a winner using Random.org.

Figure 5.7 Be Social kiosk setup at our conference to help our users sign up for various social media accounts and help answer questions

Next, we hired an intern (now a full-time colleague) to help with social media training. We scripted and produced a series of videos with assessment questions on social media. The training videos were shot outdoors using a teleprompter, iPad, iPad app called "Teleprompter+," and an HD camera (see Figure 5.8).

The teleprompter reduced our video editing time and ensured flawless delivery every time.

We also had Chinese colleagues help create content in Mandarin for local colleagues. China has a unique social media realm but except for the exceptional popularity of microblogging sites, it has the Chinese-equivalent websites for YouTube, Twitter, and so on. Therefore, many of the strategies and tactics are still transferable and applicable.

Figure 5.8 Screenshots from our internal training videos on various social media platforms (Photo credit: Leanna Laughlin)

Later that year, we formed a multidepartment team, called the "Social Media Council" to help champion our overall social engagement efforts. This team is composed of colleagues from Human Resources, Legal, IT, Professional Services, Software Development, Software Support, Marketing, and Internal and External Training departments. The council later led the Social Ambassadors initiative, which expanded best practices to all colleagues.

By the end of 2012, we observed that although a great deal of work was done with social media, there were many untapped opportunities with social learning. And thus began our next phase to integrate online social media with in-person social events.

There was more exciting news during early 2013. Our company made an unprecedented value offering to our learning subscribers: We changed our biggest sales and marketing conference to a learning conference. We renamed the event from "Be Together" to "The Bentley LEARNing Conference." We removed non-training sessions including corporate keynotes and made it a pure learning conference. This was historic for our company—and perhaps any company.

We had our trainers record videos of their sessions before the conference. Our attendees shared these courses with their colleagues and professional network who were unable to attend the conference. Because the attendees shared only the courses they really liked, many courses had amazing responses through organic endorsements.

During the conference, we set up sign-up sheets for social dinners for learners with common interests to meet later that evening. We made reservations at more than 20 restaurants near the conference center and limited each dinner table to a group of 12 people. After the first evenings' group dinner, we received suggestions that attendees would have preferred a Bentley colleague to have joined them. So at the next evening's dinner, we ensured that a subject matter expert joined each group. We received positive feedback for listening to our users quickly and enabling in-person social networking.

We also set up a LEARNing Bar, where our company co-founders and key executives participated in an interactive session with the conference attendees during lunch and the evening reception. This aspect of the event was a huge hit. We even live-streamed this event across all the monitors in the conference learning zone.

After the conference, we implemented our next social project: Virtual Special Interest Groups (SIG). Users who had traditionally met at conferences now sustain relationships via these regularly scheduled online meetings. These sessions are promoted by the SIG champion on Twitter and LinkedIn and through blogging. The SIG champion would show how to do something specific and useful for 15 to 30 minutes and then enable an interactive discussion between peers. Discussion topics were driven by what was most topical on Bentley Communities, ensuring that the agenda was relevant.

Many of our offices and conferences now feature a social wall, which displays near real-time social feeds from our various social platforms. It never ceases to impress those who tweet their picture using our hashtag and then see their message on a big screen moments later.

We later improved upon our social dinner idea from the previous year. The social dinners are now located at the conference (instead of restaurants) and feature discipline-specific themes. Conference attendees would sign up for their topic of interest during the day and later sit at the table that displayed their respective table-top signage. A subject matter expert from our company would join them to kick-start conversations and share insights but mostly listen. This format was designed to primarily enable peer-to-peer attendee conversations. Because of this initiative, our users could meet and greet new peers and talk about various topics of interest and their projects during our conference dinners (see Figure 5.9).

Figure 5.9 Tabletop signage from our conference social dinner tables was placed in the middle of the table. (Image credit: Janet Bakker)

Our next project was Social Stickers. We provided our attendees special removable labels that they could stick on top of their name badge. Most stickers would have a product or design interest and unique colors.

This enabled our conference attendees to quickly identify and interact with like-minded individuals. We also included a blank sticker with @_____, where they could insert their Twitter handle. This was yet another way we merged the online and offline social worlds.

Figure 5.10   Sheet of removable social stickers that were made available to the conference attendees (Image credit: Amy Heffner, Jim O'Brien)

We have made greater strides towards 360° Social as a team, as embodied by our social media bracelet (see Figure 5.11).

We even celebrated our social victories through specially made cupcakes (see Figure 5.12).

This and many of the previously mentioned projects are a result of tremendous teamwork by an inspired team of colleagues who are "social" and like working with each other.

Figure 5.11 Photo taken at The Bentley LEARNing Conference with a bracelet that highlights the various social media platforms with our conference hashtag. (Photo credit: Shar Govindan)

Figure 5.12 Social Media cupcakes from the Toot Sweet bakery in Exton, PA. (Photo credit: Frank Conforti)

The Most Important Type of Social and Conclusion

I continue to deeply care about and be associated with all the social (nonprofit) organizations that our company supports: Engineers Without Borders, FeelGood, Future City, United Way, The Hunger Project, Water for People, and more. Billions of people are positively impacted through the infrastructure improvements, increase in energy, food and water availability, cost-savings, and more. Most important, human lives are improved every day and night.

The ultimate form of 360° Social is when online social media, in-person social events, and social organizations are unified. It is a continuous process and requires teamwork by many people at individual levels. Technology-based platforms that enable social networking are hard to create. What's harder is enabling opportunities that aim to change human behavior and inspire everyone to be social, both online and in-person, ergo, 360° Social!

6

How to Use Social Media to Solve Billable Consultants' Nonbillable Dilemma

David Shimberg, Director of Global Services Marketing, BMC Software

Consultants are incented by their billable time, the development of best practices, and their depth of experience. Social business enables the free flow of information with an emphasis on "free," which tugs at the purse strings and normal behavior of a consultant and his or her team. This chapter focuses on social business approaches that work with consultants and their management team. When the "light bulbs go off," consultants usually top the list of the businesses most social resources.

Why?

Our forefathers tell of a time when news traveled by word of mouth, horseback, smoke signal, or even carrier pigeon. That was a time when the concept of "instant gratification" was more closely aligned with "delayed gratification." Communication was rather constrained by technology. Social technology has enabled global, high-speed, unfiltered floods of communication.

Individuals who make a living billing for their time cherish every billable minute. Professional service resources track their every minute, every task, and every activity. They are measured by the billable hour and managed by their billable utilization. Their value is tied to their ability to solve complex problems. Customers pay and expect they will deliver on time and on budget.

Time has long been the center of every professional service's business. Driving value through intellectual capital has been a desired goal, but value billing and its measure has never before had a multiplier like social business, until now.

When so much value creation can be gained by increasing communication and enabling collaboration through social technology, it should be natural that consultants would be early adopters. Let me say it in another way: If time is a limiting factor, it seems logical that value can be increased by building social webs that connect knowledge workers with those who are willing to pay for their wisdom or at least are interested in what they have to share. I long ago realized I needed to repeat the mantra "logic doesn't always apply."

Customers are starting to expect that consulting services and to some extent education services will move from a time-centered model to an outcome-based model. The consulting business that can offer to more effectively impact the value model of its clients will have an advantage. The barrier of time as the only consulting currency is being attacked, and social business has the ability to play a key role in forcing change.

Social business delivers a platform for the creation, sharing, and consumption of communication. Social business enabled by technology can also be quite disruptive, allowing different levels of an organization to equally connect with new and emerging communities. Consultants can share their ideas, best practices, tips, and tricks with their peers around the world instantly. They can solve customer challenges through a "consulting crowd sourcing" model that can then turn from an intra-organizational view to deliver value to outside clients. At these new velocities, a consulting group can deliver value faster and broader, resulting in measurable returns (and higher billable rates).

Social business value within the consulting or professional services industry is to be found in the increased productivity of accelerating access to the right answers and distributing them faster to their stakeholders. Taking knowledge content stored in individual consultants' heads, their inbox threads, and their laptop hard drives while making them community accessible is now a social technology capability, but we are just at the beginning of the journey.

In my years supporting the consulting and education teams at BMC Software, and previously at HP Software, I have come to realize that what might seem logical and natural to the marketing team does not always translate into delivery team practice. I have slowly and sometimes patiently realized that social business does really start with individuals who come to understand the personal satisfaction and potential recognition they can from sharing via social. The tipping point for an entire community of consultants, trainers, customers, and managers is much further out than the social business path of various individuals.

Social business applied to consultants and education is beginning to change a culture that was designed in conflict with our parents telling us that "sharing was a good thing." For example, we are seeing social rapidly changing the way BMC and many other technology companies deliver education. The incredible vision and execution of Sal Kahn's education model (Khan Academy), where he has "flipped the Kahn Academy classroom" and positioned the teacher as a professional in an enabler role to accelerate adoption of learning, is a paradigm we are rapidly applying to BMC Software adoption. Building communities of students and teachers so that continuous training and mentoring is today a disruptive business model but moving fast toward becoming a new norm. Kahn Academy and education approaches such as those sponsored by top universities (EdX Courses) are demonstrating that social learning works. New consulting models will emerge.

Professional services (PS) firms and groups within companies such as BMC are social entities driven by social interaction (with technology in the mix). These firms constantly invest in increasing collaboration, collecting best practice experience, and enabling and certifying their consultants. Social technology woven into the PS culture is a change agent that has significant potential to change the business model and drive business value.

Although my career has focused on consulting in the context of the software industry, it would be naïve to limit the impact of social business to this one segment of professional services. The comfort of having access to my medical professionals online, on demand without sitting in a waiting room, is an experience that prior generations could not begin to imagine. The social concept of Facebook, like it or not, is one that adds dimensions to our physically distant relationships that our forefathers (and foremothers) could never envision. Whether I want to know, I know where my friends and sometimes their friends are traveling, where they are having dinner, and how they got their haircut. Perhaps this is too much information, but you get my point. Social technology is here and changing whomever interacts with its web.

Why Not?

I would be far from honest if I didn't state loud and clear that getting a consulting group—both the delivery team out in the trenches and their management—to jump feet or head first into the social web is not an easy task. They are trained to treasure their own intellectual capital much like Midas treasured his gold. The corporate consulting model has somehow erased our parent's guidance on the importance of sharing our "things." We quarterly immerse ourselves in compliance training to retain and rightfully protect intellectual property and guard our trade secrets. We are not trained in the accelerating value of social business and the subtlety of providing just enough information so that our clients want more value and assume we have more to offer. We don't know the balance of protecting corporate IP while engaging in social business.

What we do know is our ego enjoys recognition. I believe most consultant's egos are especially proud to be recognized, just not in front of an audience. I too have lived the life of a consultant and a manager of consulting teams, so I speak from direct experience. Standing in front of a crowd is not our norm; providing wisdom in smaller controlled groups is comforting.

We know that consultants live a business life far from the "mother ship" behind customer's firewalls and on the road in hotel rooms many days and too many nights. Social business is a means to connect, contribute, and communicate. Internal communities are a safe haven for sharing and collaborating without the fear of the IP police. Social platforms that deliver external blogs, customer-facing communities are the new frontiers.

The transformation that social business promises will not occur overnight within professional service organizations. It is occurring one consultant at a time, moving toward a tipping point that will accelerate when management is willing to support the disruption to the existing business model.

How?

We have learned to approach social business within PS from these primary views:

- Internal to peers
- Internal to internal stakeholders
- External to engaged customer communities
- Thought leadership to the market place

The ease of social business engagement flows from easiest to more difficult. ("A" is easiest, but not easy.) Thought leadership (via "D") enables the services organization to build its social brand, amplifying vision, demonstrating value, and communicating a uniquely disciplined approach to meeting customer needs. Only those consultants who clearly understand the personal brand value of thought leadership volunteer to contribute. The few, the proud is better than the "we are not allowed to tell our story."

Our primary social media tools of choice include Chatter, Jive, wikis, website blogs, LinkedIn, LinkedIn groups, Twitter, and the legacy of e-mail threads. Facebook and Google+ have seen some traction but nothing of business significance. Providing enablement, best practices, and the right social and management pressures to expand the level of engagement and sharing across these tool sets requires constant pressure, not meant for those who expect instant gratification.

Content is the constant mantra that we repeat as social marketers. Consultants are seldom excited to sit down and write. They are trained to deliver technical solutions or they are busy in front of a white board architecting a solution. They have a methodology to follow and follow it with discipline. They have many ideas, but little time and energy to deliver consumable, market-friendly content. We depend on the marketing team's expertise and the resources of our Centers of Excellence to start the ball rolling so that creative writers can finish the task.

Short, small messages such as those in Chatter and Twitter are consultant-friendly. We encourage and are grateful for the small things. We seek opportunity for more, but we set expectations realistically.

Internal—Inside In

Although e-mail remains the safe default for communication, we are witnessing increased participation with the internal use of Chatter and our Services wikis. Chatter is often used by our sales and project teams to share stories about wins, success, and the impact we have had on customers realizing planned value. Our wikis are used to share best practices and lessons learned. Contributions to the wiki are peer measured, reinforcing the value of engaging by leveraging various gaming models. Providing internal social platforms to accelerate response to customer requests for statements of work or best practices is increasingly becoming a normalized behavior model. It is important to note that customer-specific data needs to be cleansed prior to posting to fully honor confidential content, even when it is for internal purposes only.

Social business is a primary driver in speeding access to internal information, knowledge, and best practices. The value dramatically increases as more and more resources actively participate in consumption and contribution. The best vehicle to drive a consultant's social business behavior is recognition.

External—Inside Out

A consulting group is in the business of sharing knowledge and expertise to empower customers. Social business platforms provide the potential for consultants to build their personal brand while increasing the reach of the group. The treasure at the end of this rainbow might be filled with perceived value, but inertia (and billable time) tends to filter the engagement level.

Our roadmap to external social business follows these primary paths (in priority order):

- BMC communities (driven by Jive)
- Blogs, podcasts, and whitepapers
- LinkedIn and LinkedIn groups
- Twitter
- YouTube (for Education Services content)

Most of the customer interaction occurs within the communities, so our strategy is to make it the hub for external interaction. We know that customers who are active in the community are typically seeking expertise that consultants can share. We also know that if we proactively engage select consultants to develop content for blogs or whitepapers, it will be consumed.

The challenge is the inertia factor. The ideal social business model should enable "natural" flow of social interaction. As a parent, you might long for the day that your children ask for veggies rather than being force fed. As service marketers, we long for the day consultants line up to share and feed the social stream. In the meantime, the best advice is to find the low-hanging fruit (willing contributors) and take full advantage. Also key in moving the masses to some illusory social tipping point is management guidance and direction. Actually, an engaged executive who is fully committed to social business is the most powerful accelerator you can find.

Effectively enable willing managers to experience the direct benefits of social business. Train them in the use of Twitter. Tweet to them with relevant content. Drive their followers. Build their LinkedIn profiles and ghost write their "thought leadership" content. Do whatever it takes, because this is the fastest path to influencing the entire team.

It is important to weave the social business platforms together. A tweet should connect to a LinkedIn profile and be visible in your community. A blog should be visible on your Services web pages, connected to the community and all related downstream social platforms. Thought leadership papers, whitepapers, awards, external presentations, and speaking opportunities are all assets of the social business stream. Produce once and use many times is the vision and opportunity.

Although profiling in our contemporary world has negative context, in the recruiting of social business champions, it is a requirement. Consultants spend hours upon hours in front of customers sharing their expertise and enabling knowledge transfer. When social champions recognize how quickly they can influence the "masses," they suddenly become the much-needed advocate. Profile consultants, architects, and sales resources who take pleasure in standing in front of large crowds. Offer to provide the needed support to make their follower count in LinkedIn or Twitter double or triple, and go to work. Your only condition with them is that they spread the news to their peers.

To succeed, it is an absolute necessity that the company's social media team helps resonate through the channels all thought leadership or related content. If a consultant is speaking at an event, we share the presentation in advance with our social media team and leverage the event's social stream to magnify our message.

Although the financial proof that social business has direct impact on the consulting's pipeline, it does have a clear impact of the retention and attraction of world-class talent. The best consultants want to know that they will receive more than a paycheck. They have sensitive and proud egos that welcome the opportunity to have their expertise recognized by their peers and clients. We suggest you do all you can to fulfill these needs, using social business as the logical vehicle. Don't stop there; make sure that your hiring needs for quality consultants is visible on social platforms where the consultant profile you seek frequents.

External—Outside In

Customers are influenced in their service-buying decisions by peers, websites, analysts, and social platforms. Even if the Services management team is not actively engaged in Twitter or blogging, they need to maintain a LinkedIn profile that reflects the professional vision and capability of the organization. Ideally, they will take the time to connect with key customers and influence their customer list. Don't assume this is happening, because we all tend to get internally focused when we need to maintain a balance that thinks "outside in is watching."

We recommend periodic audits of a manager's and consultants' profiles with suggested profiles fixes. When customers want to buy consulting services, what are the key differentiators? If it is price without the context of expertise, then best of luck. If it is a balance of expertise, experience, references, and price, then those consulting resources that are not visible in social business platforms are already at a disadvantage.

We hear constantly that employers look at potential employees' Facebook and Instagram sites to see the social view on a candidate. Naturally assume your customers are looking at your consultants' profiles. Does the background you claim for your consultants match what they show about themselves?

Social business enables many views of the consulting business that are new and unfolding. Although not every organization dives in with the same commitment, there is no turning back.

Social business has also changed the buying patterns that customers have for education services. We are in a YouTube world in which perception is that snippets of learning, generally at no costs, are sufficient for enabling technology adoption. Although you could easily argue that perception and reality do not match, the fact is that YouTube videos have forever changed the way we quickly absorb visual information. Education services are designing models so that customers who make buying decisions will get enough information to recognize that they need more. Snippets of education become perceptions of an "outside in" capability that convinces the customer that there is value to be gained from further investment.

Challenges and Direction

We envision the tipping point for arriving when new generations of consultants who live and breathe social media expect social platforms as an extension of the business model. Management will have to adjust or lose talent and customers.

Today's dominate consulting billing model based on time and materials will change, with the new disruptive model driven by open social platforms where the exchange of information, expertise, best practices, and training enablement is expected. The emerging model will be value-driven and outcome-driven, with ubiquitous access to communities of expertise.

The social web enabled by vendors such as LinkedIn, Twitter, Google, Facebook, YouTube, and Jive will continue to evolve. New players such as Asana and Evernote will enter the space and influence the means by which consultants share knowledge.

Today, consulting groups such as BMC Software's Global Services are exploring new approaches to take advantage of the best features of social platforms. Moving consultants from onsite project engagements to offshore, online, and on-demand models is just around the corner. Management is recognizing the importance of contributing to the thought leadership stream, understanding the value of leading transformation, and accepting that technology can be a vehicle for accelerating change.

Social business in our industry is nothing without the consultants' active engagement in the ways that disrupt historical interaction. Crossing this social business chasm is well underway, but it will take time and constant pressure.

7

The State of Enterprise Social Technical Support

John Ragsdale, VP of Technology & Social Research, TSIA

I first started hearing about social support in 2004, when technology companies were making initial investments in discussion forums, paving the way for full online customer communities. In fact, the first article related to social I published was in August 2005, "Social Networking Redefines Self-Service Options: Incorporating Forums into Online Self-Service," drawing on early community success stories from companies including Novell, Palm, and Canon. Unfortunately, there wasn't a lot of data available in 2005 about how to be successful supporting customers via social channels, and frankly, there is still a dearth of data available on the topic. Most books and articles seem to focus more on the lost opportunity of not participating in social media, with no actual data on what is involved, how to structure a social support program, and how to accurately measure success.

TSIA, or the Technology Services Industry Association, is all about data. In my role as the vice president of technology and social research, I help service leaders from business to business (B2B) or enterprise technology firms select, implement, and get the most value from service technology. To inform my research, I conduct a number of surveys, including annual surveys on service technology adoption and spending, knowledge management tools and processes, and leveraging social media for customer interactions. In addition, I also have an ongoing benchmark survey program to assess the health of online customer communities. This chapter draws on these surveys to provide real industry data around the adoption and pacesetter practices of social support.

As consumers, we see the impact of social media everywhere. Consumer-facing product companies have rapidly adopted new support channels and listening approaches to take advantage of customers active in Facebook, Twitter, and online communities. But what about enterprise technology firms? There is so much buzz around consumers and social media, but how much of the consumer use cases are applicable to enterprise hardware and software companies? Having been researching social support for a decade now, it is clear that supporting enterprise customers via social channels has many similarities to consumer support, but there are differences:

- **Enterprises pay for support.** When companies purchase hardware or software, they pay an additional fee for a maintenance agreement that spells out exactly how they are to receive support. Enterprise customers don't have to ask their friends or rely on Google to get product help; they have access to product experts by specified channels—traditionally phone and e-mail. There are no gray areas about how to access support.

- **Maintenance agreements include service level commitments.** Unlike consumer forums, in which posted questions might go unanswered, enterprise support guarantees a response to every question. These response time commitments are clearly spelled out for phone and e-mail support. For social support, the response times might not be defined publicly, but many technology firms have a policy in place to answer every question within a certain amount of time for customers with an existing maintenance agreement.

- **Enterprise problems are rarely made public.** The most publicized use case for consumer social support originated when customers called the contact center of companies such as Comcast and Jet Blue, found out there was a long wait for a live agent, and decided to "tweet" about their problem instead. The companies saw the tweets and responded directly to the customers, dazzling them with unexpected service and bringing lots of positive press to the brand. But this would rarely happen within enterprise support. System administrators can't take to social media to complain about enterprise technical problems.

If a system admin were to tweet, "Our payroll system crashed and no one can fix it," he or she would likely be fired for airing company issues publicly. Such public discussions of internal technology problems are typically not allowed, because a single tweet could impact a company's stock price and raise concerns for investors.

Due to these differences, adoption of social support has been slower in the enterprise world than in the consumer world, but the majority of enterprise technology firms have invested in online communities, and nearly one-half have invested in supporting customers via social media channels such as Facebook, Twitter, and LinkedIn. Let's begin with a look at adoption levels and emerging pacesetter practices for social media channels, and then move on to the more mature area of online customer communities.

Supporting Customers via Social Media Channels

TSIA began surveying companies about their use of social media to support customers in 2010, with an annual survey drilling into policies and processes for social interactions. The data in this section comes from the 2014 TSIA Social Media for Support Survey, with responses from more than 300 technology firms, and covers the most frequently asked questions related to social media support received by TSIA.

As shown in Figure 7.1, 46 percent of technology firms are now supporting customers via one or more social channels. An additional 14 percent of respondents said they planned to initiate social support in 2014.

One of the biggest surprises in the survey responses came from asking companies how their social media support program began. As shown in Figure 7.2, a surprising number, 24 percent, said the program started because social-savvy employees saw customer posts related to product issues and decided on their own to reach out to the customer to solve the problem. This might be the first time in the history of customer support that a new interaction channel was initiated without input or permission from management. Although I'm happy that these employees took the initiative to help struggling customers, it should be noted that if not handled correctly, social media support can wreak havoc for a brand. If you do not currently offer social media support, it might be worthwhile outlining the reasons why for your employees, and encourage them to come to you first before responding to any customer via a new channel.

Does your technical support organization deliver support via social media channels?

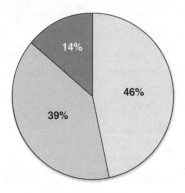

☐ Yes, we currently support customers using 1 or more social media channels.
☐ No, we do not currently support customers via social media.
■ We plan to initiate social media support in the next 12 months.

Figure 7-1 Adoption of social media support (Source: TSIA 2014 Social Media in Support Survey)

How did your social media support program begin?

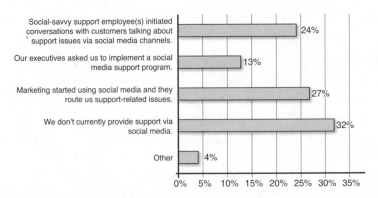

Figure 7.2 How did your social media support program begin? (Source: TSIA 2014 Social Media in Support Survey)

Note that only 13 percent of respondents seem to have proactively started the program. In addition to the 24 percent of companies whose social media support was initiated by employees, another 27 percent started receiving social media support issues routed to them from marketing—probably a big surprise for many support managers. Unlike e-mail and chat support, which typically follow a formal rollout schedule including employee training and customer invitations, many companies find themselves suddenly monitoring Twitter and Facebook threads for product mentions, without much planning or forethought.

How do companies decide which social media channels to invest in? Based on conversations with support managers, many companies look to the social channels in which their marketing organizations have already established a beachhead, usually Facebook, Twitter, and LinkedIn. YouTube is also popular, with many tech companies creating dedicated YouTube channels for videos on how to use and troubleshoot products. Figure 7.3 shows which social media channels respondents are currently using.

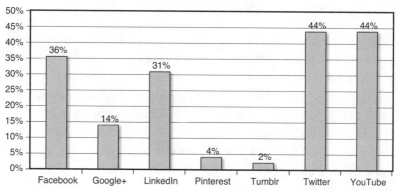

Figure 7.3 Social media channels leveraged to support customers (Source: TSIA 2014 Social Media in Support Survey)

Twitter and YouTube tied for top-used social media channels, each used by 44 percent of enterprise technology companies to support customers. Facebook came in third with 36 percent; LinkedIn placed fourth with

31 percent. It should be noted that although YouTube is a popular channel for posting how-to videos, few companies actually interact with customers or answer questions via the YouTube channel.

Service-level agreements (SLAs) are standard in B2B support operations, typically providing customers with the maximum response times, and sometimes resolution times, that they can expect for product problems. But what about social media? As new channels are introduced, you must first establish internal SLAs, so employees know that any customer interaction, regardless of channel, must be addressed as quickly as possible. Whether you want to include SLAs for social media channels in external contracts and maintenance agreements—giving customers visibility for response and resolution time guarantees—is another question, and it might be best to avoid spelling out SLAs for social media interactions in maintenance agreements until volumes grow and more customers begin listing social media as preferred channels.

For companies that offer social media support, slightly more than one-third, 37 percent, currently have an internal SLA for how long customer questions asked via social media channels go unanswered before an employee responds. Another 7 percent indicated they planned to introduce internal SLAs in the next year. That leaves 57 percent with no internal SLA.

If you are going to support enterprise customers via multiple channels, you must be sure you are delivering quality support across every channel, including social. For customers who prefer social channels, ignoring their questions indicates you don't care about them or their channel preference. If you offer support for a social media channel, at least track response and resolution times so that you can see how it compares to other channels of support. Employees should never be encouraged to ignore incidents from any channel or consider them less of a priority than phone or e-mail interactions.

When asked what the internal SLA is for social media issues, the average response was 18 hours. Figure 7.4 shows the breakdown of all responses.

Developing SLAs should involve some survey work to determine customer expectations, and although expectations are likely to be vastly different for various customers, the 3 percent of respondents with an

SLA of 48 hours or more are unlikely to dazzle customers with their performance.

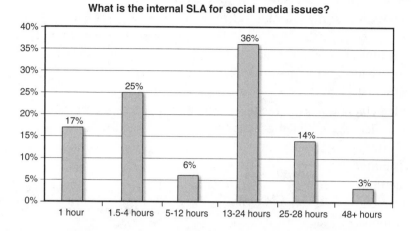

What is the internal SLA for social media issues?

Figure 7.4 What is the internal SLA for social media issues? (Source: TSIA 2014 Social Media in Support Survey)

The largest percent, 36 percent, offer an internal SLA between 13 to 24 hours, which seems a good place to start. B2B customers with existing service contracts know that phone, e-mail, and self-service are available, so hopefully any "hard down" or Priority 1 issues will not be submitted via social media. If this begins to happen, you will have to lower the SLA threshold to avoid missing any critical customer problems.

On the technology side of social interactions, the survey asked about CRM integration. Customer relationship management software, or CRM, is designed to represent the "360-degree view of the customer," and for that view to be complete, every customer touch point should be captured and documented in the account's history. Ideally, this means that a support incident (or case, trouble ticket, work order, and such) should be created for every social media interaction with customers. Having this full history not only gives insight to sales on where the customer is consuming and struggling with products, but it also provides research data for support and product development on frequency of problem occurrence—a key data point to guide bug and enhancement request prioritization or to improve product documentation or training guides.

When asked in the survey if they create incidents for social media interactions, only one-third of respondents said yes. Nearly one-half, 46 percent, said they create incidents only for social media interactions if escalation is required; that is, if the issue can't be resolved on the first interaction. Figure 7.5 shows these results.

Do you create support incidents for social media interactions?

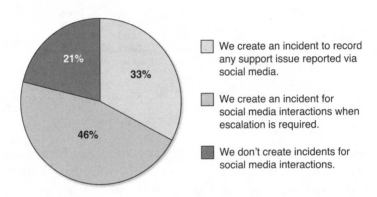

Figure 7.5 Social media tracking in CRM (Source: TSIA 2014 Social Media in Support Survey)

Support organizations should leverage the integration and rule capabilities of existing incident management systems to automatically create new incidents for product-related social interactions with customers, ensuring every interaction is captured in customer history. Companies that have invested in social media monitoring tools can be even more granular in capturing only those posts related to product problems, eliminating noise from the system.

The final set of data from the survey is regarding obstacles. The survey asked, "What are your biggest obstacles in creating/launching/ maintaining a social media support program?" and responses helped highlight areas in which companies tend to struggle the most. Respondents were asked to rate each obstacle from 1 to 13, with 1 indicating the biggest impact and 13 indicating the least impact. Figure 7.6 shows the average scores for each category.

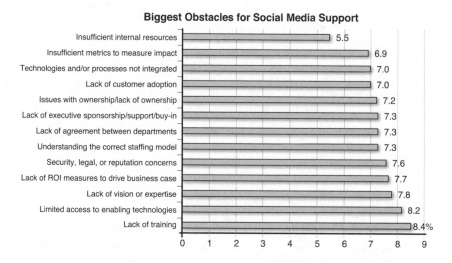

Figure 7.6 Top obstacles for social media support programs (Source: TSIA 2014 Social Media in Support Survey)

Looking at the average of all responses, insufficient internal resources was the biggest obstacle. Insufficient metrics, lack of integration, and lack of customer adoption rounded out the top four obstacles.

Not only are today's customers paying attention to which social media channels their favorite technology providers maintain a presence in, but industry analysts are also starting to monitor and measure social media support performance. In the last year, multiple analyst firms have begun monitoring product-related issues on Twitter, Facebook, and other channels to see how long it takes to get a response from the vendor and what quality of response is received. Companies with no social media support program, poor response times, or other performance issues are scolded in public reports, with company executives called out as social albatrosses or technophobes—not a label anyone wants.

Knowing that the social world is watching, keep the following recommendations in mind for your social media support program:

- **Move the conversation out of the public eye.** Don't try to solve product problems via Twitter or a Facebook thread. Move the conversation to direct messages or e-mail. You don't need the general population weighing in on each diagnostic step.

- **Close the issue out in the original public forum.** Analyst firms monitoring how well you respond to issues assume that if the customer complained via a social media channel, he or she should find out whether the problem was solved via that same channel. After you have resolved the customer's issue via e-mail, direct message, phone, or whatever, be sure to go back to the original social media channel and post some basic information about the resolution such as, "John Q Public's problem is now resolved—a quick reinstall fixed the corrupted file."

- **Survey for satisfaction across all channels, including social media.** If you are going to support customers via social media channels, you must survey them for satisfaction just as you do any assisted support channel. Be sure to capture the interaction channel as part of the survey metadata, so you can easily calculate satisfaction by channel. If social issues are not rated as highly as other channels, consider the amount of training and real-time monitoring you are doing for workers assigned to social channels—likely you need to beef it up.

Benchmarking Customer Communities

In October 2013, TSIA launched its latest benchmarking program: online customer communities. Created with input from member and partner companies, the 47-question survey covers all aspects of communities: size and growth of membership, activity levels, staffing, service levels, return on investment, and technology infrastructure and integration. The program was created to gather data to help answer common inquiries regarding community processes, as well as to establish industry averages so that tech firms could gauge the success of their community implementations. This following section reveals survey highlights for the initial peer group of technology companies with more than $50 million in annual revenue.

As shown in Figure 7.7, customers make up two-thirds, or 66 percent, of community membership, with employees representing 18 percent. Surprisingly, partners represent only 3 percent of total community members, which seems a lost opportunity for a technology firm's implementation and integration partners who likely have a lot of relevant content to share. Companies should consider special outreach programs to partners to increase enrollment and activity of partners in their online community, explaining how useful posts by third parties are a great—and inexpensive—way to boost reputation and visibility for that partner.

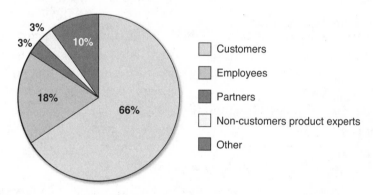

What percentage of your total community members are

- Customers
- Employees
- Partners
- Non-customers product experts
- Other

Figure 7.7 Community member cohorts (Source: TSIA 2014 Customer Community Benchmark)

When asked about the number of unique visitors to the community each month, the average represented 62 percent of community membership—a high number compared to consumer communities, in which many consumers register and might rarely return. This is an excellent proof point that enterprise technology community members are finding value in the community content and are coming back for more on a regular basis.

The survey also asks about total visits to the community each month, including repeat visits. This data indicates that each unique visitor is accessing the community an average of four times each month, showing the "stickiness" of technology communities, with members visiting frequently to read what's new and contribute to open discussions.

The number of page views per session averages 3.4, which means members are reading three to four discussion threads, on average, every time they visit the community. Average session time is a strong 24.6 minutes. For a community to hold the interest of visitors for nearly 30 minutes, on average, again proves members are interested in the content provided and are receiving value from their browsing time.

The downside to these interested browsers comes when looking at how many are active participants. According to the survey data, 87.8 percent of those who access the community are "lurkers"; that is, visitors who spend time in the community but never participate or contribute, such as posting or asking questions. Although this seems a dire statistic, multiple sources, including Wikipedia (http://en.wikipedia.org/wiki/1%25_rule_(Internet_culture)) and Nielsen Research (http://www.nngroup.com/articles/participation-inequality/), say that lurkers represent 90 percent of social media participants. If this is the case, then enterprise technology communities are actually a couple percentage points ahead of the curve. The responses received to this question ranged from 75 percent to 96 percent. Any company with a lurker rate of 75 percent clearly has a highly engaged community.

Strategies to encourage community members to convert from lurker to active participant include the following:

- **Set the tone.** Many community members feel too intimidated to post a question or comment, fearing their post will be dissed by other members. Your moderators need to set a positive tone, including a guideline that there is no such thing as a stupid question. If someone posts an incomplete or simply wrong answer to a question, educate him or her—don't bash him or her. Your support community is a business platform, not Twitter. If members post rude or intimidating comments, call them on it and point them to the rules of conduct.

- **Make it easy to participate.** Just like new users on Facebook and other online social properties, active participation starts with easy things such as clicking "like" or sharing someone else's post before the member works up courage to begin posting directly. Be sure your community is designed to offer easy ways to participate, such as "like" or "thumbs up" buttons, or options to rate articles as useful or not useful. If the only approach to participate is asking a question or adding a comment, your lurker rate will be high.

- **Reward participation.** Reputation models are designed to reward community members who participate more and offer valuable contributions. Make the threshold to move out of new-bie status low, so lurkers are quickly rewarded for participating. Automated e-mails or website recognition, thanking members who contributed for the first time, are also useful in pushing lurkers to take the plunge.

According to the community benchmark data, an average of 2.2 replies or responses is received for each new question or thread posted. Who is providing all these responses? This is a critical question, because one of the primary goals of a community is to encourage peer-to-peer support, meaning customers answer other customer questions with no corporate resources required. In general, the younger the community, the higher the percentage of issues resolved by employees. With more mature communities, customers tend to answer a higher percentage of questions. Figure 7.8 shows the industry averages for who is answering community questions.

Slightly more than one-half, 52 percent, of answers are posted by employees. Customers are resolving 37 percent of issues, which is a significant portion of community questions. In some mature communities, especially those with dedicated customer moderators, 70 to 80 percent or more of answers come from customers.

How many internal resources are required to respond to customer questions? Clearly, if customers aren't receiving answers from other customers, employees need to step in at some point and provide the information. According to the survey data, an average of 5.7 full-time equivalents (FTEs) are dedicated each week to community moderation and management. Though that might seem like a lot of resources, remember these responses are from large firms, and the 5.7 FTEs represents only 2.3 percent of the total support workforce on average.

Of the questions answered by the community, what percentages were resolved by each of these community member types?

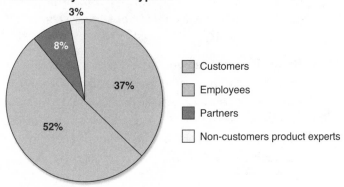

Figure 7.8 Type of community members posting answers to questions (Source: TSIA 2014 Customer Community Benchmark)

The most frequently asked questions regarding online communities are related to service-level agreements. Should we have an SLA in place, and if so, what timeframe should we use? Survey respondents indicated that more than one-half of companies, 56 percent, have an SLA in place for community postings—a bit of improvement over the 37 percent with an SLA for social media interactions. Typically, if a post goes unanswered within a specified period of time, a notification goes to the appropriate person or group to create a response. For companies that have an SLA, the average time period is 21 hours, with responses ranging from 12 to 24 hours.

One of the intents of TSIA's community benchmark survey is to help understand the return on investment (ROI) for communities. To gather this information, the survey asks a number of questions about the percentage of browsers receiving an answer to a question and the percentage of questions answered that actually deflected an assisted support interaction. Based on the responses, here are some data points:

- **Passive problem solving**: Although it is easy to calculate how many questions were posted and solved in the community during a period of time, a harder number to calculate is how many of the people who accessed the community and read discussion threads received an answer to a question. To gather this information, companies used either post-session surveys to ask members whether they received the answer to a question during their browsing session or they calculated how many "useful" clicks content received during a period of time. Using this information, the industry average for the percentage of visitors to the support community who received an answer to a question, either by asking a question and getting a response, or by reading a previous thread and getting the answer to their question, is 24.7 percent.

- **Total support volume**: The concept of total support volume is that customers receive help in a variety of ways, including assisted support (phone calls, chats, and e-mails), unassisted support (web self-service knowledge base), or by asking a question or reading a response in an online community. The survey asked respondents to estimate the percentage of browsers who received an answer to a question, multiplied by total visits to the community, to determine how many total issues were resolved and what percentage of total support volume this represented. The industry average for total support volume represented by answers received via the community is 19.1 percent.

- **Deflected interactions**: Total support volume includes many curiosity or "how do I?" questions that customers look to self-service or the community to answer, about which they would likely never contact you to ask via assisted support. Deflection, then, would be what percentage of all questions answered by visiting the community resulted in deflecting an assisted support interaction. Most companies base this data on the results of post-session surveys; though some based their responses on more informal means, such as focus groups or customer interviews. The industry average for deflected interactions across all questions answered directly, and through passive browsing, is 42 percent.

With fewer than 50 data points for these questions, I am not willing to guarantee that implementing a customer community will ultimately handle nearly 20 percent of total support volume, or that 42 percent of questions resolved in the community directly deflect live agent interactions. But this is the most detailed information available for B2B companies to date, and can be used for a "back of the envelope" approach to calculating potential ROI for a community investment.

However, it should also be noted that the value of a customer community extends beyond the numbers of questions answered, including creating a sense of community among the customers, providing a direct avenue for communicating product information and company updates, crowdsourcing the prioritization of bug fixes and feature enhancements, and so on. Multiple research studies have shown that customers who engage with companies via social media (for example, following a brand on Twitter, liking a brand on Facebook, or joining a branded community) spend more buying products and services than other customers. One example comes from digital marketing advisors Convince & Convert, who found that 53 percent of Americans 12 years of age or older who follow brands in social media are more loyal to those brands (http://www.convinceandconvert.com/social-media-research/53-percent-of-americans-who-follow-brands-in-social-are-more-loyal-to-those-brands/).

The community benchmark survey asks several questions regarding the use of technology and integrating the community into other enterprise assets. One of the key elements required for maximum adoption of an online community is to offer single sign-on, so after customers log onto your website, they are automatically logged on both to your web self-service site as well as the community. This ensures users can easily move from place to place on your website without re-authenticating, and also avoid forcing a separate logon/password for the community, which is a sure deterrent to adoption. Although single sign-on might still be on the wish list for smaller tech firms, for more than $50 million companies, 100 percent of survey respondents offer single sign-on today.

Knowledge management initiatives fared well, with 67 percent of respondents offering a federated or unified search tool across both the self-service knowledge base and the community. This means that if a customer searches the knowledge base, the search results will include related content from the community. And if customers search the community, they will also see relevant articles from the knowledge base. Bridging these two valuable content sources is important, maximizing all content across both sites.

Finally, the survey asked respondents whether they were somehow "harvesting" community content to add to the knowledge base or to leverage in some other way. A total of 43 percent of respondents indicated they were currently practicing some sort of knowledge harvesting. The most common practices follow:

- **Add to knowledge base**: One approach is identifying top-used or highly rated discussion threads in the community and adding those to the knowledge base. If a unified search tool is in place, this isn't absolutely necessary, but it is a good way to leverage useful content in as many ways possible.

- **FAQ lists**: Another approach is to take the list of most visited discussion threads and post those elsewhere on the website. This puts common issues directly in front of customers who haven't accessed the community, hopefully answering their question before they ask it. A link in the FAQ list takes the user directly to the discussion thread.

- **External FAQ lists**: Some respondents reported they have taken the FAQ list and posted it on Facebook or other social media sites to proactively prompt customers needing help with the current list of common problems.

- **Newsletters**: Some respondents said they include links to high-value posts in regular customer newsletters, which not only helps educate customers, but also entices them to access the community.

Though a large number of TSIA's more than 300 corporate members expressed interest in joining the community benchmark program, ultimately less than one-half of them participated. The reason? They were using homegrown communities or customized shareware, and when they went to their system administrators to gather answers for the survey questions, they found that the majority of the required data was simply not tracked and not available.

This is a good example of a technology area in which few internal development teams could re-create the sophisticated best-of-breed platforms specifically designed for customer support communities. If you are faced with a build versus buy decision, consider these advantages to purchasing from a support community specialist:

- **Metrics tracking**: Vendors selling community platforms specifically designed with support in mind track all the metrics included in the community benchmark survey—and often a whole lot more. If your IT or internal development team thinks it can build a community that's "good enough," make sure all the metrics you want to track are included in the requirements list for Phase 1 of the project—that will help educate your developers that you need more than shareware.

- **Integration and extensions**: Best-of-breed community platform providers have integrated their systems with the majority of CRM and knowledge management tools over the years and likely have a packaged integration to plug into the systems you use. In addition, their platforms are designed to support single sign-on with most self-service authentication tools, so no heavy lifting is required to achieve this.

- **Customer success programs**: The support community platform providers have teams dedicated to measuring customer success and helping their customers improve adoption and participation levels for community members. Based on hundreds—or even thousands—of customer accounts, including many high-tech firms, they have the expertise to make you successful, so your community hits the ground running and demonstrates value quickly.

8

The Silent Revolution: How Influencers Are Redefining Social Business Models

Nestor Portillo, Global Social Media Marketing Manager, Cisco

Why Influencers and Why Now?

It is very well known that there are some individuals who are seen by peers, friends, and families as a trusted source for product or service advice, usage, and so on. These individuals are considered "influencers" because they also drive actions and behaviors. Most importantly is the fact that they have an above-average impact on customers' purchase decisions, which is key to succeed in the new social business landscape.

Today, it is common to see how product reviews and user-generated content ranks higher on search engine results than branded content, when people are researching a product or a service, and this is forcing companies to adopt ads and paid searches to have branded content rank better in relevance and search results position.

Reviews and user-generated content are becoming popular among buyers, and they are ranking better because they normally come from very savvy and passionate users who have earned respect and recognition from their peers, communities, and other customers who share the same interests and needs.

To tackle this new trend, companies are also using gamification, ratings, and content curation techniques to harness their passion and interest. This results in an official endorsement of influencers' content and a fast track to build or strengthen their reputation as companies are realizing that recommendations coming from third parties and independent voices are more influential and effective than traditional branded content.

Sites, such as Trip Advisor, Yelp, and Amazon.com, are becoming a mandatory destination for people interested in travel, restaurants, or consumer products. It is interesting to see how influential in the purchase decision process the reviews and content coming from people who buyers do not necessarily know but respect and trust are.

What about traditional influencers, such as industry analysts, subject matter experts, academics, or business authorities? They are now considered as "topic or subject influencers" and they still influence people; however, this new wave of "peer influencers" emerging from social media, blogs, and online communities is rapidly growing and gaining popularity because they are seen as more accessible, independent, and "like me" by customers. Take as an example mom bloggers, who are more influential than any branded content for child-care products, food, and child safety devices.

How Companies Should Look at Influencers

Basic pillars such as trust, proximity, accessibility, and knowledge are still valid when looking at influencers; however, what companies need to do is a comprehensive assessment about the span of influence that an individual has in terms of these basic pillars: accessibility, credibility, and recognition (see Figure 8.1). There are famous people (such as a singer or an actor), authorities (academic and technical), and subject matter experts (savvy customers), and all of them can be considered influencers based on a specific product or market; however, the common denominator to consider is their span of influence because a famous singer with millions of followers might be ineffective when marketing some products or services not related to the music or entertainment industry.

An influencer needs to be recognized as such by customers in order to have a good span of influence; and at the same time, an influencer needs to be accessible and credible to establish trust and influence. Although social business did not introduce a new definition for an influencer, companies need to assess them in terms of the following aspects:

- **Accessibility**: Influencers need to be accessible because this makes them real and "like me." Think about the people you trust the most; they are easy to access or close to you. The same applies for influencers because they are people who spend time in a public online platform (social media, online communities, blogs, and so on), making it easier for other people to gain access to them and their knowledge regardless of geographic boundaries or time zones. In addition, you need to check the frequency of their involvement in discussion questions and answer threads or other types of content (forums posts, blog posts, reviews, rating, and so on) because a higher participation frequency means higher accessibility.

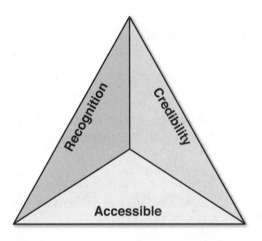

Figure 8.1   Influencer management pillars

- **Credibility**: This is an area in which some companies struggle the most because credibility is earned and not necessarily granted. The process to build credibility starts with relevance and resonance, and this includes sharing the good, the bad, and the ugly of your brand, product, or service in a timely fashion. Remember that for influencers, sharing what they know or think makes them look better, knowledgeable, and authentic so that they will share their unique point of view, and in some scenarios it might collide with yours. Normally, public relations teams (PR) and top management do not like this type of influencer behavior, and you will need to articulate very well the value of the influencer if you want their sponsorship and involvement, because their commitment and support are key for success.

- **Recognition**: We talk here about recognition instead of trust because the word "trust" has too many definitions; however, to build and earn trust, influencers need to be recognized as authorities or as subject matter experts from their peers and communities. Academic or professional credentials are a plus but not a must, whereas leadership and professionalism are a must for recognition. You want to have influencers that enjoy helping others, offer useful insights to their audience that feel fresh to them, and add value to discussions or conversations.

The Road for Influencer Engagement and Management

Like an any other important aspect in social business, influencer management starts with a clear and solid strategy. The first question that you need to ask yourself before you connect with your influencers is, "What business objective am I looking to achieve by engaging and managing influencers?"

There are plenty of business objectives that you can achieve through influencers and the most common are discussed in the following sections (see Figure 8.2).

Figure 8.2   Business objectives

Cost-Savings or Avoidance

Influencer engagement and management has proven itself as a cost-effective and scalable way to reduce support costs by enabling peer-to-peer support models via online communities. In the high-tech industry, it is common to see that a high percentage of the answers posted in technical support forums are coming from the community itself, and influencer accounts for 50 to 55 percent of the total answers provided by the community.

Influencers also play a key role in product feedback because they are active where your customers are; they can listen, translate, and aggregate unstructured customer feedback into actionable insights that your product development teams can add to your products and services. IT companies are providing access to early versions of their products and services with their influencer base, to have influencers performing thorough tests to identify and report back potential problems or functionality issues before the products or services are released to the market.

Early sharing practices translate into high-quality products, low volume of support calls post-launch, and an increase in customer satisfaction.

Content Creation Costs

Another area of contribution is in the content space (see Figure 8.3). Through user-generated content, influencers are filling content gaps or addressing the content long tail that usually companies cannot address because of scale, cost, or even knowledge.

Think about companies such as Cisco Systems Inc that provide networking and connectivity products that land in a myriad of business scenarios. It is impossible for this company to create content that fully resonates with such a diverse audience and business scenarios. Influencers and communities are filling that gap with expertise on how those products increment productivity or competitive advantage.

Finally, you should look closely at your influencer base if you compete in global markets. Influencers are a must in your product launching plans at foreign markets because they can help you to localize campaign messages and content, as well as act as an amplification channel of those because of their innate interest in sharing content that feels fresh and relevant to their audiences.

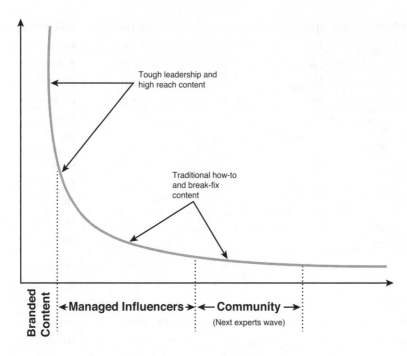

Tough leadership and
high reach content

Traditional how-to
and break-fix
content

Branded
Content
◄Managed Influencers►◄ Community ►
(Next experts wave)

Figure 8.3 Influencers and the content long tail

Multinationals such as Cisco, Microsoft, and SAP normally run campaign messages and content about new products and services with their influencers to refine the significance and impact; and at the same time have them adding relevant and suitable comments that resonates for local market making the content impactful and vibrant.

Brand Recognition/Equity

Today almost all social media and digital marketing campaigns plans include tactics around branding to strengthen brand recognition or build brand equity. Influencers are used to act as amplifiers for these scenarios because they want to see the brand that they advocate for getting advertised and recognized widely to the point that they will share your ads and messages with their networks.

With marketing budgets getting smaller year after year, companies are reorienting their tactics toward content amplification to improve their return on marketing investments (ROMI). It is well known that content is king, but if it cannot be easily discovered and consumed, it is useless. It is imperative for marketers to create ready-to-share content and provide it to their influencers on a regular basis to increase reach and impact by capitalizing on the influencer's reputation, networks, and social relationship assets. Unfortunately, sometimes shortsighted marketers do not understand the value of their influencer's networks and prefer to broadcast messages by themselves in the effort to reach a wider audience, which is an expensive and inefficient practice.

If your success metric is number of impressions, then this approach might help to achieve your desired business objectives; however, in a ROMI's driven world, this is a waste of money because you can reach the audience that cares about your product or service in a cost-efficient mode through your influencers and take advantage of your direct endorsement.

Influencers are also your most accurate, effective, and inexpensive sentiment tracker and analyzers, because they are always hanging around where your customers are and can perform a better sentiment assessment than any popular listening tool these days. (For example, influencers can differentiate sarcasms and ironies that are not easy to catch by the most popular listening tools.) If you have a formal communication channel with them, they will let you know about any situation faster and more accurately than any social media listening tool.

Another advantage is "response time" because influencers will immediately join the discussion and will provide their unique and authoritative point of view as an independent voice, which has better impact than a company's PR response. Although all of this sounds great, there is always a risk that influencers will agree with the negative sentiment and endorse or reinforce it with their reputation. This is a normal trade-off in any influencer management model. Companies need to carefully plan how to deal with it because companies might want to pass their point across without damaging the relationship with their influencers.

Market Share and Revenue

It is well known that social is changing many of the activities associated with each phase of the customer life cycle (from research to recommend) as well as making these shorter. This imposes a need to carefully map the customer journey and understand the value and impact that influencers can have at each touch point to enable and encourage them to participate and help you to move the customer forward into the next step.

Let's assume that a standard customer life cycle looks like Figure 8.4. You can see that influencers play a key role at each stage because they create content that is surfaced in the search results when customers are researching your product or service, review and rate products, blog about products and services, answer break-fix and how-to questions, offer insights and actively participate in discussions, and share with other additional functionality that they discover using the products.

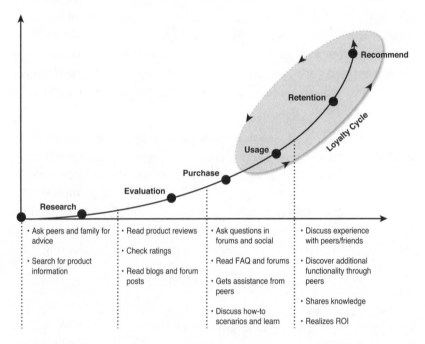

Figure 8.4 Customer life cycle

The influencer impact is present at almost every stage with higher impact on the last stages or phases (usage and retention) where loyalty is built or solidified.

Another contribution for revenue is on improving the product's time to market. Influencers can improve the time to market of products and services through content and evangelization resulting in an additional competitive advantage for companies playing in global markets, or in scenarios in which the product can easily be copied by competitors.

For global markets, your influencers can localize your messages and amplify them through their networks and communities as mentioned before. They create localized content via blogs and online communities that educate customers on new products faster than what a company can do via branded content translation or local office content creation.

As an example, high-tech companies know the benefits of engaging influencers to improve time to market. These companies used to grant access to new products in their early stage (betas) or share prerelease user-generated content in advance to have the influencers learning in-depth product's features and functionality and allow them to create content (for example, books, blog posts, whitepapers, and so on) that will be available at release or launch time. In addition, by sharing early, influencers develop the knowledge and skills required to properly assist customers with their how-to, break-fix, and installation questions, reducing support costs and improving scale.

Although there are plenty of examples of how influencers can contribute to the company's bottom line, there are some experiences in which they might "influence" customers to not upgrade or move into a new version of a product that can erode revenue or market share. An example of this adverse scenario is what Microsoft faced with Microsoft Visual FoxPro (VFP). VFP was a successful database product that reached its lifespan, and Microsoft announced its decision to not continue releasing new versions of it. Instead, it invited VFP customers to adopt a completely new product with richer functionality and scalability. Unfortunately, the announcement was not well received by VFP customers and the community, and VFP influencers started to convince customers to not migrate, making it difficult for Microsoft to move VFP customers into the new product for a considerable period of time.

As mentioned in Wikipedia, "In late March, 2007, a grassroots campaign was started by the Spanish-speaking FoxPro community at MasFoxPro[10] ('MoreFoxPro' in English) to sign a petition to Microsoft to continue updating Visual FoxPro or release it to the community as Open Source" and according to Wikipedia, a few days after, "On April 3, 2007, the movement was noted by the technical press." As a result, Microsoft decided to release Sedna (a project built using the extensibility model of VFP9) to the CodePlex community to satisfy many of the VFP community demands.

Where to Start

There is not a unique way to engage and manage influencers because this is highly influenced by the product type, strategy, business objectives, market size, and maturity. However, there are some commonalities and best practices that companies can adopt to successfully manage their influencers.

After you have identified your business objectives and strategy, the next step is to understand and map your customer journey. You should start mapping the customer journey to identify the key customer touch points and classify the venues or platforms where those touch points are taking place in terms of what you can control, what you can influence, and where you participate, as shown in Figure 8.5.

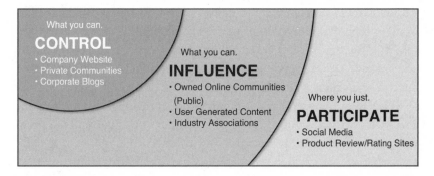

Figure 8.5   Engagement model

With the customer journey map and touch points identified, the following step is to enable a listening process (by direct participation or through social listening tools) at the mapped venues where those touch points are taking place to assess its relevance. It is important to narrow the number of venues to three to five because there are too many social networks in place today where conversations about your service and products are taking place, but their relevance might be low and it might distract resources, times, labor, and focus.

After you define your top list of venues, you can look at some other aspects such as a venue's popularity, customer engagement level (traffic, number of users, and so on), brand or product sentiment, what an outstanding contributor looks like, signal-to-noise ratio, and who are leading the most active conversations. This information can help you rank each venue in terms of impact; understand how relevant the potential influencers identified by you are to both the audience and the product or service; define your influencer criteria; and see their needs and expectations.

The next step is to assess the proximity of each influencer type (see Figure 8.6) and the contribution type or influencer behavior that better aligns with your strategy and business objectives. Although each product and market is unique as is the business model (B2C or B2B), there is an accepted standard definition of proximity that can be used when analyzing your potential influencer base.

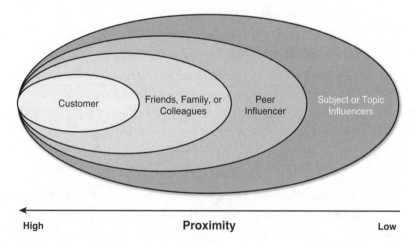

Figure 8.6 Influencer proximity model

Again, Figure 8.6 is just illustrative, and you can use it to visually identify the proximity of each influencer type and its potential impact. Proximity is important because it defines whether additional tasks around influencer discovery and how the value proposition needs to be articulated to ensure your customers can gain access to the influencer.

A common example about the importance of proximity is the subject or topic influencers access. In many cases, they need to be discovered by the customer first (via search or a reference) to start to drive influence. This doesn't happen with peer influencers because customers can proactively reach them through social networks at any time and with higher frequency.

Once all the previous steps are completed and with all the information gathered and analyzed, you are now in a position to properly define a plan about how you can add value to your influencer base in terms of the type of content that they need, frequency, tone, format, and so on, to enable them with the right content and knowledge to advocate on your behalf.

What to Consider When Implementing an Influencer Model

Based on resources available (funding and head count) and the product or market type, you might want to start managing your influencers through small but meaningful engagements, but with the mindset that everything needs to be easy and and cost-efficient to scale. Right after your initial engagement, you set an implicit expectation that you will be there all the time listening and responding.

Any first step on approaching influencers for the first time should begin with an initial meeting or communication to introduce your program or plan and set expectations. In this step, you connect with them and explain who you are and what they can expect from you in terms of engagement and benefits. Your ultimate goal is to establish rapport and set the basis for an ongoing relationship.

Once an ongoing relationship is established, the next step is to enable your influencers with content, products, access to your internal teams, readiness/training material, marketing plans, and so on a regular basis, to increase their knowledge and awareness of your plans and product. Make it easy for them to gain access to you and your content.

With influencers acquiring a stronger knowledge about your brand, products, and service, you can move them into the activation phase. In this phase, influencers can select which participation opportunity they want to engage based on their knowledge, participation preferences, time availability, and so on. In addition, this phase allows you to co-create by deeply involving your influencers in the different stages of your product life cycle and having them contribute to your business objectives (see Figure 8.7).

What are big brands learning from influencer management? The following is a compilation of successful practices implemented by consulting firms and different companies who are successfully managing local and global influencer programs as well as my own personal experience:

- **Make it easy for your customer to gain access to your influencers**. Internet and social networks are removing geographic boundaries, language, and time zone barriers resulting in a significant improvement for influencer proximity and accessibility.

  You might want to allow or sponsor a company online collaborative presence (online community, social media, discussion board, and so on) to make it easy for your customers to gain access to your influencers or advertise on your website the list of online sites where your influencers can be found (for example, third-party forums, social media, blogs, and so on). Remember, influencers feel rewarded when they get exposed to larger audiences because they can help more people, so it is in your best interest to fuel them with customers' questions and discussions by advertising where your customers can connect with them.

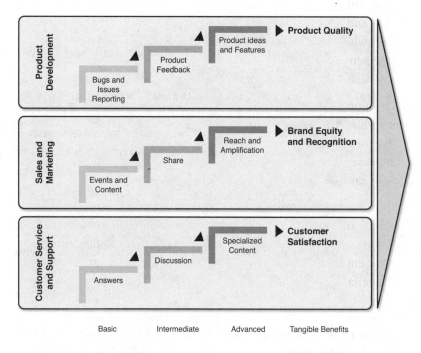

Figure 8.7 Influencer business impact

- **Help them to strengthen their authority**. Savvy customers create and share content about products and services that later are amplified, curated, and rated by a higher number of people through social media. Promote the user-generated content in your site and campaigns because this improves trust and authority of the authors. A good industry practice is to cross-promote influencer and user-generated content between social media and traditional channels such as your website, your online communities, or corporate blogs.

- **Help them to build or solidify their reputation**. Social media and online communities are the preferred destination for people who share common interests to interact and get together. Companies are understanding this fact and wisely are adding game techniques (called "gamification") to their sites and communities to reward contributions and encourage participation, knowledge sharing, revamp authority, and highlight influence by assigning badges and points to them, and featuring outstanding participation at leaderboards.

  Do this frequently and programmatically because these types of rewards are implicit endorsements of influencer leadership and authority conferred by companies.

- **Market for your influencers in the same way you do for your customers**. It is a common mistake to take for granted that your influencers do not need to hear from you as much as your customers do just because they love your brand or product and they do this on their own.

  This is a big mistake. Instead you must consider influencers as a priority audience that needs to be covered first in your regular marketing communication and campaign plans to make sure they amplify your messages and content in full alignment with your efforts. It is good practice to have your influencers refine or curate your marketing messages and content before sending these to customers.

- **Increase the influencer knowledge about your brand or product.** Share detailed information about your brand or product as much and as soon as possible. Keep them up to date and fully aware about your new products, campaigns and plans. If your top executives are concerned with this approach, you might want to ask your influencers to sign a nondisclosure agreement (NDA) to minimize leaks and lessen top management concerns when sharing confidential information. Always remind your top management team that conversations about your brand or products are taking place with or without you, and influencers are your best advocate to tell your story.

- **Market with and through your influencers.** Having an independent third-party voice on the stage (online and offline) talking about your product makes the message more compelling and impactful than your product manager talking about it. Today companies are inviting their influential customers to actively participate at product launches and industry events in a variety of ways, including keynote speakers, ask the experts, round tables, demonstrations, and hand-on labs. Your marketing mix should include an active presence and participation of your influencers at key activities because they will advocate for your product and brand in a way that resonates better with your customers. (Remember the "like me" perception.)

- **Listen to your influencers.** Influencers will tell you the good, the bad, and the ugly about your brand or products; so it is important to have an ongoing and real-time listening mechanism in place to gather their feedback or insights to refine your product, messages, and business models. They will not sugar coat their feedback, so be mindful on how you will respond and keep in mind that they want to see the brand or the product they love to succeed.

- **Track what content is being shared most and create "shareable" content.** With budgets shrinking, the new game plan is co-creation, amplification, and reach rather than the amount of content created. Check what your influencers share the most and align your content creation model with the topics, frequency, channels, and format that better suits their preferences. At the end, what you will get is an amplification machine that will significantly improve your ROMI story.

- **Review your engagement model or program and assess its validity at least once a year.** Social changed and continues changing how customers want to consume content and interact with peers and companies. Keep track of market trends and customers' preferences to evolve your influencer model or program and align it with the changing needs of your clients and markets.

- **Offer a degree of differentiation to keep them engaged.** Conduct satisfaction surveys regularly to sense their level of satisfaction with your engagement model and keep track of competitor practices to make your program different and unique. Keep in mind that your influencers advocate your brand and product on a voluntary basis; a degree of differentiation is needed to keep them engaged and active.

- **Articulate ROI to your influencer base and to your company.** Influencer management is a resource-intensive activity that requires a strong and frequent ROI articulation to ensure stakeholders' commitment and top management sponsorship. Assess influencers' contributions to your business goals and communicate it on a regular basis to not dilute efforts and secure ongoing commitment and funding.

  With the same frequency and discipline that you articulate ROI to your top management, fine-tune that ROI story and share it with your influencers. Although they do not care that much about cost-savings or cost avoidance, you might want to let them know how the company understands and values their contributions. That piece of product feedback that made it into the next version of the product or that technical support answer that has been seen by thousands of customers are normal components of the ROI story that you might want to share with your influencers. They need to feel that you know and appreciate their contributions.

- **Reward them in a meaningful way but *do not* pay them!** The basis of their credibility and the trust that they have earned from others is built from their independence. Look to reward your influencers in a way that makes them feel special, but do not pay them in any way because this will erode their credibility in front of the customers.

  Things like early access to your products, training your top executives and people responsible for product development, featuring them on your website and communications, and including them in your industry events or product launches are meaningful reward tactics that will make them feel special but at the same time will not affect their credibility.

An example in this area is Cisco Systems Inc, which organizes regular briefings with Cisco Champions to discuss a variety of topics including business strategy andproduct road-maps, or Microsoft Corp., which organizes a three-day annual summit for its worldwide influencers at the Redmond, WA, headquarters. During those days, top executives (including the CEO), product development teams, business leaders, and technical support personnel spend time with their influencers discussing product strategy, gathering product feedback, and training them on new products and technologies. This means more for them than any monetary reward.

On the same note, there are some "Don'ts" that you need to be aware of if you want to have a healthy and successful influencer engagement practice.

- **Don't drive too much sense of entitlement.** Social media has forced companies to become more transparent, to actively listen, and to a certain point relinquish control; however, your ultimate goal is to run a business, sell more products, and beat your competitors. As has been described so far, the value of influencer engagement is big; however, you have to avoid influencers' entitlement and remind them that sometimes there are business strategies that might collide with their feedback or point of view, and while it is okay to disagree you are not obligated to do what they say. Influencers need to understand that feedback is an additional piece of information to be considered by companies and not a go-do statement. So it is important to clarify these game rules since the beginning.

- **Don't dictate what they have to do or say.** As previously mentioned, the foundation of influencer credibility is their independence. Influencers work hard to gain the trust of their followers and peers, and they contribute and participate voluntarily. Do not confuse advocacy or affinity with obedience, and do not make the mistake to try to dictate what they need to say or do because it will not work and will hurt the trust established between you and them. You will get a lot of pressure from your PR or legal teams to dictate what they should say or do especially at crisis time; be prepared to manage your internal stakeholders in a smart way and avoid the temptation to dictate.

- **Don't go dark.** Influencers love your brand or your product. They have been around for a while without any engagement expectation, so it is your sole decision to engage with them. However, if you decide to do it, you need to do it consistently and be accessible because these are implicit expectations after you made the initial engagement and are an important part part of the trust model.

- **Don't drive a perception that you don't know who they are.** As part of being accessible, it implies the need to get to know a little bit more about who your influencers are. You do not need to manage all the details about each individual, but some general facts such as where they participate or contribute, top statistics on impact and contributions, geographic coverage, and general background (for example, gender, profession, and so on) are needed to demonstrate to them that you care.

A Final Note on Influencers and Innovation

There is an increasing misunderstanding in the market about the relationship between influencer engagement and innovation. Influencer engagement is the right approach for product quality and incremental improvement efforts because they will provide you with useful insights and voice of the customer about how your product or service can be improved.

If you are looking for the next disruptive idea or radical product innovation, influencers might not help and potentially could be a big and noisy barrier to overcome, because they have passion about your current product or service and how you can make it better but not about what could be a disruptive replacement.

There is a quote attributed to the famous Apple, Inc., founder Steve Jobs that says, "It is really hard to design products by focus groups. A lot of times, people don't know what they want until you show it to them." For disruptive innovation on what will be the next product or service, the best approach is to follow your instincts, go by your own, and do not center too much effort around your influencers.

A big component of innovation is the "surprise" factor, so you want to surprise not only your customers but also your influencers if you want to revolutionize your market.

9

From Modems to iPhones: A Digital Life Journey

Jerome Pineau, Director of Social Strategy Consulting, Lithium

Understanding Social the Hard Way: By Doing It

Do you know what this is (see Figure 9.1)? Neither will anyone in another 10 years at most. But in 1986, this 300-baud modem was my life line and, at times, my bread and butter. Even before my first job, I surfed IRC. I hung out on various special interest bulletin boards (BBS) until the wee hours of the night. Early on, I joined a small, exclusive, poorly understood community of programmers and computer geeks. When Prodigy came out, I signed up immediately. And for years, I lived on AOL, CompuServe, and ICQ instant messenger.

Figure 9.1 The Hayes 300-baud Smartmodem came out in 1981.

Fast forward to 2014. My FIOS fiber-optic connection at home is a million times faster than the Hayes. Connectivity is ubiquitous and airborne—no longer dispensed at the end of a traditional "telephone" handset. And I can access pretty much any organization, person, or brand 24/7 instantly from my iPhone worldwide at will. Basically, every device ever dreamed up by Star Trek's Gene Roddenberry has materialized by now. And everyone—man and machine—is now connected digitally. Exclusivity has turned into commodity. Digital is now a way of life for all humans and machines.

All this happened in a relatively short time span of 30 years. Steve Jobs once talked about looking back at the past and "connecting the dots" of destiny. Being asked to contribute to this book gives me the opportunity to reflect on my own digital journey. I started out as a programmer, a modem jockey chatting with kids and adults during late-night bulletin board system (BBS) sessions. I now function as a social media strategist. It's my job to figure out how large businesses can use and exploit social media to drive internal and external business goals.

In the Beginning, There Was BASIC

I was fortunate to be exposed to BASIC programming early in high school.

I'm quite sure my first lines of code were along the lines of

```
10 PRINT '<expletive> YOU!'

20 GOTO 10
```

This creative and exclusive skill set—not too many kids had seen a TRS-80 back then—stuck with me until college. Especially since my college (Stevens Institute of Technology) was the first in the country to require every freshman to show up with a Digital DEC-350 personal computer.

That machine ran on a subset of the PDP-11 chip and sported a "massive" 10-GB hard drive. My first roommate—nicknamed "goat man" for personal hygiene reasons—also happened to be the quintessential computer geek. Together, we quickly disassembled the machine, and he showed me how to program and hack into it using assembly language. Goat man lived and breathed software.

I was soon messing around with PDP-11 software on a daily basis and writing games for fun. More important, I got a job at the computer center, joined the computer club, and discovered I could roam the digital world as well use a simple yet effective device called a "telephone" attached to a Radio Shack modem.

I quickly realized a modem and a phone line gave me access to an underground world of "connected people"—virtual beings only discernable by the handles (online names) they had picked.

Beyond hacking, searching for information, or playing jokes on connected professors (many of which had no clue what they were doing online), I realized early on that relationships could also be created and maintained online. My girlfriend at the time studied at Columbia in New York City. We would spend hours chatting online. I also reached out to complete strangers either on other mainframes or using IRC in command-line mode.

By the time I left college in 1987, I was well versed in digital connectivity and the power of the online community. On one of my first programming jobs out of school, someone showed me how to connect to and use Internet Relay Chat (IRC). Eventually, I discovered and tried dozens of various BBS systems—most were ephemeral, but you often found the same people skipping back and forth—and understood the power and influence of online communities.

Since then, I've often heard people say, "How can you have real relationships online without ever meeting the person face to face? That's impossible!" But I distinctly remember the first time I realized the contrary having spent most of the night with a group of e-friends (some my age, some more adult) on a bulletin board trying to talk some kid out of suicide. I never looked back on the premise that emotion, love, hate, fear, and all we know in the "real" world is perfectly transmittable across digital networks. Feelings do travel over the wire. Of that I am certain from personal experience.

What a Guy Named "Guy" Taught Me

In 2008, after many years in the trenches of software development, consulting, and management, I needed to tack my career into the winds of sales and marketing. I joined a disruptive business intelligence startup as a presales engineer supporting sales teams and clients in various industries.

My role required a technical background, but more importantly, the ability to explain complex concepts and implementations in simple terms to a whole range of people from deep-diving engineers to CTOs, CEOs, analysts, partners, new hires, and folks in the marketing department.

I figured a blog would be a good way to disseminate information about the company and its offerings. Realizing most BI vendors, influencers, and practitioners were on Twitter, I also created a company account for myself. Then I started discovering and reaching out to key influencers and bloggers.

I monitored forums and blogs and jumped in at times to either learn or comment on various industry issues. I met many peers and experts in the process, greatly enriching my own learning and experience. Shortly thereafter, analysts started reaching out to me asking about the company, its products, and people.

I also believed it was important to reach out to competitors, considering them part of the community "ecosystem" for our company. Many folks are weary of communicating with competitors, and there are good reasons to do so carefully. I always encouraged social practitioners to be as collaborative and helpful with competitors as reasonably possible for several good reasons.

First, it's a small world out there and you never know where you will meet up with your competitors, or when you might also need their help or support—or at least recognition. Second, a competitor one day might be a recruiting target the next. So why antagonize people who might be on your team someday. Third, by engaging in productive talk with competition, you are validating your own brand by positioning it as a contributing peer to the industry. And that in itself is subtle PR. I always made it a point to maintain good relations with competitors and to be a *mensch* (a person of integrity and honor)—advice coined by celebrity evangelist Guy Kawasaki.

Guy was my first and greatest inspiration when first starting out in social. He worked for Steve Jobs evangelizing Apple in its early days, and invented the concept. A prolific author, his book *Reality Check* was eye-opening for me, and I recommend it to anyone evangelizing, building relationships, and marketing product or services in any industry—via social or not.

Community Management 101

The next steps in my social media travels took me along the path of community building—this time in the luxury watch industry. I learned a lot from doing it hands-on—both from successes and mistakes—but interestingly enough, I learned a lot more about community management from the hotel business than from social media. Here's how.

In 2002, tired of the IT consulting rat race, I sold everything I owned in New Jersey, packed a Jeep with the wife and dog, and drove across America to Palm Desert, California, in 5 days straight. My goal was to learn the hotel business inside out in the hope of someday owning my own bed and breakfast.

I showed up for a hotel assistant manager interview one day in Palm Springs wearing my best Tommy Bahamas shirt. And Bruce Abney, a 30-year veteran of the business who ran one of the hottest boutique hotels in town, hired me on the spot. That place was the most sought-after, desirable mid-century modern destination resort in the desert at the time. You can ask Julia Roberts. She loved the corner suite.

Here's what I learned in 2 years of intense swim-or-sink hotel experience that has served me until now building, managing, and nurturing digital communities:

- The devil's in the details.
- It's not about selling beds; it's about selling experience.
- The customer is always right. Worship him or her.
- Besides, it's not a customer; it's a family member.
- It's show business. Tell the story.
- Things can go wrong. Fess up and move on.

- You can't please everyone.

- It's not a job; it's a lifestyle.

I did everything in that job. I plunged toilets, made beds, managed housekeepers, bar tended, handled the front office, gave tours, ran the phones, pitched reservations; handled check-ins, check-outs, spa services, and customer relations; pissed off guests, witnessed guests crying at departure time; handled therapy sessions, groups, PR, press, supplies, contractors, breakfast preparation, concierge services—you name it. If the guests needed it, and it was legal, it got done. No one else was around. And you know what? That's a lot like community management.

Early on, Bruce gave me the bottom-line lecture on the job. He said, "Listen, you're always in the limelight, long periods of boredom will be interrupted by violent crises, and you're in show business now, with all the associated responsibilities. Put on the show, but be genuine. If you fake it, they'll smell you a mile away, so you might as well be yourself. You are always 'on' my friend. Forget 9 to 5. But it's all about the guests. Some are great and some are nuts, but if you ever stop enjoying it or them, you have to quit doing this job. You're married to this place, and you either love people genuinely, or you need to find another career. It's from the heart dude. Everything else is just process and grunt work."

That's a lot like community management.

You can't really teach this stuff in school. And talk about results! The people who came to stay with us weren't regular run-of-the-mill guests. These people were fanatics. They didn't come there just to party and sleep. They came there to hang out with Bruce and the team! Money was never an object. If I told you how much our 20-room hotel cleared in a year, you wouldn't believe me.

Our guests could have stayed anywhere, anytime, at any property in the world. But they chose to spend their most precious time with us. What's more, they couldn't stop talking about us to their friends, families, business associates, fellow actors, singers, musicians, models, you name it. Why? Because it was all about family. Yeah, we took care of them, one at a time, and it was personal. Very personal.

And that's what community is all about.

Social Media for a 400-Year-Old Industry

In 2009, after my product evangelism stint in the business intelligence space and several months spent consulting, I was contacted by Marvin Watches, a Swiss watch company looking for community and social media management help. I'd always liked watches, but not in any passionate way. I knew next to nothing about how they worked, or even less about the industry. So when the owner of the company called to pitch me on the opportunity, I told her she was mistaken, and that she needed someone who had a clue about watches and the luxury world.

"Au contraire," she said, "You're exactly what we need. Someone completely outside the realm who can think independently. Someone not tainted by years in the very specific niche business of high-end watchmaking."

I did some research and quickly realized that horology had no modern digital presence to speak of. In other words, this was a genuine pioneering opportunity. And a major challenge to boot. I was sold. Within 3 months, I'd sold my home in California and moved 6,000 miles away to Neuchatel, Switzerland.

It took me about 2 or 3 months to figure out who was doing what in the industry, and who and where the major players were. At the watch company, we strategized about customer relations, increased digital mindshare, reconnected with influencers and press, ran a social media PR program, and built a global e-commerce site. The brand also invested in traditional PR by hiring a specialized agency.

Six months later, having measured social media-driven exposure, impressions, articles, and buzz around the brand, the owners came to me and exclaimed, "Hey, you weren't joking about this social stuff. It really works! We spent five times as much on regular PR and got virtually no results compared to social." I smiled and nodded.

We rebuilt the website, started a blog, re-established personal relationships with customers, and even tested several VIP programs. All were unheard of initiatives from a reborn 160-year-old watch brand. We went out on the right social networks, grew an audience, got press coverage, and became the talk of the town as the "new times, new codes" Swiss watch brand.

More importantly, we built mindshare, created rabid advocates, built new blogger relationships with top influencers, bootstrapped a new e-commerce site, and got people to talk about us via word of mouth for amazing service, great content—both planned and opportunistic—and a unique way of doing business through both digital and physical means. In the industry, we became the iconoclasts many started emulating.

But it was very hard—and still is—for a four-century-old farmer-based industry to embrace social. The same can be said for luxury brands in general but horology and its traditional disconnect from customers has it particularly hard in this new 24/7 instant-gratification digital economy built on transparency and authenticity.

After a year at the watch company, I had an opportunity to strike out on my own and consult for a major power brand called Hublot. Over there, I worked more or less directly under CEO Jean-Claude Biver (now the head of all watch divisions for LVMH, including Tag Heuer and Zenith).

Mr. Biver is to the luxury watch industry what Steve Jobs was to the technology world. A Grand Master of marketing and communication, Mr. Biver was first to understand—long before anyone in his industry— the digital market shifts at hand and recognize that "the future is online as online is communication."

While at Hublot, I drew up the company's social media strategy roadmap, including social listening and engagement, social channels, editorial strategy, blogs, applications, mobile, and Chinese market penetration. Operationally, this experience was a far cry from my initial one because budgets were virtually unlimited and possibilities endless. I learned more about marketing and communication there than I could possibly have after 4 years of MBA schooling.

Mr. Biver, much like Steve Jobs, has a simple, consistent, fundamental approach to marketing. It is based on clarity, simplicity, and consistency. The premise is that every initiative one undertakes should be "either first, and or unique, and or different." Period. Under Biver, if you could make that case for any social initiative in two paragraphs or less, it would be approved and funded!

In addition, I learned several nuggets of business wisdom there. Biver says about marketing:

"The key is that marketing and branding success is never due to just one element. The key is everything must be aligned. There must be total alignment between the message of your brand, between the product of your brand, between the communication of the brand and your distribution. If any of these are not in synch, you will fail."

Here is what Biver says it takes to succeed:

"First of all you need the best people with expertise and know-how. You need a trustable and credible leader to attract the best people, and then you need to work a lot, questioning your decisions all the time: These are the three ingredients of success."

The questioning part influenced me a lot in my future social career. Because, like many people, I'd always assumed that industry captains decided on a ship's course and never looked back—not so. Most people feel that doubt and self-questioning is a sign of weakness. But, in fact, the contrary is true.

This is very important when working in social media where "social herding" and "expert consensus" can often lead to disastrous results. Lacking decisiveness, courage, or clarity is not good. But self-assurance and blind faith can be fatal in a constantly changing digital context. It is best to constantly re-evaluate one's self against cold hard data, trusted peers, and, more importantly, folks who report to you.

To benefit from this, you need to create an environment of trust, sharing, and transparency in a social team. No one is infallible, no matter where in the command structure. Always run ideas, strategy, and tactics by your closest team members. Seek advice liberally. Listen more than you talk, doubt yourself, and always question established truths. Those were some of the lessons I took along the way on to my next social adventures.

Building Global @SocialService from Scratch

The latter took me to a 3-D software powerhouse called "Autodesk." My original job description there said little about social media. It had more to do with digital content management. But luckily for me, my manager had a vision.

She realized that social could help Autodesk along several critical business goals—like brand perception, internal change management, and operational scaling. Especially as the company was pivoting from licensed to a leased cloud software model. It didn't hurt either that *her* VP boss also ran the entire division and shared the same outlook.

Within a few weeks, we explored the feasibility of a social customer care initiative at Autodesk. Working with existing service and support managers, we quickly built a business case for global social service. We then slowly put the pieces together, culminating in a final strategic proposal to upper management. It was discussed, pitched, approved, enabled, and modestly but surely funded.

In many ways, we were lucky to start building @AutodeskHelp with the most important component of enterprise social—namely, executive sponsorship and support. In addition—just as crucially—we were allowed to hand pick members of the new social service team. We knew early on that we needed to fill community management profiles, more so than traditional customer service representative ones.

Luckily, a couple of ideal candidates had surfaced on our radar early. Not because they had specific social media experience, but because they had "social service DNA." We knew this from interacting with them and observing how they dealt with customers in everyday circumstances— both good and bad. So when the green light came on, we quickly pitched them the opportunity, enlisted their support, and brought them over to the new social team.

One of the most challenging endeavors when building our corporate social is weaving the internal fabric of social collaboration because social teams and associated support staff can be configured in many different ways. There is no magic formula, and every organization is different. So we spent a lot of time building relationships, matrixing resources, and enlisting management support across departments.

We worked closely with marketing, technical support, and product managers to align on social guidelines and best practices. Whenever possible, we also did our best to sync up on metrics.

After tweaking our operational and content publishing tactics, we moved toward strategically marrying owned social (Autodesk communities) with the earned channels we were "occupying" like Twitter, Facebook, Pinterest, and others. It made sense to leverage these channels to boost Autodesk's large existing communities and to amplify community-bred content outbound using those same channels. We called it a "hunter-gatherer approach." I managed all the hunters, and my colleague and good friend Brian Kling (now at Lithium Technologies) handled the gathering pieces on the community side.

Our cooperative efforts with other departments paid off nicely on the content deployment side. We made deals with marketing, PR, and product folks: "You allow us to publish selectively on your high-reach properties, and in return, we handle your service and support traffic"—that was a win-win for all involved, especially customers.

In less than a year, we saw a small but encouraging percentage of "deflections" offloading some pressure from traditional support channels. Attribution is always a hairy problem in validating and computing social ROI, but we proved noticeable success along corporate-aligned metrics like velocity (time to respond and answer questions—known to correlate with satisfaction statistics), deflection (around 2 to 3 percent), NPS, and employee engagement (on our strategic high list).

We clocked 17 minutes or less response time on Twitter (under 60 minutes on Facebook) with a 15 percent resolution rate under that timeframe. This means that every case got resolved, but 15 percent of them got resolved just-in-time (JIT resolution) within the channel, in real time. Compare that to an existing 48-hour average and picture happy customers.

We deflected cases from traditional channels by pro-actively amplifying support content on earned channels and triaging all inbound digital service traffic volume across teams and departments.

On the NPS side, as surveying made little sense to me on streamed channels like Twitter or Facebook, we invented a "gratitude index" based on text analytics and benchmarked ourselves against peers and other industries. We hit 20 percent on that index (only superseded by Frank Eliason's @AskCiti crews at 24 percent), meaning 20 percent of our conversation traffic included words indicating thanks, praise, and gratitude.

Last, but not least, we encouraged, developed, and trained social talent across organizational departments like product teams. We worked hand in hand with marketing, PR, legal, analytics, and education to load balance social effort, coordinate initiatives, and collaborate on and govern outbound messaging and content production.

Social Experience Management in the Big Apple

I moved back to the NYC area in 2013 for—as they say—reasons of the heart. Unable to stay on at Autodesk Service and Support working from the East Coast, I started looking for another challenge.

While evaluating social media management platforms at Autodesk, I had come upon a vendor called "Sprinklr" and learned to appreciate its technology and responsiveness. Sprinklr builds and sells a social experience management platform. It's a scalable technology infrastructure that plugs into the enterprise and helps large global brands engage with customers on numerous social channels, govern and manage content publishing, and monitor social signals.

It also helps spin collaborative fiber across teams, departments, divisions, and locations, helping to break down internal silos and drive the kind of change management a modern, relevant brand needs to survive these days.

Sprinklr was on a hiring spree pending another funding round and looking for experienced folks with hands-on social chops. I figured it would be interesting to experience the vendor side of social media and joined the company in April 2013. Now, there's one really interesting consequence of moving to the vendor side: You get to see how customers—many different ones in various industries—deal with social media on a grand scale. Especially at a company like Sprinklr catering exclusive to large global brands like Wal-Mart, Nike, Microsoft, Dell, Cisco, and about 295 more like those.

Although every brand and industry clearly has distinct challenges trying to become social at scale, you begin to see common patterns and pain points emerge. For instance, everybody seeks to align organizational departments like marketing, sales, PR, service, HR, and legal.

Everyone struggles with collaboration and governance issues (especially in the financial services industry). Most companies use a myriad of tools and platforms to manage social and would prefer consolidation for simplicity and cost reasons. Editorial content strategies and associated metrics elude many companies (and agencies). Last but not least, most brands are still trying to figure out digital campaigning and how to connect social initiative to business goals and measure the success of their outcomes.

Social has progressed in great strides over the past 10 years. I believe we've reached another maturity plateau in 2014. Encouragingly, most of the time, the right questions are being asked. The pain points are well known. Rarely do you hear social validation arguments in large brands anymore. More and more social leaders and executives treat social as part and parcel of their overall strategy and not a one-off effort.

Many leaders understand how social drives internal change management challenges. And most realize their survival and relevancy as a brand hinge on their ability to analyze, define, and execute clear, consistent, and measurable social strategies across all areas of the organization.

More importantly, from my point of view, is the positive impact this shift is having on all of us as customers. Net-net results are significant improvements in overall consumer experience as expectations have risen dramatically in both B2C and B2B segments. The rising tide of social media has finally lifted all market segment boats.

Looking Ahead—Parting Thoughts

A few parting thoughts on where all this might be headed in the next years. SMMS industry consolidation for sure. The term "social" or "social media" will disappear as social will become as common as e-mail is today. Services will overtake tooling as a revenue center as "platforms" become commoditized. I've long suspected that someone will soon come up with open source building blocks for SMMS software.

When everyone is playing with identical technology, implementation, best practice leadership, and digital strategy is where the money shot will be. Selling bits and bytes is a race to the bottom in a cloud-based, collaborative technology context.

Designing and selling repeatable methodologies for implementing internal change management, connecting the right business dots, innovating, and retaining market share is likely a better proposition.

We've sure come a long way from 300-baud modems to the iPhone. And I've been more than lucky to have had an early bird front row seat to one of the most fascinating transformations in human history.

I like to say that "if you find yourself in a comfort zone, you're probably parked illegally" because change is the only constant in this business. Complacency and sluggishness are unforgiving. And in the end, that's what keeps social practitioners like us young and on our toes.

10

Top Social Business Challenges and How to Overcome Them

Lewis Bertolucci, Head of Social Media, Humana

Confessions from a Social Media Practitioner in a Highly Regulated Environment

"A good hockey player plays where the puck is. A great hockey player plays where the puck is going to be." —Wayne Gretzky

The emergence of social media in recent years has made it possible for one person to communicate with hundreds, or even thousands, of other people about brands and the products and services they offer. In light of this recent social media revolution, executives know that it becomes critical to meet consumers where they are, on social. They also realize that we're not only playing where the puck is, but also where it's going to be.

Today's consumers are moving away from traditional forms of advertising and are demanding more control over the way they're consuming media. In addition, they're connecting with brands in fundamentally new ways. We no longer live in a world in which companies closely control their brand's perception. Social media, by its nature, has produced an empowered consumer whose amplified experiences are creating a new paradigm.

The empowered consumer is now a critical factor in influencing the perception of your brand and shaping the views of other people's opinions, attitudes, and purchase behaviors. This groundswell has vastly shifted power to the consumer, who now has increasingly more control over the content and conversations that shape purchase behavior.

As more companies begin to align the consumer at the center of their business, it creates a completely new experience. Social now becomes one of the core channels to develop and establish meaningful relationships throughout the entire consumer journey. Though social media has disrupted the consumer experience, it's not the endgame, but rather one aspect of a larger marketing strategy and a means to engage and meet consumers where they are.

This chapter discusses the challenges that many social practitioners are faced with and how to overcome them. These challenges shouldn't be unique to one group because the journey in social is an evolution, in which we continually test, learn, and optimize our approach and strategies.

Social media is the new, shiny object. No matter what media outlet you follow, TV show you're watching, paper you're reading, or website you're visiting, you'll see social media at the forefront via hashtags, share buttons, or bold headlines. You're not the only one; your C-Suite is seeing the same, in addition to hearing from top consultants and thought leaders around the importance and implications social media has to big business. Your executive team is willing to invest now, to begin creating the appropriate foundation and infrastructure for the future.

Challenge: Championing and Educating Senior Leadership on the Importance of Social: Why Do You Need to Be in the Space and What Is the Strategy for the Organization?

When I first started our social media program 3 years ago, one of the biggest challenges I was faced with was educating our executive team on social media. They're a group of intelligent business professionals, but most weren't active participants in social. Where do I start and how do I explain to them why it's important, what our strategy is, and what that means to the bottom line?

Do you know the goals and vision of your organization?

- Ensure your social strategy ladders back up to your enterprise goals and vision.

- Pick up on key terms used by your C-Suite, whether that's around becoming more consumer-centric, creating a better consumer experience, impacting retention, or gaining a better understanding of the end-customer. Then align your strategy to support these key themes and goals.

How are you cutting across siloed business functions to understand what's important across the business?

- Your social strategy shouldn't exist in a silo. Whether you're developing your strategy for the first time or revisiting your social strategy (as you should, routinely), you need to ensure it's representative of your stakeholders across the business. Do stakeholder interviews to get a rounded view of what's important to each group and surface the key themes. Your internal stakeholders include Corporate Communications, Marketing, Public Affairs, Operations, IT, Customer Care, Consumer Experience, each Business Unit, Legal, Compliance, Privacy, and so on. After you create a strategy with your key stakeholders in mind, it becomes hard to refute.

Have you socialized your strategy with mid- to upper-management (directors and VPs) to gain their feedback?

- When you establish your baseline strategy and framework, begin socializing it with your mid- to upper-management (directors and VPs). Listen and pay close attention to their questions and feedback and use it to refine your strategy. Before you get to your C-Suite, vet it past this audience first to maximize the time you have with your executive team.

Are you talking in terms of likes, followers, and fans or in terms of business objectives?

- When speaking with others in the social media industry, it becomes second nature to talk in social-ese; that is, in terms of the specific terminology unique to each platform (likes, followers, fans, pins, double-taps, hashtags, virality, and so on). When you're speaking to your C-Suite, you must speak in the language it understands. When you start speaking in terms of fans and followers instead of dollars and cents, the conversation quickly turns from social strategy to Social Media 101. Your leadership's time is highly valuable; align your social strategy and conversation around what's important to them.

- Instead of saying fans and followers, talk in terms of the sales funnel. Talk about how social adds value through brand awareness, exposure, influence, engagement, lead generation, conversion, and retention. The metrics you can talk about include (cost per) visits, page-views, impressions, subscribers, incremental sales, impact on NPS, lifetime value, call deflection, and cost per sale. These are all terms your leadership team is used to hearing. Talking in social-ese will lead to confusion, a Social Media 101 course, and detract from what you're trying to accomplish, which is getting C-Suite support, securing budget, and resources to be successful.

- I've found that instead of spouting off numerous stats as to why social is disrupting the way we do business, that starting my presentation with Erik Qualman's #Socialnomics YouTube Video is an effective way to grab their attention and tee up your social strategy (http://youtu.be/zxpa4dNVd3c).

- If you run across an executive (or anyone for that matter) who thinks solely in terms of sales and social as a primary acquisition channel, I've found that the analogy of social being like a cocktail party resonated well. This helps set context around the environment that social commands.

At a cocktail party, it's highly likely that you don't know everyone, in addition to there being many conversations taking place at one time. Before you join the cocktail party, you might learn a bit about those attending (your audience) via research. Let's say you're a life insurance salesman. As you walk into the cocktail party, think about what you would do. You certainly wouldn't just barge in and tell everyone, "Hey, look at me!" and start dominating the conversation, only talking about yourself, while trying to sell them on life insurance, would you? You also wouldn't try to join every conversation either. You would first find and listen in on the various conversations to determine which one is of interest to you. When you find one of interest, you continue to listen, perhaps add a comment, ask a question, or offer useful or relevant information. Over the course of time, others will engage with you mutually, and you might attract others to your conversation. The same applies in the social space; you must listen and participate in a meaningful two-way conversation to develop trust and build that relationship. If your audience members happen to speak about how they're confused about life insurance, you now have an opportunity to help guide them in a meaningful dialogue. At the end of the conversation, you might mention that you're a life insurance salesman and hand them your card in case they have any further questions.

"We don't have a choice on whether we do social media, the choice is how well we do it."

—Erik Qualman

Now that you have buy-in from your C-Suite or business partners, it's time to begin implementing and executing your strategy. As noted previously, social is still the shiny object, and you'll garner even more interest across your business partners as you champion the strategy. I often tell people that the best thing about selling social into the enterprise is that everyone is so excited. However, the worst thing is... that everyone is so excited. Before you know it—they're all knocking down your door for a Facebook page, Twitter handle, Pinterest page, and a community! Whether you're just starting your program or already in full swing, you're likely dealing with one of two things, or both.

- You're order taking—meaning that you're not aligning the incoming requests to business objectives or the enterprise social strategy, but rather, just implementing what's being requested. This is often a result of someone in a leadership position pushing the request through or you're just "too busy."

- You have rogue sites popping up, and you end up playing whack-a-mole.

Challenge: The Excitement Around Social Has Spread Like a Wildfire

You're inundated with requests, in addition to your business partners starting their own properties without guidance—that is, going rogue.

Do you have a champion at the senior leadership level (preferably an executive or VP)?

- If you've gained alignment within your executive team, it's important to also identify an executive sponsor that can help ensure a sense of rigor and governance around the social program. This sponsor should help evangelize social at the leadership level to ensure social media activities are funneling through the "hub" or the central team responsible for social media across the organization.

Are you starting with a tactic, and have you asked yourself the following questions:

- What is the purpose or the problem we're trying to solve?

- What objectives are we trying to achieve, and are they aligned around current or future efforts?

- What key pillars of our business are we trying to uphold or demonstrate in social?

I've found the most success when you create a comprehensive project brief that's intended for your business partners to complete, to help facilitate a productive conversation around their request. Within your project brief, you can include questions like the following:

- Project overview—What is this project and what are the key objectives you want to accomplish?

- What are the key pillars you'd like to uphold or demonstrate in social media?

- Where in the consumer life cycle does this effort fall into or support (awareness, exposure, discovery, engage, purchase, retain, and so on)? What is the top priority and what value does this project bring to the consumer?

- Are you currently doing any social listening? If so, what tools are you using to understand your audience?

- Are there specific needs you're looking for social media to fulfill?

- Who is your target audience (be specific) and where on social does it spend its time?

- Do you have any active social media initiatives?

- How risk averse is your area of the organization? Can you remain authentic at all times?

- How timely can you commit to responding and engaging with your audience on social?

- What are your objectives in social media (awareness, engagement, brand management, thought leadership, lead generations, sales, and so on)?

- Do you have resources to support your social media initiatives (recommend each business unit have at least one FTE)?

- Who is the designated subject matter expert (SME) on your team to serve as a liaison to the group?

- You want to change your current relationship with members and or prospective members by _____.

- What types of content does your team create (that is, photos, blog posts, videos, and so on) and how often do you create and upload this content?

- Is there a demand for content from your business unit?

- What type of content would you like to create?

- Do you currently require legal or compliance or any other approvals before syndicating content?

- Identify project assumptions, issues, risks, constraints, and critical success factors and key performance indicators (KPI) and how you will measure success.

After your business partners have completed the Project Brief, ensure they have an Executive Sponsor (typically at the director or VP level) to sign off on the brief or have them copied on the e-mail they send back to you, stating they are aligned. The last part is critical. When the requestor is faced with explaining the project to their leadership team, they will think through whether the project is a priority or just a "nice to have."

Having your business partners fill out the Project Brief forces them to think through whether it makes sense for them to pursue the project, while helping you gain a better understanding of the project prior to having an in-depth conversation. Lastly, the Project Brief allows you to track incoming requests and mitigate the "order-taking" mentality we often fall victim to.

In most cases, you'll have rogue social properties pop up or a business unit goes against your recommendation to not leverage social for its stated objectives. If this occurs, just ensure you're clearly stating why, document it for future reference, and focus your energy toward what's providing the most value. What you might find is they'll learn through their experience that social requires a significant amount of time, effort, resources, and budget to sustain and meet business objectives.

By asking the right questions upfront, you can help educate your business partners while also providing a sense of rigor and governance around your social media program to ensure consistency and that it aligns with your enterprise strategy and framework.

"No man is an island."

—John Donne

As your social media program gains momentum within your organization, you'll soon feel a sense of being utterly overwhelmed. You're likely still spending at least one-half your time meeting with business units and educating stakeholders, while your other one-half is spent consulting, moderating, curating, managing, measuring, leading, and optimizing your social efforts. There's so much more to accomplish, yet not enough resources and hours in the day to get it all done.

Remember when I said the best thing about selling social into the enterprise is that everyone is so excited; however, the worst thing is... that everyone is so excited?

Challenge: You've Perhaps Bitten Off More Than You Can Chew

Begin to realize that there's so much more to accomplish beyond social marketing. You might not have the budget or resources, and you feel that social needs to be more evolved and integrated across your business.

Do you have a short-term and long-term (three-year) plan and roadmap?

- You should have a good idea of where you want to the drive the social program in the near and long term. You've established the foundation and now it's time to evolve the program and become more integrated with the enterprise, but you can't do it alone—you'll need help.

- Build your organizational plan.

  - Remember the Project Brief we spoke about previously? Leverage the Project Briefs and determine the following: How much volume via the intake process did you receive, what are the key themes within the business unit requests, can you handle all the incoming requests, and do these requests require more people to effectively implement and execute upon? As you begin to ask yourself these questions, you'll find that you don't have enough resources to not only support your core enterprise properties, but also your business units. Use this as justification as to why you need additional budget or people.

  - What is your plan for the coming year? Whiteboard everything that comes to mind, and then begin prioritizing.

  - Social is evolving from an art form to a numbers game, and you're going to have to pay to play. Across your social properties, what budget is needed to reach your qualified audience?

  - Do you need to invest in technology solutions to create operational efficiencies or to fill a gap? For instance, do you need a Social Media Management System (SMMS) to automate workflows, reporting, and publication across your social properties? Do you need a Social Intelligence platform that enables you to more effectively listen to the social space to make insightful and actionable recommendations? Do you need an Enterprise

Social Network (ESN) solution to facilitate your journey to becoming a social business?

- Talk to your business units. What budget is needed to support them in social to meet their business goals and objectives?

- Is enterprise training and certification in social to create ambassadors for our brand a priority? If so, what's needed to make that happen?

- Is there a need to develop an external community (if so, an external community platform is needed) or an enterprise blog? What's the platform cost and effort to implement and maintain it ongoing (content creation, moderation, marketing, and so on)?

- Are there gaps in expertise where you'll want to bring in a social media or consulting agency?

- Do you need to integrate with IT, customer service, or other teams? If so, what amount of effort and budget will it take?

- What's needed to ensure you're part of the integrated marketing plans and not siloed in your social efforts?

- How do you become more integrated with your customer service department to ensure you're meeting consumers where they're at and creating an exceptional consumer experience?

As you answer these questions and prioritize, begin thinking about the budget and resources needed to execute on your roadmap; whether that be an agency augmentation model or staffing full-time employees. Try not to limit yourself in how you're going to accomplish your vision. If you've done a good job to date, your leadership team is likely willing to help make social a success. When you have a dollar amount and the people needed, you'll need to tell a compelling story of how going from "A" to "B" (B, being your roadmap) can move the organization forward. Be ready to articulate what's below the line (or lost) if you don't get the budget and resources requested. Let's say you're asking for a total of $100 and two additional people, but your leadership team can give you only $50 and one person; you'll need to reprioritize and set expectations around what can be delivered based on what you receive.

Setting expectations is critical to ensuring your success and to protect you from any backlash, should anyone feel you're maturing the program quick enough.

Also consider that you might not always need "new" resources or a budget to execute your plan. Social isn't an island; you should be intersecting with and integrating across your business. If you've showcased the value that social can bring, or in some instances, the lost opportunity, you might just get your business units to help provide the resources and budget. Lastly, though your team might be the "hub," you should enable your business units to effectively deploy social. Social by nature is not confined, so make certain you're not centralizing efforts if not necessary.

"If you're not measuring it, you're not marketing."

—Unknown

If we're not measuring it, we can't control it, we can't get better, and we'll never know what success looks like. It's time social media practitioners stop dancing around the value that social brings to the table and begin embracing the age-old question, "What's the ROI of social media?"

Challenge: Comparatively Speaking, Social Media Is Still in Its Infancy for Channel Maturity

Unlike traditional media, like Direct Response (DR) and web banners, where there's a clear measure of success, like impressions, clicks, or acquisition, social adds the complexity of human interaction. Social media is heavily relationship-based and has many touch points where the consumer can engage with your brand, thereby creating many different metrics. It's estimated that there are more than 600 different engagement metrics in social. The challenge then becomes how do you simplify the hundreds of social metrics into something that's meaningful and makes sense.

Have you ever tried to explain what you do professionally to your parents or grandparents? It's tough, isn't it? The same applies to social;

it's difficult to explain, but it's our job to simplify it so that it makes sense.

"If you can't explain it to a six year old, you don't understand it yourself."

—Albert Einstein

As noted previously, are you speaking in terms of Likes, Followers, and Fans or in the language of your C-Suite?

- Aligning your objectives to the sales funnel is the easiest way to simplify social for your C-Suite. It's true that the sales funnel is no longer linear; the customer life cycle is quite complex with many touch points across numerous platforms. Given that there's no single solution across the complex customer journey, we must understand and measure the role that social plays in getting prospects into the path to becoming customers.

- As social media practitioners, we must stop surfacing new metrics to measure, like, return on conversation, or return on engagement; it will only confuse and become ignored. Think in terms of the sales funnel (see Figure 10.1).

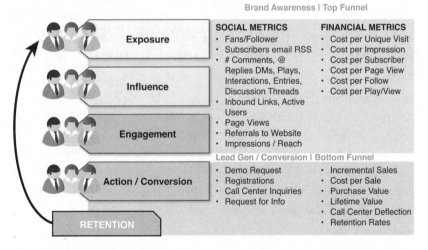

Figure 10.1 Social and financial metrics examples in relation to the sales funnel

- At the top of the funnel, you have Exposure. How many impressions are we receiving or what's our overall reach. Exposure is a direct result of either paid amplification or the qualified footprint (fan or followers) you've acquired across your social properties.

- Next is Influence. Influencers are often associated with media outlets, friends, family members, bloggers, public figures, or customers who have built a trusted following. Influencers play a key role in amplification of your content, in addition to providing a higher conversation rate because it's coming from a trusted source and not directly from your brand.

- "92% of consumers trust recommendations from friends and family more than any other form of advertising and just 10% trust brands today." (http://www.lithium.com/pdfs/infographic/lithium_nine_big_reasons_for_serious_WOMM.pdf)

- Engagement follows suit and is summed up by every action a consumer takes to engage with your brand and includes clicking through to your website, commenting, retweeting, or sharing your content. The difference between Exposure and Engagement is that with Exposure, end consumers might have just seen your content; with Engagement, they took an action to engage with your brand.

- At the bottom of the funnel, you have Lead Generation and Conversion. After they've progressed through the funnel, from seeing your content, then engaging, they might then opt to give their e-mail in exchange for ongoing content (like an e-mail newsletter, an e-book, or whitepaper). This is considered a soft lead. A hard lead is when a prospect requests additional information for your product or service offering. This is considered a qualified lead because they're taking an action to learn more about your offering, as opposed to an exchange for something free or a piece of content.

- Finally, there's Retention. We often forget that retaining a current customer is often far less expensive than attracting new ones. In addition, you might find that prospects who convert or engage via social tend to have a higher life-time value and remain customers much longer. Therefore, it becomes critical that you're isolating this group and measuring items such as retention rates, life-time value, NPS, cross-sell, and overall spend.

- After you begin tracking and attributing the engaged user to social, the next step is to benchmark the customer journey through social to other marketing channels. If you don't have benchmarks in place today, that's okay. Use this exercise as a means to benchmark and optimize your activities moving forward. How did social compare? You might determine that social is the most effective channel within your integrated marketing plan. If so, that's awesome! On the flipside, you might find out that social was the least successful channel in fulfilling the business objectives but don't be discouraged—understanding what works and doesn't work is essential to optimizing your social efforts in the future.

If you're still feeling intimidated about picking the right social and financial metrics, here's a simple matrix that can help you get started. Figure 10.2 isn't inclusive of everything, but should definitely help get you started and determine what makes most sense for your campaign.

	EXPOSURE	ENGAGEMENT	LEADS / CONVERSION	ADVOCACY / RETENTION
SOFT / SOCIAL METRICS	• Search Rankings • Social Shares (Web) • Referrals to Site • Unique Visitors • Reach • Impressions	• # Fans / Followers • # Subscribers (email, RSS) • # Comments, Interactions, @Reply, DMs, Plays, Bookmarks • #Discussion Threads • Inbound Links, Trackbacks, Pingbacks, Entries • # Active Users • Poll Votes • Page/Video Views • Return Visits • Time on Site • # UGC Uploads	• Referral Network • Call Inquiries • Brochure Requests • Coupons Downloaded • Hand-raiser Registrations	• # Bookmarks • # Status Updates Shares by Member • # Tweets / RTs • # Inbound Links • Influence Ranking • Media Coverage + Blogs • Video Installs • Spin-Offs (Videos)
FINANCIAL	• Cost per Unique Visitor • Cost per Impression	• Cost per Subscriber • Cost per Page View • Cost per Fan/Follower • Cost per Play (Video)	• Incremental Sales • Cost per Sale • Frequency of Purchase • Average Purchase Value • Call Center Deflection	• Lifetime Value • Cross-Sell Value • Revenue • NPS Score • Retention Rates • Cost of Service

Figure 10.2 Matrix of social and financial metrics, relative to the conversion funnel

- Taking a look at Exposure, you can measure:

  - Impressions—say you pushed a Facebook Status update and promoted it to your key geographies and target audience (27- to 35-year-old males interested in the outdoors that like hiking, fishing, or are fans of Cabela's)—how many times did your message show in newsfeeds: impressions or reach?

  - Reach is typically lower because it's the number of unique persons who have received impressions from your page post.

  - Financially, you can measure that Cost per Impression by dividing the total number of impressions the ad had by 1,000. For example, if your ad had 10,000 impressions, you would divide 10,000 by 1,000 to get 10. Next, divide the total cost of running the ad by 10 to calculate the Cost per Impression (CPM). So, if the cost of the ad were $160, you would divide $160 by 10 to find the CPM equals $16.

  - The key is to compare how your results stack up to other channels. Is your CPM lower than traditional display ads or other placements? Given Facebook's targeting capabilities, perhaps your CPM comes in higher, but at the same time, you're more confident that your message is reaching a qualified audience—as opposed to casting a wide net. This approach isn't to showcase that social trumps other channels—but rather, how it plays a role in the integrated marketing plan. Social works best in tandem with other channels and shouldn't be thought of as a replacement.

- Along the same lines, if your Facebook post had a CTA on it, like tell us your story or you point them to your Blog post titled "5 Tips to Create a Memorable Family Camping Trip," you can measure the engagement via:

  - Comments on your post (which also amplifies overall Reach or Impressions)

  - Visits to your blog post, blog comments, story submissions, trackbacks, or even time on site

- On your blog, you have a clear CTA for visitors to "SUB-SCRIBE." Now, they've opted in for future communications, you have a soft lead. Also, as part of your blog post, you have direct links to your products like a family-friendly tent for four, and you're offering a special discount of 20 percent off. Your customer clicks through, adds it to his cart, and makes the purchase. CONGRATS! You just converted a customer from social media! But not just that, you added Share buttons to his purchase and he decides to share it with his network, Hashtag BOOM—you have an ADVOCATE!

As we talked about previously, there are many touch points for customers in their path to purchase, so attribution to social can get tricky. Attribution is assigning credit for a conversation. The most common type of attribution is called "last-click attribution," which means that all the value associated with the conversation is assigned to the last click; this is common with Direct Response marketing. Technology has now enabled us to better track the individual marketing activities that lead to a conversation. This is important to note because your potential customer will be interacting with your brand far before conversion occurs.

Think of attribution like an assist in basketball. One player ultimately scores the goal, but along the way other team members help to score the goal. As a marketer, you'll want to understand not only who scored the goal, but also those that assisted along the way, as a team, to enable the goal. Similarly, within digital marketing, each channel plays a role in the path to conversion. That said, perhaps you'll want to measure first-click attribution, which assigns all the value to the channel that initiated the conversation or linear attribution, where each channel is assigned a value based on its role to conversion. Ultimately, attribution is all about understanding each channel's role in the customer's journey and to help make better marketing decisions on budget allocation.

To help visualize this, say your organization deployed an integrated digital marketing campaign that included search, paid search, e-mail, direct response marketing, and social. You then track the path of consumers across the various marketing channels in their path to purchase.

The best way to measure each channel's path to purchase is via a technology solution, such as Google Analytics. You can set goals and custom URLs to track their journey from engagement to your website and their behaviors when there. You might not be able to measure everything; it all depends on the website, mobile app, or device you're trying to measure and might require IT integration to implement the tracking solution to capture all the data points.

Afterward, you analyze the results to determine marketing effectiveness, by channel. Based on the traffic sources report (search, display, e-mail, social, and so on), what was the amount spent relative to the number of visits and conversions (purchases) and the revenue generated by each channel? This can help you determine which channels were most effective.

Remember, it's imperative that you're driving users to your home page where you have control over the experience; whereas you don't have control on social platforms such as Facebook and Twitter.

"It's failure that gives you the proper perspective on success."

—Ellen DeGeneres

This chapter covered a wide range of topics, all of which I hope are relevant and useful to where you are in your social media journey. Each journey is unique and not all businesses are alike; so remember, we don't always succeed and failure is nearly inevitable. If you do fail, fail smart, quickly, and learn from it. Keep calm and social on, my friend.

11

Social Support in a B2B Environment: Lessons from Xerox Corporation

Sandy Puglisi, Manager of Customer Tools and Social Media, Xerox

Regina Estes, Former Director of Internet & Remote Services, Xerox

In the Beginning...

Entering the world of social support is challenging regardless of who you are, but understanding and meeting your customers' needs in a B2B environment can add some complexities that require expert advice. Although Xerox had successfully been delivering a wide array of technical solutions to other businesses for more than 100 years, we were virtual newbies in the world of social media. Based on feedback we received during the audits for the J.D. Power and Associates Certified Technology Service & Support Program, we knew we were barely scratching the surface—we needed a strong strategy for social support and an integrated solution to deliver a superior customer support experience.

To understand what we did going forward, you probably need to understand a bit about where we came from. We developed our initial strategy for unassisted support in the year 2000. We called it our Move to the Left strategy. With an over-arching goal of moving the solution as close as possible to customers and providing them with the quickest, most cost-effective solution, the program was kicked off with membership from virtually every operating company and every business organization within Xerox. Everyone brought specific requirements for both assisted and unassisted support service. All requirements were reviewed, evaluated, and when required, tested to reach consensus on global specifications. Our results, measured in the percentage of solutions provided remotely to customers, were reported monthly to the CEO.

As the years moved on, we continued to expand our strategy. Our Move to the Left strategy was no longer just a Xerox Technical Service initiative; it became pervasive throughout Xerox and turned into a core strategy that spanned the product development teams, engineering, and our research groups in Rochester, Palo Alto, and Grenoble.

The strategy helped define our support initiatives. Between 2000 and 2009, we launched a global customer knowledge base, translated content in multiple languages, enabled customer e-mail globally, consolidated supporting infrastructure, and updated the tools used by both our internal support help desks and our field technicians.

It also played a key role in the design and development of the product. For example, if you are designing a product that enables a superior customer support experience, you want to make sure the product can identify problems and direct the customer to the best course of action. If it is something simple, such as changing ink, you want to display the steps on the device interface. By working together, the knowledge base team and the product engineers displayed current knowledge base content right on the device. If there were a more complex issue that required technical service, the machine could automatically place the service call and alert Xerox of the service issue.

A Change Is Needed

Although the work effort of all this was extensive, the remote solve rate had improved gradually year over year but certainly wasn't impressive. Then in early 2009, based on the results of our monthly scorecard, our then CEO, Anne Mulcahy, requested a review of remote services. Her final question was, "What is needed to make a step function improvement in remote services?"

Hmmm—we had to think about that one awhile. We gathered our experts together and, after much conversation, finally decided we needed to restate our objective. For several years, our objective had been to "improve the remote solve rate," and we had "succeeded" every year. We had improved our remote solve rate either 1 or 2 percentage points each year and showed a positive ROI associated with the improvement. But to achieve a step-function improvement, we needed to get a bit more aggressive. We needed a Big Hairy Audacious Goal (or, as we called it "a BHAG" because for any effort to become mainstream, it must first become an acronym). Our new goal: Turn the current remote solve rate around. Instead of solving 60 percent of customer problems onsite and 40 percent remotely, we would flip it and figure out a way to resolve 60 percent of customer issues without going onsite.

So we did what all good business people do. We brainstormed, prioritized, drew affinity diagrams, and projected the solve rate improvement and associated the cost of each initiative. And in the end, we identified multiple initiatives that would improve the remote solve rate. One of those initiatives was offering product support via social media channels.

It Is Never Easy...

Of course, operationalizing a strategy always has its challenges, and implementing a social support strategy in a B2B environment was no exception. Even though the CEO was behind us, we still had to garner other executive commitment. From a Xerox service-perspective, customer service entitlement was a big question. If we weren't collecting a serial number, how could we tell whether customers were entitled to support? The answer, of course, was...we couldn't. But did we care? Well, we kind of did and kind of didn't. Although we feared the loss of control and the ability to track and measure the interactions with our traditional metrics, we could live with it. One of our goals was to divert calls; therefore, sharing knowledge via social media channels allowed us time to focus on more complex customer issues.

To validate that we were going down the right path, we did a quick survey of our customers. We had 258 participants; they came from both large and small companies and had a variety of products and user profiles. We learned the following.

Social Media Use

Our survey results identified our customers were engaged in different social media channels.

- 45 percent read blogs (10 percent read vendor blogs and 9 percent read Xerox blog); 15 percent write blogs.

- 38 percent participate in some type of online community; 19 percent in printing/production.

- 22 percent have a Twitter account.

- 31 percent are LinkedIn members.

- 58 percent are Facebook members.

Interest/Participation

The survey results also identified a significant percentage of customers engage in online self-help.

- 65 percent use knowledge bases.

- 25 percent comment on blog posts.

- 43 percent indicated they would be interested in joining a Xerox User Group to interact with other Xerox customers and provide feedback on new support offerings.

We were pleased with the results. It looked like there was significant awareness and readiness for social programs and a high interest in participation. This gave us a base to move forward and gain the executive commitment we needed.

Another challenge we had to tackle was how we would coexist with marketing. The marketing organization had already launched a Facebook presence, a corporate Twitter account, and some specific product marketing Twitter accounts. We didn't want to confuse the customer, and we didn't want to disrupt any organizational processes either. Through research and benchmarking, we found that one of the main reasons social support efforts fail is because companies don't adequately promote the various support channels and make it easily accessible to the customer. We needed to coexist on Xerox.com with marketing in a sensible manner that made it easy for a customer to find our support social media channels.

It was a simple thing to make the community visible after the customer had entered the Support section of Xerox.com, but we struggled with an integrated presence throughout the website. This continues to be a challenge for us today. Customers should easily access available support channels regardless of where they are on the site.

We were also challenged with implementing social support in a global environment. Our award-winning knowledge base was available globally, and depending on the product, in up to 23 languages. How would we manage non-English requests in a forum or twitter channel?

And, of course, we needed to provide a solid ROI analysis before moving forward. Although it might be simple to create an ROI from a marketing-perspective, it is significantly more challenging from a support-perspective. Marketing ROIs look at increased brand recognition, awareness, and conversion rates. For a social support ROI, we need to focus on cost-savings. We determined our key ROI levers were case deflection, support efficiency, better voice of the customer, and customer satisfaction. To get to a realistic ROI, we broke down the cost of a "solve" at every point in the solution delivery process. We then developed conservative assumptions on potential call deflection through social channels. It wasn't a compelling case, but it was enough to move forward.

Getting Started (and Getting Help!)

At last, work got underway.

We started by offering a customer forum that would allow peer-to-peer conversations. Our customers work in a world in which they are specialized and proud of their product knowledge. The forum would give them an opportunity to share their knowledge, communicate with similar businesses to share best practices, and build content that others visiting the site could use.

Of course, we didn't know where to start, but because marketing seemed to have more history and experience in social media, we looked to it for guidance. We also did some benchmarking with other companies to get a better understanding of the different applications available, staffing requirements, and work processes. When we thought we knew what we wanted, we engaged the leading vendors to determine which one best fit our needs. We selected Lithium Technologies as our vendor of choice and scheduled the kick-off meeting.

The kick-off meeting was one of the best decisions we made on two counts. The social support team was a virtual team; we lived in New York, Texas, California, Oregon, Tennessee, and Georgia. So the formal kick-off meeting brought us all together for a rare face-to-face meeting. And Lithium sent Joe Cothrel, its chief community officer, to help guide us through the process. Joe was awesome! Even though we had done our homework and were well prepared for the meeting, he addressed our challenges and provided his expertise to help us develop a good solution.

For example, we had spent considerable time trying to sort through the 200+ Xerox products and had headed toward a product-based forum structure to match the Xerox offerings. During the workshop, we learned that when you start a new community, the broader the topic, the better. So instead of one forum per product family, we ended up with only a handful of support forum boards based on solution topics (for example, printing, scanning, security, and hardware). This created a few robust boards instead of hundreds of boards with a small number of discussion threads.

Our team developed a good plan, but the road to an actual launch got bumpy at times. We struggled with branding guidelines...and the lack of branding guidelines. We were the first customer community on Xerox. com, so some policies and guidelines just didn't exist. This spawned the creation of a Corporate Social Media Strategy team that brought together representatives from marketing, public relations, advertising, IM, and service. A few external experts were also brought in to work with the team. The creation of the team did not slow our momentum but instead provided a vehicle to communicate our progress and share issues we were working on. More importantly, it provided a cross-functional workgroup to address new social media considerations... like listening. More on that in a bit.

Another obstacle was Single Sign-On, or SSO. To be honest, SSO slowed us down a bit. Xerox offers several applications that enable customers to log in with their credentials to manage their account. To keep a customer from having multiple Xerox.com login IDs, we needed to figure out a way for each of our secure portals to work together. It seemed overwhelming at first but turned out to be a simple solution. We needed to figure out the key information to pass from our Xerox-secured login system to the Lithium solution. The SSO solution enabled our community members to easily navigate from one application to another without having to be revalidated.

A Funny Thing Happened on the Way to the Forum

Well, actually *two* funny things…. Global support turned out to be a non-issue. We knew we couldn't justify multilingual support structures for our social media channels, so we compromised. Because we were launching the social channels on the U.S. portion of Xerox.com, we didn't expect too much non-U.S. activity, so those requests would be handled by the North American support organization. They would provide a "best-effort support experience" and direct the customers to their local support resource, if needed. As it turned out, though, we *did* have non-US activity, and it was a non-U.S. customer that became our first super-user helping customers on a global basis!

Then, after we launched our customer community, we discovered there was an internal need for the same type of support. The service organization had reduced the second-level escalation teams that supported the field, so we built internal, private boards for our technicians and analysts. This enabled them to submit their questions and get answers from headquarters support or from their peers. More important, it allowed the content to be reused. It's been successful; our technicians can resolve their questions 70 percent of the time within 15 minutes or less.

You Can't Create in a Vacuum

If there is one thing for certain in life and in business, things are always changing. Sometimes the changes present opportunities to improve or expand your work. This was one of those times.

Concurrent with our efforts to launch customer user communities, Xerox.com, with support from the Corporate Social Media Strategy team, launched a corporate blog site. Anyone at Xerox that met the writing qualifications stated in the guidelines could write a blog. There was a good fit for service and support, and it was a good opportunity to share knowledge. We focused on the most frequently asked questions at our support centers and on product How-To's and created a new support blog called "At Your Service." We got a lot of support on identifying topics but struggled with finding authors to write the articles. We finally identified an individual who enjoyed writing, was good at it, and actually wanted to blog, so we created a permanent position (support social media program manager) responsible for authoring and managing the blogs.

When It Rains, It Pours; Right?

Social media channels were rapidly expanding. YouTube had caught on, and when we started to look into it, we discovered that many folks were using YouTube as a search engine. We had Xerox queries coming from Google and Bing and now on YouTube. It was a perfect venue for How-To's. Because we already had a lot of videos on hand from our customer training, we thought this could be a quick win. Our corporate direction, however, was to focus on marketing messages within the Xerox Corporate YouTube Channel.

Further investigation led us to discover a large library of Xerox product support videos already available on YouTube being posted by customers and authorized Xerox dealers. We used this discovery to help build our case for a support play list within the Xerox Corporate YouTube Channel. When we had a home on the YouTube play list, we prioritized our content with the most frequently accessed videos from our customer training, many of which contained links back to solutions within the knowledge base. And it worked! Not only did we see an increase in views, but we also started seeing activity coming from YouTube back to our corporate support site on Xerox.com.

And We Still Weren't Done

We had work underway on the user communities, blogging, and videos. But we knew there were conversations taking place without us. We wanted to gain a better understanding of what our customers were saying and how we could use their own words to improve their support experience. So we started listening.

Probably everyone knows what "listening" is in the social support environment, but just in case, it is basically an automated eavesdropping on social media sites—a way to hone in on things you might be interested in knowing. For example, you can use listening tools to "listen" for specific words. We weren't sure what to listen for or how to listen, so we joined forces with the Corporate Social Marketing team. It had already launched PR listening streams. When we started listening, too, we discovered that listening for marketing and listening for support were two very different things. We were focused on general service sentiment so we had to change the key words to pick up on service and support conversations. The marketing team listened for Xerox brand and image, general perceptions of Xerox, and any discussion on our product or our competitor products. We listened for words like "help" and "install" or anything that sounded like a customer in need of help on a problem with a Xerox product.

As we listened, we noticed tweets cropping up with a distinct support flavor. Although we weren't exactly sure what to expect, we figured if our customers were talking to us (or about us!), we should join in the conversation. So we added Twitter to our social support offerings. We created a Twitter handle (@XeroxSupport) and started interacting with our customers. It became obvious that any support dialog had the potential to either boost or deflate Xerox sentiment. By "being there," we could hopefully drive a more positive sentiment.

Customers tweet about all sorts of support issues, from a specific product problem or frustration at not finding the right support resource, to just having a general question. They don't want to call or e-mail, so they tweet. And because we know customers appreciate a response in their chosen support channel, we tweet back.

Then there are some customers (and competitors) who seem to enjoy posting and spreading negative sentiment. When we are listening and responding, we can typically dispel any concerns, get to the root of the problem, and turn the situation around.

Again, we assigned a single individual to monitor and tweet. And much like our blogger, our tweeter had multiple resources to help get the answers our customers needed. Sometimes it was a support question, sometimes it was a complaint, and sometimes it was completely out of our control and we had to engage other organizations. More often than not, we found that customers were using Twitter to express their frustration when we failed to resolve their issue within our traditional support channels. We found this interesting and did some further research. An article from the blog ExactTarget identified that less than 1 percent of customers choose to use Twitter as their first engagement when trying to resolve a problem.[1] So instead of developing robust escalation processes within our support backend systems, we focused on improving sentiment.

We launched a Twitter broadcast campaign aimed at generating positive sentiment by linking to our blogs, KB content, and corporate marketing messages. We saw some improvements and increased our followers but have come to realize that Twitter is not the channel of choice for B2B support issues. It is, however, another channel to promote new product and service offerings, to notify customers of security alerts and software updates, and to share product features that enhance the user experience.

We Learned a Few Things Along the Way

Hindsight is 20-20, and it sure would have been nice to have a little hindsight when we started this journey. We certainly would have focused on some standards related to content creation and optimization for search results. We hadn't been launched too long when we realized

---

1 ExactTarget Twitter X-Factor Report (http://www.exacttarget.com/subscribers-fans-followers/twitter-x-factors.aspx)

Xerox Support search results sometimes got lost in the web clutter. We got a better grip on Search Engine Optimization and developed some operational guidelines to help prepare content for each social channel. For example, on Twitter, we used short URLs, avoided acronyms, and utilized hash tags (#) for our top keywords. For our blog, we used keywords in the titles and headlines, created keyword-rich content (targeting at least 5 percent keyword density), added relevant links, and optimized multimedia objects. For videos, we created strong, but short, video titles and used effective tags and descriptions. And we figured out that we could tie them all together, so regardless of where customers started, they could easily access any support channel we had available.

Other Lessons

We learned several lessons on this journey. A few of the most significant lessons are outlined in the following sections.

In a B2B Environment, You Need a High-Level Corporate Plan

If social media offerings are not properly executed, you can confuse customers by creating too many places for them to go. In a large corporation, it is easy for multiple organizations within a company to take similar paths. At a time when social media was growing in leaps and bounds, it was a topic all over Xerox...not just in support. It was critical that we put a solid governance process in place. Without it, we could have potentially created multiple, community silos with duplicated content on multiple platforms. Our governance process created standards and provided a vehicle for all organizations to learn from one another and leverage areas of expertise.

ROI Is Always a Driver in Business Decisions

In a B2B environment, though, it is difficult to capture true ROI. How do you assign a value to "the customer is there, so we should be there, too"? We did develop an ROI, and it was a positive one, but it was so small, it was hard to justify the work effort. Nonetheless, even though the ROI was not compelling, we felt the value to the customer was. Social media engagement has become a basic customer expectation and is continually growing and changing. You might not have a tangible return on your investment, but the intangible customer interaction is invaluable.

Interpreting What We Heard

By listening and following our customers, we learned some valuable lessons. We found that our B2B customers start looking for answers right on our corporate support site or within our forums. However, when our tools fail to address their question or problem, they start looking for support on third-party forum sites, YouTube, Twitter, and sometimes Facebook. Understanding this helped us to prioritize our work efforts and staff each effort appropriately. We still play in all these social support channels, but we focused the bulk of our work effort toward improving our knowledge base content, creating useful videos, and encouraging activity in our user community.

Understanding the Limits of 140 Characters

In a B2B environment, Twitter is effective in capturing the voice of the customer and his or her concerns, but it is not an effective vehicle to support the customer's specific product issue. For example, we recently received a tweet that stated the following:

> @XeroxSupport I am facing problems with services from Xerox in my country, can you help? #Xerox

Tweets of this nature do not contain enough information to validate the customer's service contract or contain the necessary information to even begin to troubleshoot. Roughly 98% of the tweets we receive do not identify the product model. With the minimal information we receive, the best thing we can do is to engage in further conversation or point them in the right direction to open a support ticket with our technical support. A typical response would look something like this:

> @Company Please DM me your serial number, company name, and contact phone number and I have will someone from your region contact you.

Tying It All Together

To get a 360-degree view of the customer, integrating social support platforms within the organization's CRM is required. Visibility to the multiple channels and discussions that can span across phone, e-mail, forums, or other social media enables a better understanding of the customer's situation and helps to identify best practices to resolve issues.

An effective support delivery process should center on a cohesive, well-connected flow of knowledge. Think of it as a wheel where the spokes are the various support channels available to you and the core knowledge repository is the hub. Regardless of which spoke of the wheel you choose, you still get to the hub for a common resolution. In other words, no matter how a customer chooses to engage us for support, it should be a good experience with consistent results. There is no need to replicate the knowledge captured within the support organization; just determine how to best share that knowledge in all channels. It is equally important to identify and make available valuable customer content that cannot only be shared with customers but also internal users as well.

In our B2B business, we are still driven by phone support requests, but our efforts to move to web and social media are making progress. Our activity level doesn't compare to those in a B2C environment, but we know there are customers out there and we need to be with them, listening and effectively supporting them via their channel of choice.

12

Knowledge Management and the Social Media Revolution

Lynn Llewellyn, Sr. Director of Knowledge Management, ServiceNow

Knowledge Management and the Sharing of Information

I've been in the technical support world for close to 20 years, and over and over I've heard both colleagues and customers lament about how difficult it can be to find the information they need. With the ever-increasing complexity of the products we work with, it is impossible and unrealistic to expect anyone to have all the answers. Having access to the right information at the right time, then, is critical. Relevancy, not volume, is key.

In the past, we peeked over cubicle walls and picked a buddy's brain or we waded through manuals, and although these remain valuable resources, it's not enough. More to the point, it's not fast enough. We have become accustomed to getting answers at the click of a button and we're vocal when we can't find what we're looking for. After all, by now, isn't everything available on the Web?

If Only That Were True

The reality is that although you can find a lot of information by searching online, and even more information by searching a dedicated knowledge base, so much valuable knowledge is trapped in the heads of subject matter experts. And when you know the answer, it can seem more expedient to tell someone rather than take the time to write it down. In the short term, this might be true. In the long term, we are missing out on the opportunity to share the vast amount of knowledge we have accumulated in the trenches and make it readily available for others to use.

The Social Media Revolution

The bad news is that we aren't always sharing knowledge, even when we have a mechanism like a knowledge base in place. The good news is that a whole new world of knowledge sharing has opened up in the form of social media.

Social media tools such as Twitter, Facebook, blogs, and LinkedIn have transformed the way we communicate, both personally and professionally. They have changed the way we interact with our customers and have provided a direct route from us to them, and them to us. We can ask and answer questions, provide updates, make announcements, and post alerts, and we can do it in a way that reaches our audience in seconds.

Traditional knowledge management programs are formalized and metric-driven. We measure things like how many new knowledge base articles have been written, how many times an article solves an issue, how customers are rating the content, and so on. These metrics let us see the impact of the work we are doing. The communication done through social media can be harder to quantify (more about that later), but that does not mean it is without value. On the contrary: Social media has provided an invaluable channel through which we can engage customers and exchange information and has been a logical and transformative extension to knowledge management.

I recently read in the *Globe* and *Mail* that more than 6 billion hours of video are watched each month on YouTube—almost 1 hour for every person on Earth; Facebook has more than 1.28 billion active monthly users, and 500 million tweets are sent per day.

When I was first introduced to Twitter, it was completely foreign to me. How could I rationalize the need to jump into this new world? At the time, we didn't advertise that we were listening to social media channels and didn't set any expectations that we would respond to tweets, so I was surprised that people were using it as a mechanism to contact a software vendor. Yet, that's exactly what they were doing, in droves. Numbers alone provided the rationalization I needed. In my mind, even if one or two customers a day were asking for help through social channels, that should be enough of a reason to respond. In my opinion, it's like not answering the phone or responding to an e-mail from a customer.

Anyone in a support organization can relate to the increase in case volume that accompanies a feature or product release. I've seen spikes as high as 20 percent during a new release. Historically, we took a reactive approach to this increase. We prepared agents for the influx of calls, increased staff (if this was even an option), and braced for impact. If a problem occurred, recovery was slow because the support center was the only mechanism available to handle the issue. If you were fortunate enough to have a good website or a knowledge base, customers could find out about an issue and its resolution, but the onus was still on the customer to find this information. Social media has allowed us to swiftly, effectively, and, perhaps most important, proactively communicate with customers. Instead of taking weeks or even months for information to disseminate, one tweet has the power to instantly reach millions of people. I recall one case in which we knew that an issue had the potential to impact thousands of users, but rather than dealing with the issue one at a time, we used social media to get the word out with a workaround. The result was that we saw few actual cases into the support organization. Best of all, our customers become responsible for this content and retweet on our behalf, reaching further than we ever could alone.

Social media forums have become a savvy customer's preferred communication channel and companies that fail to take advantage of this are destined to fight negative issues reactively. I am more forgiving if I can get a response to an issue in a timely manner and appreciate the transparency that announcing issues through social media provides. After all, there is nothing more frustrating than waiting on the line to get an issue fixed only to eventually get through to an agent and find out that it's a known issue with no resolution.

Setting Up Your Program for Success

The Internet has spoiled us and has become the de facto place we look for almost everything, both personally and professionally. For example, I no longer use my many cookbooks when looking for a recipe. They seem a little outdated now, and I don't want to waste time looking through indexes or table of contents. Instead, I hop onto Google and browse the endless options, many of which are complete with reviews and comments.

And like I'm willing to search for a new recipe, people in the technology industry are willing to search online and engage in self-help. What they aren't willing to do, however, is spend a lot of time searching. Speed is the problem, and if you're willing to participate, social media is, in many ways, the solution.

That's not to say engaging in social media is without challenges. It isn't your typical Customer Relationship Management system or Enterprise Resource Planning roll out. Lack of understanding is why a lot of companies tend to roll out social media programs as grass roots initiatives, at least initially. And why not: It's straight-forward to set up a Twitter account or Facebook page.

The challenge is integrating the new program and getting it operationalized. Many peers have told me that they are interested in implementing a social media program but that they have been met with hesitation and reluctance. They have found it difficult to get agreement on strategy or support for funding. This resistance has made it difficult to get started and often the program has fizzled out.

I am writing this chapter not to create step-by-step instructions (sadly, there is no one-size-fits-all approach) but rather to share my experiences. In my time implementing social media programs, I have seen what has worked and what has failed. Hopefully, it will give you a bit of insight that you can use to shape your own program.

So Where Do You Start?

First, you need to understand the demand for social media in your organization. Does your business lend itself to social media? If your company does not share a lot of information publicly, then social media might not be for you. However, if your company does already share information, perhaps through a website or a knowledge base, social media is a perfect opportunity to extend your reach.

It works best when information flows freely. For example, if you send out a tweet to your customers but have your website or knowledge base locked down, your customers reach a dead end, which results in a negative experience. You don't necessarily have to share everything, but think about what you do want to share and make sure this information is readily available. Further, social media is a two-way street. You need to be willing to respond when contacted, either by engaging directly with the customer, or indirectly, by making information accessible.

Having a well-defined business case can go a long way if you are just starting to think about social media and how it can work for you. Be prepared for a lot of discussions about the financial viability. For example, you might need additional staff, you might need to purchase software licenses, and so on. Many will be skeptical that it's worth the investment. As I mentioned previously, social media isn't for everyone, and it would be wise to resist the temptation to participate simply because everyone else is doing it.

Identifying the problem you are trying to solve is crucial and knowing what you hope to accomplish will shape how you use social media. For example, if you want to get early access to customer feedback, you can monitor Twitter and Facebook posts. If you want to spread news quickly, you can post your own Tweets and Facebook posts. If you want to provide a more in-depth look at issues, you can run a blog.

Similarly, you want to identify your customers' needs. It can be beneficial to hire a firm to do user studies and get feedback directly from customers about the type of social media they are looking for and what they hope it will do for them. Their requirements are as important, if not more so, than your own. This initial investment could save money in the long run and prevent you from implementing things that customers aren't interested in. If funding is an issue, try free forums such as a blog or Twitter poll to gauge interest.

Your maintenance plan is also something you need to consider in the early stages. Running a social media program is a big commitment. You could potentially have numerous public-facing and internal channels that need constant monitoring, so you need to think about the resources required to run the program. I recommend resisting the temptation to immediately hire the youngest person in the room: She might, in fact, be the best person for the job, but you require expertise as well as enthusiasm, and a seasoned professional might be more suited to the role. Having a social media presence is more than playing around on Twitter and Facebook. It requires the ability to anticipate needs, put out fires, and measure impact.

However, a social media expert (or two) might not be all you need for success. Some people will be excited about the prospect of participating in a social media program, but many others might not see the value and will be reluctant to participate. Because of this, adoption can be a slow and frustrating process. I recommend using those who "get it" as advocates: Their passion can be contagious, and a champion on the call floor can be invaluable. For example, enlist support engineers, either part time or full time, as subject matter experts. We called these folks "knowledge champions." Their role was to review and create content, and respond to questions internally and externally. They also took a lead role in monitoring our collaboration groups. And even as adoption increases, remember that not everyone will participate to the same degree. Some will lurk and simply consume information, whereas others will be active contributors. In time, as lurkers begin to see the value, they might find themselves participating and your program will gain forward momentum.

Even though a social media presence is becoming expected, it might make sense to start with a small pilot project. Think about your business and determine whether there is a logical starting point. Do you have a product release coming up? Is there a crisis that you need to deal with? Do you have a promotion you would like customers to know about? Narrow your focus to one of these events, and then as the program picks up steam, you can broaden your horizons. You might even want to start in listening mode to see what, if anything, customers are saying about you. There are numerous tools that allow you to monitor Twitter for any mention of your company. You might be surprised at how many of your customers are tweeting about you, and this will allow you to find out the good, the bad, and the ugly. They might even ask direct questions, and if you aren't listening, their questions are falling on deaf ears. And if you are a small company that isn't being talked about, maybe you can start the conversation.

I will say this again because it bears repeating: Before going down the social media path, understand what you hope to achieve, how you plan on achieving it, and how you plan on managing your social media profile. The temptation to play with all the cool tools is strong, but document your requirements before thinking about the tools that will help you get there.

Social Media Tools

Simply having an online presence isn't enough, and an understanding of how each of the social media channels works is of paramount importance. My intent in this section is not to provide an exhaustive description of available social media tools so much as provide a high-level overview of some tools and how they might work for you.

Many of the free tools available, such as Twitter, Facebook, and LinkedIn, already provide robust functionality. There are, of course, limitations to these tools that you need to consider. For example, free tools might not have analytics available, and you might not have the ability to customize. There might be fees for upgrades, which is something you need to factor into your budget.

Twitter is a great tool for both engaging customers and monitoring what customers say about you. However, time is of the essence, and I do not recommend using Twitter if you can't commit to responding quickly. Twitter is also a good tool to use for broadcast messages. The 140-character restriction does mean that you are limited in what you can say, but it's perfect to let customers know that a fix is coming or that you are anticipating certain issues. Think of tweets as express push messaging, and take advantage that you can instantly reach your customers.

I remember an instance a few years ago in which we needed to let customers know about an internal infrastructure issue that was impacting our ability to communicate via telephone. We sent out a tweet with the details, and our customers rallied around us as we worked through the problem. By retweeting the message, our customers helped us share this information around the world. It showed us what Twitter was capable of and helped us avert a crisis.

Never forget the speed at which tweets travel and that there is an expectation of a timely response. Setting up a Twitter account and not using it is bad, if not worse, as not having one at all. I'm not saying you can't try new things, but everything you do can be seen and screen-captured, and ensuring that you can support the channel before setting anything up will save you from an embarrassing misstep.

Multimedia can also be a great tool for sharing information. In a previous role, we started a YouTube channel and a video blog to host quick how-to videos. Sometimes, a quick visual was all our customers needed to understand how to implement a resolution, and feedback was overwhelmingly positive. Producing the videos is relatively straightforward—although it's important to strive for quality and consistency so the videos don't seem amateurish—and there are quite a few vendors that sell video capture software. There are, however, a few things to consider. For example, you need to decide whether you are going to host the content on internal systems or whether you are going to use YouTube. Both have their advantages and disadvantages, and you might need to overcome obstacles such as internal limitations or firewalls blocking access to YouTube.

You also need to think about video maintenance and decide how often to update video content. In my experience, the knowledge base articles that are often the impetus for videos are updated fairly regularly, which can cause videos to become out of date. You also need to decide whether you will translate video content into different languages, which can be a huge undertaking in its own right. And of course, you need to decide who will actually create the videos. I suggest working with your marketing department to see whether guidelines for multimedia creation are already in place. Taking advantage of an existing framework saves you from doing work that's already been done, and it ensures that you are operating within an accepted standard. Working with your marketing department will also ensure that what you are creating will both complement and enhance the corporate brand.

Although it's a great way to interact with customers, social media doesn't always have to be external-facing. You can also think about internal communication channels and collaboration tools such as instant messaging, collaboration tools, internal wikis, and internal blogs. But just as with external-facing tools, you have to be prepared to commit to internal tools. You can't expect them to run themselves, especially when they are fledgling and the initial adoption rate is slow.

Instant messenger was my first experience with an internal social tool, and most of you have probably used an IM client at some point. The real-time interaction proved to be a lifesaver on more than one occasion and the ability to create groups allowed for even more collaboration. Best of all, in a global company, instant messaging breaks down geographical barriers and allows colleagues from all over the world to exchange ideas, debate each other, and provide validation. One example comes to mind when we rolled out a new customer-facing portal: Questions coming in internally from our sales organization were fast and furious because we had set up a collaboration group prior to the roll out, and we instantly addressed all the questions that were coming in. Eventually, it became a peer-to-peer group with other sales folks answering questions.

Most support organizations run a 24/7 operation. With calls coming in around the clock and from around the globe, issues can arise at any time. To tackle this, most support organizations should have one or more collaboration tools in place. Tech support engineers in EMEA might discover a problem and start to document it, but as other centers come online, they can join the conversation and provide their input. By the time centers on the other side of the world are open for business, the issue might be identified, documented, and even resolved. And if it's not, they can help get it there. Could you use e-mail for this? I suppose, but e-mail communication does not flow as freely as a collaboration tool, and interested parties will get bogged down in endless e-mail threads.

If you do not have internal collaboration tools in place, it might seem daunting to set this up, especially if the corporate culture is not in itself overly collaborative. Luckily, there are a lot of tools and options to choose from. If there is a lot of resistance to sharing information, you might want to start out small (with, for example, an IM client) and work your way up to more robust tools. There are too many to mention here; it might be worth taking the time to talk to the people that will be using the tool to get their perspective. After all, you require their buy-in for the tool to be successful.

Once You Select Your Social Media Tools, It's Time to Put Them to Work

In the past, I've used events as a trigger for initiating communication through social media. For example, during beta testing of a new product or feature, early adopters are often interested in finding out more. A Twitter account could be a useful forum for having an open discussion. How open you make the discussion depends on your company policy and your comfort level with revealing potential issues. And although it can be scary to make yourself vulnerable, I have seen a negative situation turn into a positive one by the way it has been handled through social media. Never underestimate how much customers appreciate the transparency that social media provides.

Although you can't control customers talking about their experience, you can control your involvement and ultimately help shape that experience. For example, say you pay for a product or service and for one reason or another, you are unhappy. You go online to vent a bit and other customers chime in with their experience. But if the company never responds, you would not only be wasting your time, but also your issue wouldn't get resolved. That negative experience could extend to your impression of the product or service or even the company as a whole. If the company does take the time to respond, it shows that it values you and that it wants to help. The bonus is that it also shows everyone in your social media sphere the same thing. In this way, social media has the capability to reach beyond a single customer.

Ignoring your customers is a surefire way to alienate them, and it is good to remember that the pen, or in this case the computer, is mightier than the sword. Customers are more than eager to share their negative experiences online, which means that the reputation and brand that you worked so hard to build can be tarnished instantly, and in just 140 characters or fewer.

Measuring Impact

Sooner or later, you will be asked to prove the benefits of the program and articulate why it's worth the investment, so you need to think about how you will measure the success of your social media program. Common metrics include number of followers/subscribers, retweets, clicks, and so on, and although these statistics can tell a story in their own right (if nothing else, they tell you how popular you are online), you might need to go a step further and extrapolate what this actually means to your business. For example, because you started engaging in social media, have you noticed a decrease in call volume? For example, if you have promoted a topic, have you seen a decrease in that topic coming into the support organization? On the flipside of that coin, have you noticed an increase in case deflection? Did you increase attendance at an event or have you noticed an increase in revenue? Remember that your social media program was put in place to enhance your business and measuring your impact is necessary to defend your program, especially if you face resistance.

There are plenty of free tools available for measuring results, such as Google Analytics, Hootsuite, TweetDeck, and TweetReach, just to name a few.

Joining the Revolution

When I was introduced to the concept of knowledge management, it instantly made so much sense to me. Sharing information was something we were already doing in our support organization, albeit on a small scale. Even though the benefits of pooling our knowledge seemed so obvious, there was a lot of resistance to formalizing our ad-hoc processes. Many were protective of the information they had acquired—after all, it hadn't always come easy—and others were willing to share but didn't actually see the value. We've come a long way, and knowledge management is now accepted as a worthwhile pursuit.

Fast forward 20 years to the advent of social media, which can face similar resistance, perhaps more from those who don't understand the technology. But make no mistake, the nature of support and the expectations of our customers are changing rapidly, and if we are to have a chance at success, we must consider how people want to communicate electronically and apply it to our businesses.

13

Creating a Culture of Social Care: Using Social Media to Enhance the Customer Experience

Genevieve Gonnigan, Former Social Care Manager, Infor

By the time you read these words, many things will have changed in the social space. A new social network will have emerged; a few existing social channels will have disappeared or reinvented themselves by amending, adjusting, and improving their terms of usage, privacy tools, and layouts. In the span of just a few years' time, social media has become more a part of our social fabric by making us all accessible to each other, nearly instantaneously, from wherever we are in the world. As consumers, we expect to have that same access to the companies that we do business, and expect the same ease and speed of receiving a response from them as we do when we Instant Message a friend. For businesses, social media has quickly changed from something that was a "Nice to Do," to "Something We Should Have Started Doing a Long Time Ago."

Businesses provide so much more than a solution or a product. In addition to delivering traditional customer care and support, we are now deliberately making efforts to develop and nurture the customer relationship and deliver a personalized customer experience. We aim to purposefully and successfully cultivate the human-to-human aspect of our business-to-business relationships. This chapter discusses how creating a culture of social care can facilitate this cultivation.

In this new age, being social means being open to being transparent, to sharing information, to collaborating, and to having authentic interactions with each other, be it our friends, our family, our colleagues, or our customers. Although we might be a bit more forthcoming in our personal interactions, within our organizations we still hold on tightly to our information, guarding our intellectual property, ensuring our corporate privacy, and avoiding the legal pitfalls that can arise from oversharing. However, we are all in business to serve and exceed the expectations of the customer. This is our mutual cornerstone, to do what we can to make the customer happy, not only in the initial delivery of the product or service, but also in delivery of customer support. However, it is not enough to deliver the service of support within the constraints of our corporate firewalls; we now must be prepared to provide exceptional care and deliver timely support to customers wherever they are, whenever they ask. That is what social care is all about.

Most organizations look at social as a marketing tool, a way to increase reach and brand awareness (outbound marketing) and to source leads that can lead to new customers (revenue generation) and with good reason. Companies who use Twitter generate twice as many leads as those who do not. As well, of companies using LinkedIn, 6 percent have acquired new customers via the social channel. Thus, the primary responsibilities for utilizing social, including developing corporate social strategies and utilizing social monitoring and social community tools will usually be managed by the marketing organization. However, when a consumer reaches out to a business on social media, a majority of the time it is to receive customer support. Customers expect a response to a tweet, Facebook, and LinkedIn post just as they would expect someone to pick up the phone if they were to call the business directly. Just as an organization would not have a customer support phone number if they did not have someone on the other end of the phone available and capable of assisting a customer, organizations are tasked with ensuring a knowledgeable representative is at the other end of a social channel, ready to provide direction to a customer when requested. That is the customer's expectation, and it is a reasonable and fair expectation. Customers will "Like" and "Follow" an organization if they have had a good experience with the company and have brand loyalty, with the hopes that as a part of the organization's social circle, they will receive the "hear it here first" news about new products and services, or a live feed of real-life events such as a conference or trade show. However, primarily, what they really want is to receive a quick answer to a right-now question. Responding to customer inquiries, putting out fires, smoothing ruffled feathers, providing a fix are duties that are managed by customer support. Therefore, collaboration between marketing and customer support and every department in between becomes paramount for true success with social care.

Steps to Creating a Culture of Social Care

The following sections discuss a process outline for getting started.

Identify Your Evangelists

Rallying the troops is the best way to get a fire burning under a social initiative. There are folks in every organization who seem to have been born socially savvy. Perhaps it is the first person who suggested the company blogs, or maybe it is the social butterfly constantly posting something somewhere, or the company cheerleader igniting the social grassroots efforts. These are the people who are passionate about getting the company onboard the social train, passionate about helping customers, and providing an exceptional customer experience. These people exist in your business. Spoiler alert: It's not the intern. Yes, you want someone with fresh ideas who is socially adept, and yes, he or she should have an established social following because it demonstrates an aptitude for social tools and the know-how required to communicate effectively within these channels. However, your sanctioned evangelists should have intimate knowledge of the business. They should be or have direct access to the key contacts within the organization that can help resolve social inquiries. They should be knowledgeable of the company's goals, mission, messaging, and direction and demonstrate a sense of stewardship in the organization. They should have the ability to cultivate an awareness of what collateral is good for public consumption and what announcements are internal or for targeted audiences only. This enables them to know what can be shared and when, what cannot be shared, and when to consult the legal team. Find these ambassadors, crown them, and let them evangelize!

Provide Training and Mind the Multigenerational Gap

In the workplace, we all face the challenge of blending different methods of interacting and engaging with each other. Many of us work in organizations with employees that span the generational gamut: from Baby Boomers to the Millennials and Generations X, Y, and Z. Mature workers are more professional and traditionally structured, preferring face-to-face or phone interaction, whereas newer generations are casual with most of their interactions being done behind a digital screen.

Although business leaders recognize a need for a social presence for the organization, getting seasoned employees, particularly managers and executives, to actually use social tools will be another challenge. A particular obstacle for employees who are not digital natives is just figuring out the basics of how social tools and channels work. Fill this gap by providing social media training. This is the first step for getting seasoned employees to even want to use social tools; they need to know how it works, the benefits, and the cautionary tales before they can be expected to fully participate and incorporate these social mediums in promoting brand awareness and enhancing customer interactions.

By providing basic training on the major social tools best suited for the enterprise (Twitter, Facebook, YouTube, LinkedIn, and Corporate Blogs), you help demystify social media for senior members of the workforce, giving them the confidence and building blocks to, eventually, strategically use social media in their professional interactions. In my former support organization, we produced a monthly #SocialSeries where we invited novices and "experts" to a 30-minute session that focused on a particular social channel demonstrating how the tool could be most effectively used within our specific roles. These events were live with time at the end for Q&A. We used the hashtag #SocialSeries so that participants could continue the conversation about these sessions within our internal online employee community boards. One of the best things about these sessions is that it became a wonderful way for people from different departments to collaborate and identify different ways the teams could use social to care for our customers from lead to sale to support.

Each session focused on five modules:

- **The basics**: What is this social tool and how is it used? At the beginning of the session, we presented a quick demo of that month's social tool (for example, Twitter) and defined the commonly referenced terms associated with the channel: What is tweet? What is a retweet? What is the difference between Following versus Followers? What are hashtags and how are they used? This is an important first step. We could not assume that everyone in the audience was familiar with the social channel and its associated terminology. The rest of the session could not be as effective without this initial review.

- **Getting onboard**: How do I set up a profile and control privacy settings? For each social tool, we walked through the steps of creating a complete profile and setting privacy settings. We stressed the importance of having a good profile picture, one that could be used across multiple social channels so that your personal brand could be easily identified. We discussed the value of an intriguing tagline and how it helps to attract like-minded associates into your social circle. Newbies to social media are often extremely concerned about privacy issues, so we explored how to "lock down" certain information from the public eye and how to define a digital line between your personal and professional persona. This gave the participants the confidence that they would have control over how they presented themselves to the world. This made delving into the social waters a bit less unnerving for those who were apprehensive at the onset of the training.

- **Content**: What do I post? This is the number-one question people ask when they are encouraged to join a social channel. It is also the deterrent for newbies to stay engaged on a social channel after they create a profile. We discussed using the Share button on websites, including our own corporate site and corporate blogs, to post content to various channels. We also introduced our own Corporate Gaggle with messaging created by our corporate and departmental teams that could be used to easily and automatically share corporate content to our individual social channels. (This is discussed further in the "Create Customer-Centered Content" section that follows.) The participants were more likely to stay active on social media if they had messages crafted for them in advance to share. This also helped to guide employees on how to create their own messaging.

- **Network engagement**: Establishing a network can seem daunting if you don't know who you're looking to add to your network or why it would be of value. Here we emphasized the importance of "listening" to our customers and finding opportunities to provide proactive customer support and enhance the customer's experience. We encouraged employees to connect with customers and colleagues as much as they felt comfortable doing so. For example, we suggested connecting with key account clients and immediate team members on LinkedIn as a starting point; we suggested joining LinkedIn industry and user groups to listen in and participate on relevant discussions; also we encouraged Following our customer's corporate Twitter handles and Google+ pages and setting up Google Alerts to easily stay current on their clients' businesses. Last, we also encouraged promoting goodwill by sharing our customers' social content on our own social channels.

- **#DoOneThing Challenge**: Each session ended with a #DoOne-Thing Challenge. Because we presented a good deal of information in such a short amount of time, we wanted to make sure participants walked away with an action item that would connect them to the specific social channel as soon as possible. We offered three to four options from which the participants could choose one (or all) to complete before the next month's session. Options included finding a good profile pic for your social channels, adding five new connections to your LinkedIn network, tweeting a corporate blog post, posting a customer's YouTube video on our Facebook page, and so on. When participants completed their challenge, they posted their action to our internal social community with the hashtag #DoOneThing. This simple challenge made the experience of getting active easy to do and added an element of fun to our #SocialSeries.

Providing training and exploring social channels in easily digestible chunks was a simple way to increase employee engagement and increase their comfort level with social media. These sessions created internal brand ambassadors who were eager to connect with customers in a different way and added a new dimension to the customers' experience.

Create a Cross-Functional Social Team

Every department appreciates the need to participate in social to accomplish its customer-centered objectives. The marketing department knows that social is a valuable tool to market to new and existing customers; the sales team sees the opportunity to source new leads and provide a personal touch when closing deals with new customers; the human resources team sees the opportunity to gain a broader reach for announcing job opportunities and proactively sourcing qualified candidates (who are often current customers); the customer support teams see the opportunity to provide care to the customer, turn a complaint into a compliment, and provide an enhanced customer experience. At the core lies the customer, so it behooves us all to be united and collaborative in our efforts to interact and engage with our prospective and current customers in a unified voice under an umbrella of a unified mission.

At my current organization, like many other organizations, we have a social council composed of the social evangelists and ambassadors from each department. Within our council, we are focused on collectively creating the framework that outlines our social best practices and developing the social pipeline of handling the customer from the point of a lead to selling the solutions to providing consistent care for that customer after it is onboard. Collectively, we can also identify the super user customers who are often the best candidates for spearheading customer user groups, participating in focus groups and product development panels, as well as filling open job opportunities within our organization. Within the social council, we openly discuss our corporate social campaigns and strategies and also share our plans for individual departmental campaigns so that we can identify ways we can support and collaborate with each other in making our efforts mutually successful. In this forum, we are actively finding ways to collectively care for the customers.

Identify Your Brand Ambassadors

With a team in place and a well-trained workforce, you have the human resources in place to actively monitor the social space for your customers and the conversations related to the company and its products. Certain individuals will emerge as frequent contributors who talk about or talk directly to your brand. These contributors are your informal brand ambassadors. Usually, these are actively engaged customers who are passionate about your product and your company and will gladly spread your company message, promote your products, and remain proud super users.

It is important to recognize these contributors because in any space, real life or virtual, customer word of mouth is still the best and most successful advertisement for any company. These contributors are invaluable, and a bit of recognition can go a long way in the customer maintaining that excitement and willingness to promote your organization. Simply telling a customer, "Hey, we see you and we appreciate you being our brand ambassador" can be a powerful reward. A Like on a Facebook or LinkedIn post, a YouTube Comment, a retweet, and a +1 are all simple yet effective ways of recognizing an informal customer brand ambassador. Sending private messages that include soon-to-be-released collateral such as videos and product announcements gives the brand ambassadors a sense of V.I.P. privileges, which further deepens their brand loyalty and encourages them to continue to spread the message of your brand happily and willingly. Again, promoting goodwill is a tenant of true social care.

Create Customer-Centered Content

Work is beautiful. That is the theme and message of a current marketing campaign of my former organization, highlighting the different ways its solutions help customers continue to do meaningful valuable work, no matter the job, no matter the industry. After this campaigns' first appearance in *The Wall Street Journal*, the hashtag, #WorkIsBeautiful, organically emerged and became integrated and embedded into all the messaging associated with the organization. Employees highlighted customer successes by sharing their #WorkIsBeautiful stories across multiple social channels. This campaign has been completely centered on customers, the work that they do, and the beauty that is found in it. I love this campaign because it is refreshing. Most company campaigns are about the company and what it can do for you. This campaign is about customers and what they do for you. The company not only cared that customers used their solution, it sincerely cared about customers and wanted to highlight what it is doing in its industries to keep our world moving forward. Internally, it ensured that this message is well crafted and easily distributed by the employees by providing key messages that can be promoted on various social channels. For those that are still getting their feet wet with social media, providing verbiage that can be edited or posted as-is helps diffuse the frustration that comes from not knowing what to post. It makes participating easy for employees and helps magnify the reach of the campaign.

Provide an Engaging Forum for Your Communities

Most organizations have basic customer communities and dedicated forums where customers are encouraged to participate by connecting with other users, posting and answering questions so that others can benefit from the collective knowledge of the community members. Communities are a great way to create a crowd-sourced knowledge base that can be accessed on-demand. If the organization does not provide this forum (and sometimes even when it does), customers can organically create forums independently via LinkedIn Groups, Facebook Groups, or Google+ communities. In either forum, both positive and negative conversations happen about your organization and your products, so communities provide a great view into the needs and wants of customers. Listening to the conversations in these social forums can give a keener insight into what customers truly want from the relationship with the organization, where the shortcomings exist for product delivery and customer support, and identify opportunities where organizations can turn an unhappy customer into a satisfied customer and possibly turn a satisfied customer into an enthusiastic brand ambassador. Also, incorporating gamification elements into the communities such as points for levels of participation, competitive leaderboards, and awarding community badges provide incentives for customers to ensure continued participation in the communities.

Be Responsive

Conversations happen, customers ask questions, and competitors provide answers. Of utmost importance is to respond when a customer reaches out, no matter the channel. The customer must be acknowledged publicly. If the matter is too sensitive or too involved to be resolved in the public eye, the conversation can be moved to another channel such as e-mail or telephone. Directing a customer to the appropriate resources requires someone who has the knowledge or the ability to quickly find the valuable resources the customer needs. Therefore, employing your evangelists within support to monitor the social conversations allows the support team to provide a timely response and get customers the information they need. In the instances when a customer is publicly complaining, we have the opportunity to turn customers into brand ambassadors simply by acknowledging their posts, validating their feelings, and making a sincere effort to satisfy the need of these customers. But timing is key. Customers expect a response within 2 to 4 business hours. Most businesses are responding within 14 hours. Two to 3 days delay is as good as no response at all. The longer the wait, the harder it becomes to "wow" with an exceptional customer experience.

The customer experience is the great differentiator. It is why we fly with one airline over another, prefer one hotel chain over the other, and choose to sign with this vendor versus another. Trust leads to transaction, and one of the most exciting benefits of this new social age is the opportunity to get close with our customers and develop connections with the people with whom we do business—learning about their needs and providing solutions before they even ask it of us and making our transactional interactions transformational. Not only do customers treated like human social beings remain loyal, they also willingly become your strongest and most compelling brand ambassadors.

Creating a culture of customer care is a collective effort of the entire organization. A social organization has become the expectation of customers. By embracing social media and integrating these channels into customer support offerings, you can take full advantage of the opportunity to create authentic connections with your customers. You can meet, greet, engage, and support them where they are, deepen your customer relationships, and add an interactive and engaging dimension to customers' experience.

14

Arming your Advocates: Formalizing the Social Media Advocacy Program to Activate Your Biggest Fans

Michelle Kostya, Customer Success Executive, Hootsuite Media Inc.

Think about how you make a purchase decision on your next book. Certainly, we judge a book by its cover, the description, and the reviews and claims regarding "bestseller" lists. Perhaps even more often we pick books through word of mouth, reviews, and thumbs up. We look to our friends, and "people like us" for recommendations. With the Internet and in particular with social media, this broadens our access to recommendations from people we view as similar to us, and in this example, who influence our book-buying decisions. Working in the early 2000s at a Canadian book publisher with limited budgets and miniscule print runs meant we had to harness word of mouth to drive purchases, so publicity activities were the primary tactics on our marketing plans. Book tours, PR, galleys, or advanced reading copies were key to most book launches. Only a few books had the print runs that warranted advertising dollars. Had social media been around at that time, I am certain we would have jumped on that bandwagon!

Leaving book publishing, I took on a role as marketing manager for the Canadian arm of a small appliances company. As the regional office of a U.S. company, we were given our print and TV ads, and our collateral and products were largely dictated by the head office. When it came to PR, however, we ran the show, so we could be creative without the significant oversight of our counterparts in the United States. Our brand had a premium place in the market, and our advocates included everyone from home cooks to more influential TV personalities. Our product was aspirational and recognized for quality, and due to this we had plenty of existing fans. This is circa 2006, so again we focused largely on offline word of mouth and engagement with our fans. At this time, many blogs had gained readership, so we also started to look at opportunities to talk to our target audience—moms—through this increasingly vibrant space. In our most successful program, we worked with a high profile mom-blog, Urbanmoms.ca, to create a regularly sponsored column on cooking, and then leveraging the fans of the blog and column, we held cross-country Kitchen Parties with our products and a charming chef. This program gained media coverage, influencer coverage, and best of all word of mouth from our advocates!

Word of mouth and advocacy for products aren't new. Social media has simply given consumers greater reach to share what they love (and what they don't).These brand advocates and brand detractors can now broadcast their love and hate across the globe not just to those close to them. Because of this, brand advocacy has become a critical part of a brand's marketing mix. However, brand advocates not only support the goals of marketing—they can also support the business goals of many other parts of an organization.

What Is Brand Advocacy?

Simply put, an advocate is a person who talks positively about a brand or a product within his network: online or offline. He has his own trusted network and has various levels of influence. The reach of one advocate can be minimal, but as an aggregate the total reach of your brand advocates can make a strong business impact.

There is a distinction between advocate and the term *influencer* that marketers banter around. Having an influencer outreach program doesn't replace the need for a brand advocacy program. Influencer marketing is where a brand identifies individuals who have strong influence over potential buyers, and the brand then orients its marketing or particular tactics around these people. The brand's advocates might not have 5,000 followers and a Klout score of 60, but they do hold influence within their own social circles. Yet, the influencers you reach out to as part of an influencer program might not be advocates; in fact, they could be detractors or indifferent to your brand or product.

Understanding this distinction: It is equally important for brands to define strategies to reach out to your influencers and to connect and empower brand advocates. As Jay Baer states in his post "Why Online

Influencer Outreach Is Overrated and How to Fix It," we often "overrate audience and underrate advocacy" and "You can't live on audience alone, you need true advocacy, too." Influencer programs can help you drive awareness and increase the reach of your messages, but tapping into the excitement and passion of brand advocates can drive *action*—from purchase to loyalty and even cost-savings. If you aren't speaking to your advocates, who are your current customers, you should start doing this before putting resources against influencer outreach.

Brand Advocacy in the Role in Customer Support

Brand advocacy can support business goals beyond those of marketing. Often brands overlook the opportunity brand advocacy has to scale customer support and foster loyalty through peer-to-peer support.

In 2007, I joined Twitter and as a new mom, I started a "mommy" blog, and eventually as my obsession with social media grew, a blog dedicated to what I was learning about in this space grew. In 2009, I was given the opportunity to work at BlackBerry. I had tried for a few years to get my foot in the door in the marketing department, but it wasn't until a community manager role in the customer support organization came up that I actually managed to get that foot in. If it hadn't been for my obsession with my BlackBerry 8700, I might have turned the role down because I couldn't fathom what I could do as a marketer in customer support. The truth is customer service is marketing. By delivering great customer service, you drive loyalty and encourage new customers.

BlackBerry launched its Support Community in April 2008, and I joined less than a year later because it recognized the need to have a dedicated community manager to engage with the community, actively solicit feedback, monitor conversations, and remedy situations by feeding information back to the business. This role helped to show the commitment BlackBerry had to its fans and existing customers, and because of it the community flourished.

For years, BlackBerry primarily had a person-to-person support model with its existing Enterprise customers. But with the launch of its first consumer device in the 2006, it was necessary to support end users. Although this was done primarily through its carrier partners, it had to find a way to care for its customers who didn't have an IT department and whose questions were largely low in complexity. The customer support organization offered self-service options on the website, including documentation and technical support articles. But, the support community allowed peer-to-peer responses and a more agile environment for information transfer.

A vibrant support community, whether owned or external, can have many benefits for a brand. For BlackBerry, it assisted in deflecting support calls to its carriers and to use by helping the customer at the time of need, and it helped search engine optimization and content creation efforts with relevant and timely threads. But, for a support community to be successful, it requires not only the support of the business, but also the support of its brand advocates, or as it called them in its community, "super users" or "super fans." Without these ambassadors, the community would have stagnated with unanswered threads.

BlackBerry grew and maintained its Support Community through key pillars, which broadly could be identified as: Listen, Speak, and Embrace.

Listen—Offer Opportunities for Advocates to Share Their Feedback and Recognize They Are Also Providing It Without You Asking!

- We gave community members a voice by having employees actively gather feedback and insights and route this information into the business. We developed a list of internal partners that supported these efforts and who also came to us to get a pulse check from our members.

- We analyzed topics and trending conversations within the community, especially around product launches or software updates so that changes and necessary communication could be implemented quickly.

- We recognized that listening requires acknowledgment, but not always solutions. Sometimes saying "we hear you" is enough.

- We refrained from getting defensive when a member was unhappy. We did not delete or censor these posts but when the situation warranted, we escalated.

Speak—Be Present and Add Value to the Conversation

- Created a genuine connection with our community. Humans create connections, not company logos—so we focused on one-to-one connections between our employees and our customers.

- Our team was empowered to not only provide technical support but also talk about sports with our super users, if that was the topic of conversation!

- We consistently had a presence in the community. We would welcome new community members and had dedicated staff in the community. However, we restrained ourselves from answering questions to allow customer experts or super users to emerge. Instead we supported threads that hadn't been answered in more than 48 hours, or helped our super users answer the question by giving them the knowledge they needed.

- We always aimed to offer value to the community. There were other places our customers could find support and how-to assistance, but we had the capability to give them direct access to our staff and we used this advantage. As an example, we held "Insider" events where internal specialists engaged directly with our community.

Embrace—ALWAYS GIVE BACK to Your Fans Not Just When There Is Something in It for You as a Brand

- We gave members a reason to visit, and visit often. We discovered that our members came back often when they had friends within the community. We created a VIP space for our super fans where they could have off-topic boards and build friendships with other community members.

- We thanked community members for their positive contributions. Not only did we have the gamification of levels through the platform, but we also regularly thanked members for going out of their way to help a community member. These tokens of thanks were often intrinsic—giving them added abilities within the community (for example, the ability to move a thread or post a video or giving them a new badge or title). On occasion, we gave members branded gear, devices, and at least once, Canadian maple syrup to thank them for the work they did.

- Our brand advocates were so important to us that we gave them VIP access to special events. Sometimes, these were fan events in their city of residence, but other occasions we flew them to events. For the first event, I brought a select group of super users was to a BlackBerry conference. The members had known each other online for more than 1 year but had never met in real life. When they met, it was more like a high-school reunion.

- We gave them inside access to our experts. We often held conference calls with select group of super users to discuss community issues, concerns, and provide product information as required.

Was our community successful? Absolutely! The community had a 93 percent answer rate (the percentage of threads that received a response), 32 million accepted solution views (posts that were acknowledged as solved), and our super users had in some cases spent more than 20 hours a week participating in the community. We had members who had been dedicated to supporting our customers within the community since April 2008. As an example, one community member had spent nearly 1 million minutes online and had authored more than 5,000 solutions (posts accepted by the original poster as the answer to their question) and they had read a whopping 1-million messages. The loyal brand advocates on the support community contributed to more than 30 percent of all interactions in the community. Not only were many of these members active in the owned community, but they were also spreading their love on other social networks such as Twitter and Facebook!

Brand Advocacy: The Role in PR and Marketing

"Brands speak in sales language, advocates speak in the language customers can relate to and, thus will always be more trustworthy; any brand that doesn't embrace its advocates will fall behind the competitors that do." —C.C. Chapman, author of *Content Rules*

Harnessing the passion of fans and advocates for increased word of mouth, driving brand awareness, positive sentiment, and purchase is nothing new. This predates social media and the Internet. But the reach potential with social media is vastly greater over offline opportunities when a brand leverages the natural affinity a customer has toward a brand.

Mack Collier, author of *Think Like a Rock Star*, has a great visual on his blog to describe how brands repeatedly focus on acquisition of new customers rather than concentrating on the much smaller but potentially more valuable group of brand advocates. Of course, the potential market for new customers is quite large in comparison to the number of existing customers a brand might have, and certainly it is much larger than the number of advocates a brand might have. But, brand advocates are vocal, positively passionate, and trusted in their network and consequently enormously valuable for brands. Often, a small number of really adoring, passionate, loyal fans creates a large impact (and a positive one) for the brands they care about the most.

These fans are not only vocal but they also are trusted within their social networks. Edelman produces a study called the "Trust Barometer" every year, which explores trust in industry, government, and organizations. Since 2009, experts (both academic and technical), "a person like yourself," and regular employees have had significant gains in trust for consumers. As marketers, we often get stuck talking about "optimization" and "key messaging" that we forget to look at the situation from the eye of the customer. What value are you providing? How do customers talk about your product? Who are customers asking for information when they are making a purchase? Sometimes, simply taking a step back and thinking about it from the standpoint as the customer is all you need to gain perspective. How do you make purchase decisions? Chances are that your friends and your social circles impact your choices quite a bit.

Given the impact brand advocates have in social media, and the increased trust in experts and peers, coupled with always-on, real-time social media, we can easily understand why many brands are creating advocacy programs to support marketing and PR.

Advocates can't be summoned or conjured up at the time of need. Brands need to put in the time to build the foundation for brand advocacy before they need them. Don't wait until you are in the middle of a crisis or product launch to try to activate your brand ambassadors or you will find it ineffective. Contrarily if you have done solid groundwork, your brand advocates can deliver authentic and trusted messages with incredible reach in social.

BlackBerry has vocal advocates—they say when they love something and when they dislike something, too. They have blogs, they tweet, and they have BBM groups dedicated to their love for the BlackBerry. A few years ago, we noticed a hashtag trend forming where people were self-identifying which side of the smartphone market their loyalties lay. In the last week, 1,200 tweets (at the time of this writing) included this initially fan-created hashtag.

The customer support organization was first to formalize the relationship between BlackBerry and these brand advocates, while the PR teams focused on online bloggers and influencers in addition to traditional media. Thinking back, I suspect this was largely because these fans were in our support community, and, quite frankly this initial group didn't like to be ignored! Joking aside, these fans helped us do our job better, and without them the community wouldn't be what it is today. The social marketing team engaged with these advocates within our social properties, but it wasn't until 2010 that the social marketing team reached out to this audience offline. It was the first, but certainly not the last, major product launch that included device "seeding" to enthusiasts and global fan events.

In 2012, BlackBerry formalized its advocacy program: BlackBerry Elite. The members of this elite force were given frames for their social avatars if they wanted to use them, and many did—proud fans even during times when it was tough to be a fan. Prior to the Elite program, there were teams across the organization that had identified advocates. As discussed previously, there were the support super users. There were developer advocates and those the social team had identified for seeding and fan events. The Elite program brought these streams together to help advance the business goals for the 2013 launch of BlackBerry 10.

In December 2012, some Elites were flown to Waterloo, Ontario, to the BlackBerry head office to meet with employees and execs, and in January they were invited to fan events globally for the launch of BlackBerry 10. Of course, on launch day for BlackBerry 10, these fans were the first to get their very own! It wasn't only the extrinsic rewards, however; these advocates had inside access through BBM groups, through regular communication, and through conference calls with the internal employees. It was fascinating to watch from the sidelines, as my friends, the super users, posted pictures of the trip to Waterloo, and the fan events—all with incredible excitement and anticipation for the launch!

Just to show the incredible impact brand fans can have tied to marketing and communications, take a quick look at BlackBerry Live, the annual company conference in Orlando, Florida. This event was previously called "Wireless Enterprise Symposium" and was the event I had taken my group of super users to in 2009, 2010, and 2011. In 2013, again there were a number of Elites in attendance at the conference, and these Elites were a driving force in the social conversation around BlackBerry Live and #BBLive. As can be expected, those in attendance tweeted a lot—about 12 times more than non-Elites. But even those Elites who didn't attend wanted to share what was happening and they posted 6 times more than a non-Elite member about the conference. These Elites, whether attending or not, had influence within their own social networks—the average Elite was retweeted six times!

Again, I believe the key pillars for a brand advocacy program for marketing and PR are to Listen, Speak, and Embrace. Listen to the feedback they are providing you on your advocacy program, your products and services, and, of course, ask questions. They love the brand—and they want more reasons to validate that love, so this is a group that will always want to share their opinion. Speak with them, and share with them as much as you can. This can be tough in competitive markets, but open up as much as you can when you can. They will start building a sense of buzz around new products as early as you start providing them information. Finally, embrace them as though they were an extension of your company. Instead of getting caught up in what is in it for the brand (fans, impressions, or click-through), remember advocacy is a mutually beneficial relationship—and to keep your fans and advocates, you need to go above and beyond to delight your customers.

Brand Employees = Brand Advocates

A chapter about social media advocacy programs would not be complete without discussing brands leveraging their employees and partners online.

Your employees are diverse, with different interests, knowledge of your products or services, and with a varied social footprint. If you facilitate and encourage their sharing in social media, chances are they will reach a different audience than your official brand properties. Today, some forward-thinking companies are providing their employees governance, training, tools, content, and rewards for being active in social media.

Mitel is one of these companies. Mitel originally wanted to create, share, and amplify its customer success stories. In January 2014, it started Customer Success Friday where it published a blog post discussing customer achievement. At this time, Liz Pedro, the director of customer success marketing at Mitel, said that there were only a handful of active employees on social media. To encourage participation and sharing, she started a contest called #TeamMitel where she would award a daily winner who used the hashtag with a gift card. This drove participation up and Liz decided to look at technology to scale the program and help to continue to drive engagement. She started a pilot with advocate marketing software Influitive. She wanted a product that was easy for staff to use that she could customize with challenges and content. In three weeks, Liz had 750 employees signed up on the Advocacy Hub, and these advocates shared 6,720 posts, far exceeding previous months for the brand. She set up challenges in the platform, everything from sharing a tweet to writing a case study to providing sales with a referral or testimonial. Asked what lessons she has learned from the program, Liz says, "Don't underestimate the power of employee engagement. Employees want to help your company grow and you have ones that just need a little push and an easy way to participate."

Just like a customer advocacy program, an employee program requires new skills and training, business processes, infrastructure, and measurement capabilities. If you are considering launching an employee advocacy program, I highly recommend reading *The Most Powerful Brand on Earth* by Susan F. Emerick and Chris Boudreaux, which runs through in detail how to plan, implement, and measure employee advocates.

The Four (or So) Steps to an Advocacy Program

Whether for customer service, marketing, PR, or leveraging your employee advocates, there are a few key steps to any advocacy program.

Define Objectives

Define clear objectives from the outset. What are the expected business outcomes for your advocacy program? Understand your goals and key performance indicators so that you can optimize as you go along.

Identify Advocates

Consolidate and review existing lists, and look inside your organization and outside to find your brand advocates. There are social technologies and vendors you can use as advocates as well, but chances are you can find them on your existing channels as a first step.

Build the Infrastructure

How will you manage listening, speaking, and embracing your advocates? You need to identify resources internally who can help support your efforts and determine where, how, and when you will communicate to your advocates. This could include a channel plan, editorial plan, communication plan, and depending on the size of you program, a technology plan.

Measure and Improve

If you did your homework on "Define Objectives" measurement, it should be simple. But, measuring and collecting data is only one part of this equation. Use the data to continuously improve your program, and your products or services. Although this is identified as the fourth step in this approach to build a formal advocacy program, it should be always on. Always be piloting your program.

A Final Thought

Just a few years ago, brands looked at social media in fear. Companies were afraid employees would squander away their day surfing the net, posting on Facebook, and watching cats on YouTube. They worried that customers would talk about them on social media, and they worried that they wouldn't talk about them on social media. Social networks were considered a security threat in many organizations. Policies were put in place at companies to restrict use of social media at work and to control what employees could say about their employer online (often nothing). I can recall a time when it was perfectly normal to have a significant review process for every tweet that official brand channels posted.

Today, however, brands are recognizing that to scale social engagement, they need to mobilize fans and employees as brand advocates. Advocates are not only scalable, but they are also more trusted. Brands that don't find ways to activate fans and employees will be left behind. There is an incredible amount of noise in social media, with more and more content created every day. Technology has both enabled content creation and a rise in content consumption. But can this continue? Certainly content creation will continue, but what about content consumption? There is not an infinite amount of time to consume content. Mark Schaefer writes in his post "Content Shock: Why content marketing is not a sustainable strategy," "Like any good discussion on economics, this [Content Marketing sustainability] is rooted in the very simple concept of supply and demand. When supply exceeds demand, prices fall. But in the world of content marketing, the prices cannot fall because the 'price' of the content is already zero—we give it away for free. So, to get people to consume our content, we actually have to pay them to do it, and as the supply of content explodes, we will have to pay our customers increasing amounts to the point where it is not feasible anymore."

Think about this from a brand perspective—content marketing is essentially your "owned" content. It is the content you create on your blogs, your dot com, and your social channels. In the past, having quality content meant you got noticed; today great content is just the price of admission. To amplify your content, you have two opportunities—paid and earned. Paid of course is the money you put against your content to advertise it. Content marketing efforts now and even more so in the future will likely need paid behind it. One needs to only look at changes to Facebook's algorithm on organic content to see that dollars will be required to gain eyeballs on content. What other strategies can a brand implement to break through the "content shock?" Schaefer offers 10 strategies in his follow-up post, "10 Strategies to Battle Content Shock." And one is leveraging "citizen influencers," or brand ambassadors.

The truth is that advocates are your customers first. If having customers is important to you, then having brand fans should be equally important. Looking ahead, chances are good that customers and employees will continue to be vocal online and in social. If you aren't recognizing your advocates by listening to them, speaking to them, and embracing them, you want to start right now or risk getting lost in social noise of the future.

15

It Takes a Village: Building, Training, and Leading Community Teams

Caty Kobe, Head of Training, FeverBee

Job openings for community managers and other roles involving the use of social technologies tend to attract a special type of person. These people are smart, funny, analytical, creative, hardworking, compassionate, clever, and data-driven—a harmonious mix of both left-brain and right-brain thinking. These qualities combined with the roller-coaster nature of working in social require a new type of management and training style to ensure these employees are engaged and well prepared to succeed.

Though community and social media-focused positions often attract younger candidates, this chapter isn't about managing different generations. Instead, it discusses how to hire, train, and inspire employees that spend their careers deeply rooted in social technologies.

Building Your Team

A great recipe requires the finest ingredients. A strong house requires a strong foundation. A top-notch community initiative requires brilliant, experienced individuals that can bring your brand to life online. Putting together the optimal team to meet your company's community needs requires strong planning and thought. Fight the external pressures to move at the speed of light, and put together a cohesive plan before slapping a job description online.

Why Do You Need a Community Team?

One of the most common mistakes that businesses make when executing on a community or social initiative is not having enough people involved to ensure success. Few business initiatives are successful solely through the work of a single person, so why would your community and social strategies be different? You don't need an army, but depending on the size of your organization and the scope of your initiatives, you likely need more than one person to help with getting the work done. And if you don't have more than one person involved, your personal expectations must be in line with how quickly milestones can be achieved.

According to the 2014 State of Community Management report, best-in-class communities employ an average of 5.4 community managers and are also almost twice as likely to measure the value of the community than that of an average community.[1] Having multiple community professionals on your team helps to ensure that your milestones can be met and that the workload is reasonably balanced for the team members. There's an unfortunate stigma in the business world that community managers are supposed to be available 24 hours per day, and even remain on call when they're on vacation.[2] I'd like to argue that might have been the case for an unfortunate few during the infancy stages of our industry, but we have matured greatly since then. As a testament to the industry's stability and structure, I'm pleased to share that I took a 3-week vacation to Europe last year. I spent 21 days exploring life in the United Kingdom and Italy, and when I came home, everything was fine! All emergencies had been handled gracefully, and our metrics didn't suffer as a result of my absence. As an added benefit, my own relationships with my customers and my energy toward my role improved after I returned as result of having time off to recharge.

Having a staff, even if it's small, can ensure a better balance for your employees involved, offer redundancy and appropriate coverage in the event of vacations, sick time, or role transitions, and ensure your community and social initiatives are as successful as possible. It's

---

1 Slide 22: http://www.slideshare.net/rhappe/the-state-of-community-management-2014

2 http://mashable.com/2013/01/27/community-manager-qualities/ and multiple in-person conversations

important to take this into consideration when planning the budget for your social strategies and initiatives.

Plan Your Team Structure

As crucial it is to have multiple people on your community team, it's also equally important that you don't rush too quickly into the hiring process. As Winston Churchill said, "He who fails to plan is planning to fail." Take the time to map out the ideal structure of your team as it relates to your broader community vision and timeline. Even if you don't have specific headcount available, think through what you want to achieve, and by when, and then document how these goals align with your broader corporate objectives. Building out your team's structure and plan ahead of time can ensure that both you and whoever signs off on your additional headcount will have a clear understanding of where the team is headed.

A community team structure can look something like this:

- Community manager
- Associate community manager
- Community moderator

The community manager is typically a high-level role that reports upward in an organization. This role is responsible for carrying out the community strategy, managing the team, consolidating community data into actionable insights, and ensuring cross-functional coordination related to the needs of the community. In small organizations, the community manager might also take on the functions of an associate community manager.

Associate community managers report in to the community manager and have more of their hands in the day-to-day community operations. They plan events and build relationships with your top community members and other partner sites and might also have a team of moderators reporting to them. In smaller organizations, an associate community manager might also play the role of community moderator himself or herself.

Community moderators are responsible for enforcing set guidelines and policies for the use of the community. They're responsible for identifying patterns in the content that's submitted, as well as managing the behavior of users. To manage costs, many organizations often outsource moderation capabilities to third-party vendors or enlist the help of community volunteers to manage the work. Regardless of where the moderation capabilities come from, it's crucial that they understand your community's guidelines and terms of services policies so that they can moderate quickly and fairly.

The daily responsibilities of a community moderator tend to remain consistent, whereas the responsibilities of an associate community manager or a community manager can vary with the needs of the community. In addition to understanding the work of a community moderator, community managers and associate community managers need to look for ways to improve processes and must become fierce advocates internally on behalf of community members. Bigger organizations might even have a community department, where multiple community managers (and related staff) roll up under one community department leader who interfaces at a departmental or executive level.

The number of people that you need on your community team depends on a variety of factors, including the following:

- Specific goals and milestones for your community initiatives
- The size of your organization
- General size of your potential community
- Age of your organization and recognition of the brand
- Available budget

If your plan is to focus the community on peer-to-peer conversations and self-moderation, you won't need as many moderators on staff. However, you should understand that if you go this route, the community manager cannot be expected to manage and respond to every post. In some communities, moderators are expected to moderate 60–100 posts per hour, but the quantity of the content moderated can be greatly higher than the number of conversations that have an employee's response. Conversely, if your vision is to have more company influence in the community, you need more staff to actively participate.

When planning for the size and scope of your team, it's always smart to future-proof as much as possible. Think about the full requirements for the experience that you want to provide with your community and plan for that from the start. If you don't have the headcount available, work with your HR department to determine how you can earn additional headcount and adjust your expectations and milestones accordingly.

Common future proofing scenarios to consider follow:

- What coverage are you expecting in the community?
- Will your community team be serving community members in different time zones?
- What happens if your community experiences viral growth?
- How many events will you want to have after you're fully ramped up?
- How often do you want new knowledge base or blog content added to the community?
- How involved do you want to be with your customer champions?

After you have your team structure and plan mapped out, start drafting your necessary job descriptions. Clearly articulate the details that each individual role will be responsible for, and be mindful of the overall tone. I've found that boisterous and annoying job descriptions (you know, the ones that say "ninja" somewhere on the page) tend to attract candidates of the same nature. Job descriptions that are dry and full of corporate jargon will likely turn off the creative minds that you'd like to interview.

If you're nervous about writing a job description for a community manager, or maybe you've never done it before, I'd recommend looking online for some examples. There are community management jobs posted on LinkedIn, Mashable, Indeed, and other job boards pertinent to the social industry. See what others have written, and then make it your own. A Google search for **Community Management Job Description** will also yield some useful blog posts on the subject. It's better to err on the side of specific details as opposed to vague responsibilities. Sure, you might want to keep the role open-ended, but a lack of clarity on what actually needs to be achieved often leads to mismatched expectations about the job that you're hiring for. Don't forget to check Glassdoor so that you have a realistic sense of current salary expectations.

Finding the Right People

Believe it or not, community management wasn't a profession that I chose. It chose me. I had recently been promoted from an entry-level inside sales representative to a web content manager when my boss brought me into the main conference room and proceeded to tell me that we were going to be making a few changes to our team. The room quickly began to feel small and stuffy as I watched her present my new opportunity. It sounded interesting but was *very* different than what I had been working on prior to our meeting. I didn't really know where to start, but I knew that if I wanted to keep my paycheck, I would need to embrace this new position and try to do the very best that I could to succeed.

Long story short, it worked out well. My management team could have quickly decided that I wasn't a fit and opted to bring in someone new, but instead it saw qualities and experience that it could work with, and I was willing to invest time in shaping my new role. Depending on the stage of growth that your company is in, you might also consider looking at internal candidates along with external applicants to fill roles on your community team. Even if an internal candidate might not have direct community experience, her knowledge of your product and internal processes, along with written communication skills could prove to be an incredibly valuable combination.

When evaluating external candidates, look at their experience and extracurricular activities to help narrow down the list. Checking out candidates' participation in other communities can give you great insight into the caliber of their writing, as well as how they carry themselves online. It's difficult to tell how abrasive people might be in online communications simply by reviewing a resume. I do this when evaluating candidates for roles on my community team, and it has saved me from wasting time on face-to-face interviews with someone who simply wasn't a fit.

Also, some of the strongest brand community managers that I have seen are those who have a true passion toward the industry that their company serves. For instance, if your company manufactures kitchen tools, take a look at folks who are into cooking or maybe have a food blog. If your company sells bicycle parts, it might make sense to hire a cycling enthusiast. When community managers and community members share the same passions, powerful connections, influence, and bonds form.

In-person interviews are the "make it or break it" point for you, just as much as it is for the candidate that you're interviewing. Many companies overlook the importance of a positive candidate experience, and yet, that's one of the primary criteria that I, and other community managers I know, will evaluate a company on. If a company doesn't treat me right during an interview, it's hard to know whether it will have my back after I sign on as an employee. In addition, I won't bother risking my professional reputation on, or refer my peers to, a company that doesn't treat candidates well. Did you know that one-third of candidates today feel comfortable going public about a bad candidate experience?[3]

Treating your candidates well is simple—simply treat them the way you'd expect to be treated during a job interview. Have the day planned out and the meeting rooms booked in advance. Give them a heads-up on who they will be interviewing with so that they can adequately prepare. Be on time to greet them, offer a beverage and a quick office tour, and after you settle into a meeting room, try not to have to switch to a different room mid-discussion.

Because so much of successful community management hinges on a community manager's ability to create cross-functional relationships, it makes a lot of sense to have that person interview with representatives from several different departments within your organization. Not only will this give your potential hire great insight into the company and show that you recognize the importance of interdepartmental collaboration, but including other department team members in the hiring process can also help the potential hire to feel more connected to the role and community strategy as a whole.

---

3 Source: http://datamonk.com/mobile-targeting-in-recruiting-the-importance-of-the-candidate-experience/

Training Your Team

Providing your new community managers and moderators with a strong onboarding experience allows them to contribute value to your organization faster than they could without training and also realigns their personal commitment to the company. After a good first few weeks at the office, your new hires will likely be singing the praises of your organization to their friends, family, and anyone on the social web who will listen. You couldn't ask for more than a happy, engaged employee who proactively spreads the word about your brand.

First Impressions Matter

Many people assume that community managers have extroverted personalities and will hit the ground running at a new company with no hesitation. However, that's a chancy assumption to make, which can easily lead to missed expectations for both you and your new employee. I am actually quite shy, and having to walk into a room full of new peers can be a bit terrifying, but it would be hard for anyone to know this based on my online presence and interview skills.

When you've been at a job for a while, it's easy to forget how uncomfortable it is to start fresh at a new company, and that simple oversight can cause a lot of trouble for your new hire. I, too, am guilty of this. However, the first few days on the job often set the tone of the next few months for a new employee. Learn from my mistakes, and take measures to ensure that the start of your employee's experience is a good one. Here are my tips for an enjoyable first few days:

- Ensure your employees' equipment is set up with the proper software and permissions and is available to you the day before they start.

- When setting up their e-mail address, take care to monitor how many distribution lists they are on. It's overwhelming to open your inbox for the first time to several emails without context.

- Set up their desk for them. Be sure to wipe the surface with a cleaner, and make sure their filing cabinet has been cleaned out. There are bonus points if you leave a small welcome package with a pen, notebook, stickers, or other company swag.

- Walk your employees around the office, and introduce them to the other departments. Do this even if your HR department gives a tour of the building because it's more comfortable to be personally introduced to your new colleagues. Plus, you can clearly point out who your new hires will need to work closely with better than your HR counterparts.

- Set up introductory meetings. You know who your community managers and moderators need to work with, so set up a few meetings on their behalf to ensure that they're moving in the right direction. You don't even have to join them!

- Have a plan for the first couple weeks. Detail who they need to meet with, and what specific tasks that you'll want accomplished and when. This way, your employees will know what they're supposed to be doing while you're in and out of your daily meetings, and they'll feel like they are contributing to the business from the get-go.

Initial Training

Much can be said about the value of a great onboarding experience. Studies show that employees will typically spend 60–90 days getting acclimated to a new company and culture, if not more. That's at least 60–90 days that they're earning a salary, though they might not be contributing as much value to your company as you'd like. A well-thought-out onboarding program can easily shorten the time-to-value for new employees and also helps to improve employee retention and loyalty. It's important to provide training on your company's vision and purpose, your product, and on the expectations around the required writing style and tone to ensure a well-rounded community onboarding experience.

Community managers almost always end up becoming the face of a brand in one way or another. This happens because we spend a lot of time interacting with our customers online, as well as at offline events. When we're off the clock, we meet up with other community managers and attend our own conferences and meet-ups to better ourselves as professionals and push our industry forward. Whether I meet with customers or my own peers, one of the first questions that I'm always asked is, "How do you like working for your company?" It's much easier to answer that question when I understand and am fully aligned with my employer's mission, vision, values, and goals, so share these concepts with your community teams early.

Along with training on your company's culture and message, focus a good chunk of time on getting your team a baseline level of product knowledge. In most branded customer communities, community managers and moderators spend a lot of time talking with customers about the product. Your team must talk intelligently about the product and have more than just a surface-level conversation to ensure maximum levels of productivity. It's not efficient if your team constantly has to check with a product manager before posting a response. If you don't have product training readily available and don't have time to create any, make sure your new hire has access to a test instance of your product along with some time to do his or her own testing. Don't forget to add an entry to your to-do list to develop product training before you hire anyone else!

It's also important to provide some guidance on your company's overall style and tone. Work with your marketing or public relations team to uncover what words and phrases are not recommended for use, and put together some examples that help to illustrate the voice of your brand. Style and tone is not something that's typically perfected overnight. It takes time and a lot of attempts to get it right, so give straightforward feedback on how your team's writing can improve. You don't want to get into the habit of having to approve each tweet, response, or blog post before publication.

Providing training for new community managers brings a lot of value to your organization, including stronger job satisfaction, better job performance, a greater commitment to the organization, and reduced stress—all of which can save your company money over the long run! For some companies, it might not be possible to put your employees through as comprehensive as a training program as you'd like. If that's the case for you, focus your initial training on the areas in which you're less confident in your new employee's understanding and abilities to ensure you get the basics covered.

Keeping Them Current

One of the final pieces to consider in your overall onboarding experience is how you'll handle continuing training for your team. In silo organizations, it's easy for decisions to be made and changes to be put in place without communicating to the rest of the departments. This behavior puts your frontline employees, like community moderators, at risk for being caught off guard during their daily work. In addition, as a manager I've found that continuously providing training to existing employees helps to improve job satisfaction and keep up morale. Too often employees find out new information too late and slip into the, "Well nobody told me," mentality. Those negative thoughts can fester, which puts your leadership and investments in your employees at risk.

Ongoing training doesn't have to be determined from the start, but it is something to think about within the first 3 to 6 months of an employee's start date. Here are some things to consider:

- How often will you provide new training for your existing employees? Every quarter? Bi-annually?

- How will you train for updates to existing products? This includes functional product knowledge, along with how to position the information to customers without sounding too corporate or unauthentic.

- How will you train for new product launches?

   What happens when policies are changed? For most web-based services, policy changes, especially privacy or terms of service/terms of use policies, can wreak a lot of havoc with customers. Plan to communicate to employees and customers around these changes early.

- How can you help your employees further their career? We talk more about this in the next section of the chapter, but it's worth thinking about as you ponder the types of training you need moving forward.

Leading Your Team

Management has to do with control and coordination, whereas leadership focuses on inspiring people. Management is something that employees expect from department heads and team leads, but leadership is the emotional hook that keeps them engaged in their roles and loyal to you. Though your job title might say "manager," your team is really looking for you to be both a manager and a leader at the same time. You have a team of highly skilled professionals who are clear about their purpose and goals and have been trained to execute on their goals properly. There should be no need to control anyone. Instead, you need to use your innate leadership skills to inspire and influence your team on a daily basis. Your team members need to know that you support them, you trust them to do their job, and that you care deeply about their professional development.

The Buck Stops with You

Part of being a strong leader means that you might need to stand up for your team members, or otherwise protect them during challenging times. A couple years ago, I had the unfortunate experience of having to deal with a mild case of cyberstalking. A community member had taken screen shots of the avatar by one of our employees and began to create many duplicate accounts under his personal likeness across a variety of social networks. We had never experienced something like this before and had no idea how to best to handle the situation.

The experience clearly illustrated that community managers and moderators risk their online reputations and identities when engaging with other users as a representative of your brand. By simply being affiliated with your organization, community team members are susceptible to being targeted and harassed online by angry customers or by those with nothing better to do. As department and team leaders, we have a responsibility to anticipate these risks and enact policies to help protect our team members. If something does threaten the safety or security of your team members, you have to take ownership of the situation swiftly and work tirelessly to find a solution. Personal privacy is a fragile thing, and you risk losing the trust and respect of your team if you don't take concerns of privacy breaches seriously.

Invest in Relationships

When I think back to the bosses and leaders that I've worked for over the years, the common thread in the leaders who have had the most impact on my career are those that understand the value of investing in employee relationships. The relationships that they have established with me have helped to grow and shape my career in ways that might not have been possible, and I'm grateful for what I've learned along the way.

Along with insight, these relationships helped to establish loyalty and commitment toward my manager, and those bonds helped me to push through the hard days. When it became my turn to begin managing people, I also made it a point to connect with my team. As with my own experience, these small investments in relationships paid dividends, and I built a team of community managers who were dedicated to me, who helped us deliver on the commitments that we had made to our broader management team.

Investing in relationships with the members of your team matters. It doesn't mean you have to be friends with them, but you do need to get to know them. In Patrick Lencioni's *3 Signs of a Miserable Job*, one of the first pillars of workplace misery is the notion of anonymity. If employees don't feel that their managers and leaders know who they are, they're likely to be disengaged from the company and from their roles. Employees who don't feel connected to their work, or their leadership team, do not often deliver incredible customer experiences and are only steps away from leaving the organization.

The Return on Employee Engagement

One of the things that strong leaders have in common is that they're good communicators. They check in with their teams regularly and listen to their stories. They celebrate successes and proactively address concerns. Are you doing that with your team today? When was the last time you asked your employees whether they are happy, or whether they're still enjoying their role? Identifying issues early gives you the opportunity to make the necessary changes to keep that employee interested in coming to work for you every day, and it also plays a part into the whole "invest in relationships" bit that I just talked about.

Another way to keep stellar employees engaged is to find ways to offer them new learning opportunities. If you have someone that is a natural leader, work with her to develop those skills. You might consider sponsoring her to take a leadership development workshop or introduce her to a potential mentor. Maybe you have an employee who has an incredible knack for design. Get him some online classes on graphic design, and offer the opportunity to create new banner images and graphics for your communities. Offering more responsibility to your team as its skill levels increase is another way that you can prove that you trust and believe in the team's future.

Finally, recognize when transition might be inevitable. Managers are just as susceptible to burnout and fatigue as employees are, so recognize when you might be ready for something new. In a previous role, I had a wonderful junior community manager who was working for me. We were a solid team and in line with our organizational responsibilities and with each other. One day I realized that my employee's skills and engagement had plateaued and that the only way for him to up his personal development would be to take on a role similar to the position that I was in. At that point, I opened up the dialogue with him and shared my observations. I was also nearing a point in my role where I was considering other opportunities, so I wanted to feel out his thoughts for taking on additional responsibility. The timing was right, and a few months later, I stepped aside and have watched him flourish from outside of the organization.

Community is one of the few functions within an organization that transcends departments and can affect organizational change. Executives have argued for the past few years about the value that a community team brings to an organization, but with a great strategy, thoughtful planning, and solid execution, that value can quickly be recognized.

If you want your community strategy to be successful, be sure to clearly plan and articulate the current and future needs of your team before moving into the hiring phases. After you have hired a few folks, take care to give them enough training to ensure they're off to a good start. Finally, don't forget to step out of your role as a manager every now and again to focus on your role in being a leader who can help to shape the career experiences of your direct reports.

The team running your community will be as excellent as you plan for them to be. As a leader, it's up to you to decide whether your plan is for short-term or long-term success.

16

Social Support UNtruths—
When Received Wisdom Is Not Wise

Francoise Tourniaire, Owner, FT Works

As a consultant, I help technology organizations improve their support and customer success operations, and projects often include communities. When my clients ask me whether they should do X or Y, my go-to answer is, "It depends."—and I understand how frustrating it is to hear that.

Aren't there best practices for support and social support in particular? Of course there are, and I'm always happy to expound on them, but over the years, I've found that even best practices that seem so self-evident might not be so true, at least in specific situations. So I thought I would gather a few real stories that are exceptions to commonly accepted best practices.

The three stories I tell here do not prove that the best practices are entirely wrong. Best practices do apply in most cases, and that's why they are best practices to begin with. But the stories illustrate that there is no such thing as a universal truth for social support.

Because I must protect the privacy of my clients, I give no names, but I strive to provide as many details as possible about the type of business, customer segments, the nature of the technical issues, and the support organization processes to give a rich context to each story.

I hope that the stories are helpful as you develop your own strategy for social support and that they inspire you to get educated on best practices while always maintaining a critical mind and a desire to experiment outside the well-worn path.

Untruth: Communities Are an Add-on to Support and Cannot Stand Alone in the B2B World

Truth: It is possible to deliver *all* support through a community in some circumstances.

Case Study

A vendor of a portfolio of 3-D animation software provides all its technical support through a series of online forums. There is no case management system because there are no cases. There is no hotline because there is no phone support. There are no 1:1 communications between support contacts and support engineers because all conversations take place on the forum. But there are service-level agreements (SLA) for response time, as would be expected for a standard support program. There is a cost for support, and yearly renewals. There are productivity metrics for the support engineers. And customers are happy with the support they receive!

How does it work? After all, we are talking about B2B customers here. Don't they expect some kind of personalized, or at least private service, out of the public eye?

First, this has been the setup since day one, so it's not a matter of migrating customers from a standard 1:1 support model to a 1:n support model. Customers are used to support being delivered in discussion forums and whether they like the format (and I will show that they do, in fact, like it), they have been conditioned to use it.

Second, the service level is impeccable. The response SLA is 2 hours and is met (and exceeded) consistently, and responses are technically accurate and well researched. Indeed, because all communications are exposed for all to see, support engineers have a clear incentive to provide high-quality answers, both technically and professionally.

Third, the community is relatively small and is gated, so there is a real sense of safety in knowing that all the actors on the forum are known and can be trusted. There are no lurkers with unclear intention: Everyone on the forum is there to exchange technical knowledge.

Fourth, because of the nature of the product line, issues rarely involve confidential data or processes. In a past life, I worked for several database companies, where support engineers routinely accessed confidential customer data when performing complex troubleshooting. (And I signed a respectable number of nondisclosure agreements each week.) There was no way that the database customers would expose their data on anything resembling a public forum. In contrast, in this case, issues can be reproduced without using confidential data and without exposing any confidential projects.

For this vendor, delivering support exclusively through the forum brings precious benefits, in particular the leverage of 1:n support because all questions and answers are available for all to see, and the frequent contributions of peer customers who often manage to beat the tight SLA for a vendor's response and provide excellent answers. And peers are not shy about pointing out when a question has already been asked, further reinforcing the self-service capabilities of the forum.

To deliver fast and complete answers, the support team is organized in a way familiar to case-oriented organizations: Support engineers are scheduled to watch the forum during specific time intervals and are expected to confirm with the thread creator that the solution works rather than just posting it and moving on. However, compared with standard organizations, there is more of a team approach. Support engineers routinely comment on each other's posts, so there's a looser concept of case ownership and much more of a collegial approach. This seems to bring positive dividends in the form of a faster resolution time and more diverse resources collaborating on tougher issues, just because it's easy to see what everyone else is working on.

Is it perfect? No, some larger customers are agitating for personalized support because they feel some of their questions require a bit more privacy. (And perhaps they should, indeed, get the personalized support they want, for a fee.) Without the ability to conduct live troubleshooting sessions, it's sometimes difficult to reproduce the toughest cases. It would certainly be possible to add that capability, although the vendor has not chosen to pursue it. Still, customer satisfaction is high, and there's no need to conduct surveys to find out: The forum records high numbers of accepted and liked answers.

One more thing, I chose this case study to illustrate the UNtruth that communities, at best, are an add-on to support, but it illustrates another UNtruth: Communities can solve only easy problems. This community solves hard problems including multivendor problems and questions about product best practices because of the collaborative environment. Specifically, although the support organization might not be aware of how to use the products to solve a specific business issue, chances are that other customers are. And for multivendor issues, other customers might also be the best resource—or several support engineers and others within the vendor's organization can easily collaborate because the issue is right there in front of them instead of hidden away in a case-tracking system.

And one last comment: This community also illustrates that gated communities, communities that are restricted to paying customers, can be successful and meaningful despite the UNtruth that open is always better. Here it works because all serious users of the products are paying for support, and they can form a meaningful community within the gated space. (The tools are mission-critical for their users, so access to assistance is prized, and the lure of new releases and new features also helps!)

It could be argued that the community could be opened to all users, with less attention placed by the vendor on threads posted by nonpaying customers. The vendor's rationale against opening the community is that paying customers would feel less safe in sharing their experiences with individuals that are not as tightly dedicated to the product. We can only guess at whether opening up the community would help or hinder its success, but it's certainly working well in its gated state.

Net/Net

With the right product line, it is possible to deliver all support, or a great deal of it, through a forum. The critical requirement seems to be the commitment to deliver fast, guaranteed answers. In other words: Treat the forum as you would the almighty support queue.

Untruth: Small Support Communities Are Not Viable; Bigger Is Always Better

Truth: Vibrancy, not size, is the critical success factor for communities.

Case Study

A hardware vendor is considering establishing a support community but has been dissuaded to do so by industry colleagues and by community tool vendors because the customer base is quite small: only about 150 customers. The received wisdom is that a "rule of 10" applies—about 10 percent of customers will visit a community, and 10 percent of those will contribute. Following this logic, a community with 150 potential participants is just too small to succeed.

But the support director is stubborn: She feels that her small group of customers is very dedicated to the product and will make the community successful despite its small size. Indeed, customers are asking for a community on a regular basis. And the customer base is expanding, so the numbers will only get better.

After a 6-month trial period, it turns out that the instincts of the support director were correct. The community is thriving, with multiple posts everyday and lively debates. What went well and why is the rule of 10 seemingly irrelevant here?

First, the numbers were not quite as small as initially thought. Sure, there are only 150 customers, but in the B2B world, this translates into many more interested parties. The vendor had been restricting support *contacts* to two per customer (for a maximum total of 300 individual contacts), but the community is open to all employees of customer organizations, and entire teams are now participating. It is a registration-required community, but anyone with an e-mail domain that matches existing customers can register. In some cases, dozens of individuals from given customers have signed up.

Second, the level of interest in the products and in the community is high. Many participants are using the vendor's tools (specialized measuring instruments) as an essential part of their job, and they are eager to communicate with each other about how best to use the tools. Individual threads quickly grow to dozens of replies as community members rival to show off their tricks of the trade. With that, the rule of 10 is handily surpassed. Most members visit the community more than once a week, and the proportion of active members (who post in addition to reading) is much more than 50 percent.

Third, the vendor made a concerted effort to nurture the community during the initial launch. A couple of part-time support engineers read the posts daily and made sure that all unanswered threads got an answer. Because of the rapid success among the customer base, today it's the rare thread that does not receive a speedy answer from a member of the community, so the support team has had few threads to answer recently.

Interestingly, in this case, there are no true MVPs, individuals who make outsized contributions to the community. Instead, there is a large group of committed contributors. Perhaps this more egalitarian model of contribution is a consequence of the small size of the community, and it will transition over time to the familiar MVP model as the community grows?

Note that there might be another UNtruth that applies in this situation: Knowledge is concentrated in the vendor's organization. In fact, customers often have more expertise on how to use the products and how to get value from them than anyone else inside the vendor's organization, including professional services. Customers are a fount of knowledge about best practices and innovative uses of the product, and vendors can learn a lot from them—through the community.

Net/Net

The rule of 10 is only a guideline. Small but enthusiastic communities can be successful and function without much involvement from the vendor, after the initial launch, which always require some investment in people resources. If your customer base is clamoring for a community, and especially if you have good candidates for MVPs, you can launch a successful small community.

Untruth: Make the Community Go/No-Go Decision on the Basis of an ROI Analysis

Truth: It's hard to get to a hard metric for community ROI, but the exercise is worthwhile.

Case Study

An established, large software vendor would like to start a support community. The immediate impetus is the launch of a cloud version of its main software line and the realization that cloud vendors typically maintain vibrant customer communities.

The support executive starts by creating a back-of-the-envelope calculation showing that the cost of the community software, plus implementation, would be quickly recouped if the community can reduce the caseload for the new product by a small percentage. The CFO is not impressed by the small saving generated by the investment and denies the purchase.

Chastened, but undeterred, the support executive hires a consultant (me!) to create a "benchmarked ROI" for the community initiative. It's quickly apparent that the total investment will be significantly higher than initially planned. In particular, a community manager needs to be assigned to the project, as well as several part-time contributors, while the community develops its own customer-contributors.

On the other hand, the savings are not as obvious or immediate as one might want—who knows if customers will use the community at all? And will the incident rate benefit from the existence of the community? (After all, we don't know much about the incident rate for the new product because we have no experience with it.) Still, after developing several forecasting scenarios, we find a range of less blithely optimistic but still nicely positive ROIs based on reduced caseload. We also create a reasoned justification that notes the requirement for communities in the cloud space, the current customers' clamoring for them, and how community content can be used to quickly build a knowledge base.

Hurrah! The CFO approves the ROI analysis and signs off on the purchase, sternly enjoining the support executive to report back on actual performance.

The epilogue? After many months and a much higher total price tag than planned, mostly because other product lines decide to piggyback on the deployment, the community is live and functioning well. No one ever looks at the ROI again.

So was the ROI analysis worth it?

- Yes, it led to the approval of the purchase—but we don't know whether the CFO weighted the ROI analysis itself higher or lower than the well-thought-out justification blending numbers and intangibles that accompanied it.

- No, the purchase might well have been approved purely on the basis of the requirement for the cloud product—but again we do not know that for sure.

- Yes, it forced the support team to think through *all* the resources required for implementation—but the ROI analysis was more of a chore rather than the engine of that reflection.

- No, it was never used after the initial justification—and that's a shame because it was cunningly constructed (if I dare say so myself) to be usable post-implementation. What a wasted opportunity to test the assumptions we used against the very real world of deployment!

- Yes, the ROI creation process and the spreadsheet that was created as a result are now used as a model for other decisions, so the usefulness of the exercise exceeded the initial, one-time use. It now enables the support team to weigh any strategic initiative, whether process-based or tool-based, against its likely benefits such as productivity increases.

Note that the vendor has not only neglected to measure any case deflection benefits of the community, but has also not attempted to measure benefits beyond it. It's certainly not easy to measure loyalty or product improvements, but it would be a worthwhile enterprise. (And if you recall in this case, I took the easy route of mentioning those benefits as soft benefits of communities, specifically avoiding the issue of measurement.)

Let's start with loyalty. People like to belong to something larger than themselves and helping their peers generates much pride and, perhaps strangely, loyalty to the vendor. Fans (I'm talking about the MVPs here, not the garden-variety lurkers) identify with the product and with the vendor even as they change jobs, thereby providing instant, and ardent, internal referrals! And, of course, they are much more credible than vendor employees at defending the product against critics. How do we measure loyalty?

We could start with simply capturing the revenue expansion (add-ons and referrals) coming from the fans, the MVPs. It's still a small piece of the iceberg, but that would be a start. I worked with a (completely different) client who captured add-on purchases made online as a result of an MVP recommendation. It made sense in the B2C world and perhaps could be adapted to B2B.

For product improvements, communities are known to surface issues early, and they are effective as quantifying the impact of issues. So many times, I have been in an executive meeting where well-paid individuals wondered what customers thought of this or that idea. Depending on the issue, reaching out directly to the community or to the MVPs would solve the problem. The MVPs are a wonderful customer advisory board—and someone smarter than me can think of good ROI metrics in this area.

Net/Net

Capturing an exact ROI for communities is difficult because many benefits don't lend themselves to easy, let alone meaningful, quantification. At the same time, the process of researching ROI encourages the organization to consider the entire process of implementing and managing communities, and that kind of planning and brainstorming is immensely useful. It is also useful and beneficial to validate the ROI analysis after the fact, against actual data and experience, to validate the many assumptions that are made in the course of creating it and better understand and manage the business.

I hope that these stories and the UNtruths they illustrated will be helpful in your own journey toward social support. Keep questioning received wisdom: It does not always apply!

17

When Online and Offline Collide: Harnessing the Power of Mobile and Social

Annie, Tsai, Chief Customer Officer, DoubleDutch

Over the past seven years, smartphones have increased tremendously in global popularity, with the digital and physical worlds colliding in unavoidable and exciting ways. Our day-to-day activities are intrinsically linked to our mobile devices. We use our phones for everything from engaging with our friends and family, to conducting business, to tracking our schedules, interests, and even our health. When was the last time you used a physical, printed map to navigate to your destination? Do you ever go to a restaurant without consulting Yelp or Google? The smartphone has bridged the online and offline divide—and the possibilities are endless.

It wasn't that long ago when we lived our lives in a very different way. We memorized phone numbers, spoke with our friends on the phone, took notes in notebooks, sent each other messages in pager code, and we had to hit the numbers on our phone's dial pad multiple times to get to the right letter when saving a contact in our mobile phone. I remember in 2002 when Sony Ericsson launched the P800, one of the first joint ventures between Sony and Ericsson, and felt for the first time that smartphone design had come together with the right combination of form, function, and timing (see Figure 17.1). It was also one of the first camera phones on the market, which was an exhilarating consumer proposition, given that handheld 4.0 megapixel digital cameras were barely reaching mass popularization at the time. For some reason, in the U.S., one could only buy the P800 on eBay when the phone was first released, so I ended up in a bidding war with someone from Louisiana. When I finally received and started using my beautiful light-blue smartphone, I recall being distinctly underwhelmed in what the promise of a connected future delivered. Sure, I had my telephone, camera, and PDA combined into a single device, but technology was still too far behind the grandiose vision of what a smartphone could be.

Figure 17.1   Sony Ericsson P800, released in 2002

Fast-forward more than a decade and we see a dramatic shift in how deeply rooted mobile technology—specifically smartphones—have become in global culture. With smartphone adoption growing from under 20 percent in the beginning of 2010[1] to 71.6 percent in mid-2014[2] in the U.S., it's safe to say that most business professionals are equipped with a smartphone in their pockets and are using it to conduct business dozens of times per day. With the massive improvements in wireless bandwidth, processing power, and network speed, the trend is continuing with U.S. adults spending an average of 23 percent more time on their mobile devices in 2014 than the prior year.

---

1   http://www.clickz.com/clickz/column/2071614/location-marketing-convergence-social-mobile

2   http://www.marketingcharts.com/online/us-smartphone-penetration-tops-7-in-10-mobile-subscribers-in-q2-44667/

Further supporting the mobile revolution are the activities people are engaging in through their mobile devices. Processing power has dramatically improved from the first 10 million applications downloaded during the opening weekend of the Apple iTunes store in 2008[3] to the 85 billion apps downloaded in October 2014 (see Figure 17.2), which means that the types of activities smartphone users can engage in have also evolved dramatically. In fact, 2014 marked a significant shift in how U.S. adults engaged with online social networks, with a majority of this activity being done through mobile devices.[4] This "always connected" world is not only changing the way we use technology, but is shaking the very foundations of well-established social norms surrounding how people engage with each other in the physical world; online and offline are colliding.

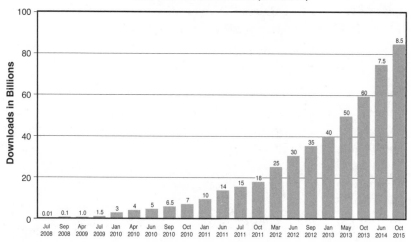

Figure 17.2 Statista results on # apps downloaded in Apple App Store (in billions): http://www.statista.com/statistics/263794/number-of-downloads-from-the-apple-app-store/

---

3 https://www.apple.com/pr/library/2008/07/14iPhone-App-Store-Downloads-Top-10-Million-in-First-Weekend.html

4 http://www.emarketer.com/Article/Mobile-Continues-Steal-Share-of-US-Adults-Daily-Time-Spent-with-Media/1010782

The reality companies are faced with is that most young adults entering the workforce in the U.S. today have spent the majority of their formative years exposed to a "Mobile First" way of life. In ExactTarget's 2014 Mobile Behavior Report, 85 percent of respondents said that mobile devices are a central part of everyday life.[5] When segmenting for 18–24 year olds, the response rate went up to 90 percent. Companies today, including DoubleDutch, are facing the distinctive challenge of integrating the right blend of mobile and social technology into our internal and external service offerings. Because the outcome is to ultimately drive higher revenues, enhancing individual experiences will help companies better understand how businesses can leverage these new social norms.

Over the past five years, although companies have made the significant investment shift from powering their workforces with basic mobile devices to Blackberrys, and now to smartphones (see Figure 17.3), users now have immediate access to an unprecedented amount of information and people at the tips of their fingers. And providers of these social and mobile services have the ability to better understand their audience by collecting massive amounts of data based on their interactions with the technology.

Today, this kind of information is heavily leveraged in B2C marketing to influence consumer spending and build brand loyalty, but the possibilities to create engaging experiences and use data to measure ROI for marketing spend in the B2B world are in many ways even more intriguing.

The global investment is still very much an offline world of events, and event production is particularly intriguing, and represents an interesting and largely untapped opportunity for companies to integrate well-established consumer habits around mobile and social technology to significantly improve the event experience and one's ability to achieve desired outcomes. In 2014 alone, companies will have spent an estimated $565 billion on organizing, exhibiting at, and attending events worldwide.[6] What's perhaps most surprising about this statistic is that the enormous portion of companies' marketing budgets—on average, 20

---

5 http://www.exacttarget.com/sites/exacttarget/files/deliverables/etmc-2014mobile-behaviorreport.pdf

6 Frost & Sullivan, "A Survey of Meeting and Event Planning Professionals and Hotel Operators," July 2013

percent of a company's total marketing spend[7]—by and large does not have effective ROI measurement capabilities. With millions of people coming together for days at a time for events around the world, there's a unique opportunity for companies to layer well-established consumer habits around social and mobile technology on top of existing event infrastructures and begin to deeply understand ROI from a completely untapped perspective—interest and engagement derived solely from attendee activity during an event. Similarly to tooling an email, product, or website so marketers clearly understand key performance metrics like email click-through rate, website abandon rate, or most used product features, marketers can and should be leveraging technology to understand how they benchmark against key metrics for event marketing spend.

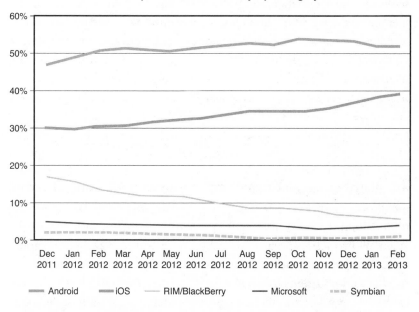

US Smartphone Market Share by Operating System

Dec 2011, Jan 2012, Feb 2012, Mar 2012, Apr 2012, May 2012, Jun 2012, Jul 2012, Aug 2012, Sep 2012, Oct 2012, Nov 2012, Dec 2012, Jan 2013, Feb 2013

Android ■ iOS ■ RIM/BlackBerry ■ Microsoft ■ Symbian

Figure 17.3 U.S. smartphone penetration across smartphone operating systems—2011 to 2013 shows the already small market share of Rim/Blackberry dropping dramatically while IOS and Android continue to steadily rise; http://www.theregister.co.uk/2013/04/05/android_market_share_slipping/.

7 B2B Marketing Budgets Set to Rise 6% in 2014: Forrester; http://adage.com/article/btob/b2b-marketing-budgets-set-rise-6-2014-forrester/291207/

Over the years at DoubleDutch, we've had to do a lot of testing around how to derive ROI for the events where we power apps for our clients. The unique perspective we offer is that being a social mobile technology company, we've been able to be our own customer and attempt to quantify ROI for ourselves with our own products. But, that's not to say that we haven't faced many of the same challenges as our clients when it came to ROI measurement.

In our experience, the most critical place to align when organizing an event is in understanding how the event team defines success. We've seen countless events take place where internal stakeholders are not involved in the early conversations around expected outcomes. It's not uncommon for those creating the vision for an event to have conversations revolve around "We need to build our brand" or "Our competitor is doing it, so we need to prove we're bigger and better" without a clear understanding of what it takes to prove that spend was worthwhile. As a result, the reasoning around why budgets should be allocated towards event spend, how much to invest, and how to measure whether or not that investment was effective are often misaligned from the beginning. This misalignment can be avoided when event organizers, their executive stakeholders/sponsors, and the event team can quickly come to an agreement of how success is defined prior to selecting the tools to measure these success metrics. Companies organize events for several reasons—incentivizing your sales force to sell your product on-site, building relationships and brand recognition, or connecting merchants to buyers to name a few—and defining success early on includes not only understanding the type and goal of your event, but also understanding who your attendees are and why they are attending your event. Your metrics of success and the way you measure them should be guided by all of these factors. Table 17.1 contains two examples of metrics and programs by event type. Organizers can use these to begin formulating a holistic view of event success and how mobile social technology can be leveraged to measure that success.

Table 17.1   Event Types: Metrics and Programs to Define Success

Event Type and Goals	Mobile Social Metrics and Programs to Define Success
Internal Sales Meeting: Generate excitement for the upcoming year, build relationships, reward top performers.	**Metrics** ■ Greater than 100 actions per user within the mobile app ■ Polling results tied to specific content
Association Trade Show Conference: Connect attendees with exhibitors, deliver educational content, overall association engagement (networking)	**Metrics** ■ Leads by exhibitor, potentially also segmented by sponsorship level (depending on the size of the trade show, these goals will vary) ■ Session survey results and speaker ratings (four-star average and above) ■ Percent of attendees with more than two logins per day ■ Social media sentiment and buzz **Programs** ■ Hashtag incentive programs ■ Lead scanning as a part of points attainment for giveaways ■ Polls and surveys integrated into session content

With an internal two-day meeting with 200 of your top employees for example, your goals might be centered on ensuring content stickiness and relationship building. Overlaying a social mobile digital layer at this kind of event becomes a matter of aggregating content and creating a closed social network to allow for freeform conversation in a secure setting. Capturing data around the kinds of topics that generate the highest engagement and conversation among the attendees in real time then gives the event team an indication of what content is resonating most powerfully with the audience. Leveraging online polling accessed through mobile devices to test or get feedback from attendees on how well they recall important information and the overall event experience enables the event organizer to immediately benchmark how well the event meets the goals around content stickiness (see Figure 17.4).

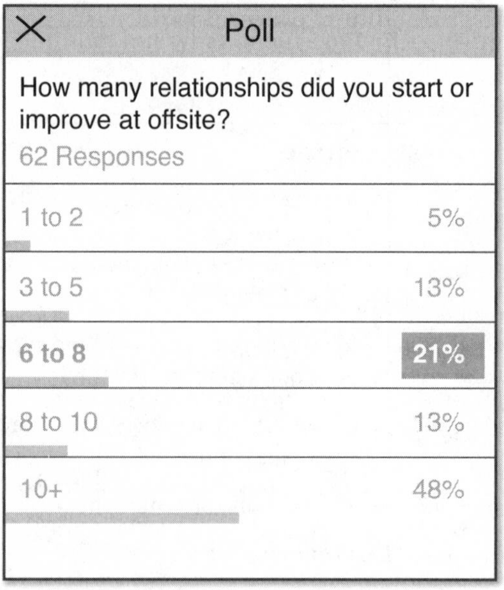

Figure 17.4 Poll taken from recent DoubleDutch internal company offsite through a social mobile app; poll was integrated into the CEO's closing statements and results were delivered in real time to the audience.

On the other end of the spectrum such as with a large expo with thousands of attendees, the event organizers might be more interested in ensuring attendees are able to find the things they traveled there to get, whether it's an item to purchase, understanding trends in the space, or connecting with a specific person. To achieve these goals, leveraging an open network and existing social channels might be more effective at driving overall awareness around the event. In this case, it might be more important to use mobile and social tools to track leads generated for exhibitors, event influencers (see Figure 17.5), hash tags (#) and mentions (@), and general social media buzz.

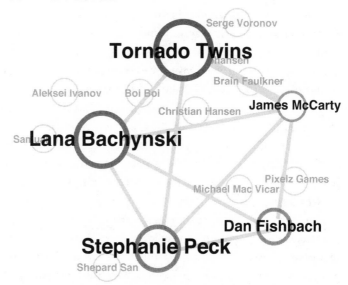

Figure 17.5   Post-event engagement report showing the most influential attendees at the Game Developer's Conference 2014 based on activity in their mobile app

Regardless of the goals being set to define event success, it's absolutely critical that someone either on the event team or close to the project champions a holistic view of technology before, during, and after the event. At events, organizers can quickly go overboard in the various ways in which the digital layer can be applied to the physical world of their event and the overall physical space. As with all technology and software spend, it's easy to overinvest in technology and underutilize it. And it's also very easy to purchase technology just to check the "in with the times" box without having a good enough understanding of exactly what it is you're investing in—and how else you can leverage that technology to do several things to improve and measure ROI at your event. When this happens, attendees often feel the resulting misalignment caused by a disjointed and under-integrated event technology.

Circling back on the event goals will also help your champion retain clarity when it comes to deciding what kind, how much, or how little technology gets implemented both in the event space or in the attendee's personal space through his or her mobile devices. For instance, encouraging social interaction and networking through a Vine video wall is not as effective as an activity feed stream of closed network content (or depending on your event type, open network hash tag feed) on large screens. Or, using large billboards to convey key messages might not be as effective as personalized push notifications through a mobile app to attendee smartphones when your audience represents a variety of segments within your customer base, and a broadcast message might not apply to everyone. If an event technology is to be successful, it is crucial that the event technology champion understand deeply how to best apply the digital layer to the events in order to create the best experience for the attendees. When your technology champion has a clear understanding of what you are investing in and what that technology portfolio can help you deliver and measure upfront, your attendees will only benefit from a well-thought-out and integrated experience.

A great example of technology championship was seen with Forbes, one of the world's top business media outlets with both online and offline publications, and its use of event technology at both its Women's Summit and its 30 Under 30 Conference. In addition to its ability to draw concrete learning from one event to the next, much of its success and ability to be so responsive and quickly implement ideas is because it became an exceptional technology champion. It learned how to use the app and maximize its features, and as a result it gained an in-depth understanding of the best ways to apply it to its specific audience. This combined with its keen understanding of its audience created a strategy that it knew would foster a whole new level conversation. The outcome? With nearly a thousand active users, almost 4,000 photos and nearly 8,000 status updates were posted. Most impressively, data pulled from the app reported a massive amount of networking that took place through the mobile app with nearly 14,000 attendee profile views. By using technology to seamlessly play into its audience's mobile-centric behaviors, Forbes successfully created a closed social community that actively lives on.

Once your investment in social mobile has been decided and the team members have a clear understanding of how they are going to integrate the tool into the overall experience to support attendees getting the most out of the event, it's critically important that the attendees themselves also perceive that they will both gain value from interacting with the digital layer and have more fun at the event as a result of doing it. To easily encourage adoption and usage, deeply integrate social and mobile into how the event is executed at a foundational level. A simple example of this is if you have content breakout sessions as a part of your event, encourage your speakers to run polls or have questions asked through the mobile app to get immediate and very public feedback. With our clients, we've found that events that integrate polling through their mobile app into session content generates 4–6 times the engagement of events that do not utilize this single feature. Once attendees get into the mobile app, they are more apt to continue engaging with the content and each other through that channel. There is an added benefit for everyone involved— attendees see in real time what others around them are thinking, event organizers are able to collect data in a centralized place to better understand what is happening at the event, and speakers can create a significantly more engaging experience by understanding in real time what the people in the room are thinking without having to sidetrack the presentation with open discussion.

Attendees can have significantly better experiences when event organizers are listening to their audience and making adjustments in real time. With the Partyforce 2014 mobile app, a fun networking tool built as a companion to the Salesforce.com Dreamforce 2014 conference (see Figure 17.6), the negative sentiment around missed networking opportunities at the 20,000 person Dreamforce conference became apparent after the second day. To address this concern being voiced through activity posts in the app's social feed, a "Missed Connections" section was added on day three in the app so attendees could post notes and find each other from prior evening events (see Figure 17.7).

Figure 17.6 Salesforce.com blog post highlighting Partyforce 2014 as a must for navigating the massive conference located in San Francisco, CA

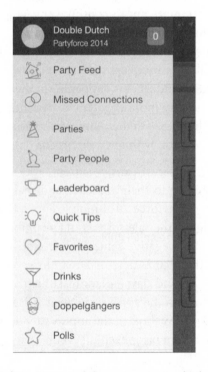

Figure 17.7 Partyforce 2014 mobile app content, which was customized to be a networking event companion app to Dreamforce 2014

With the event itself, it's easy to apply basic online and social marketing best practices to your social mobile experience to supercharge results from your mobile app investment. For instance, a cardinal rule with social media marketing is that you shouldn't be afraid to ask your followers for what you want—more likely than not, those already engaged with your brand will be more than happy to meet your request if it is within reason. Driving engagement within a social mobile environment is no different—don't be afraid to ask your attendees to perform certain activities in the app, like post photos highlighting great moments, submit nominations for an award (see Figure 17.8), engage in creative ways through social media (see Figure 17.9), or crowd source the best content by posting the quotes that resonate most powerfully with speaker audiences. That content then serves as a virtuous cycle to get more attendees engaging with the posts by liking, commenting, or posting new related content.

Figure 17.8 Forbes 30 Under 30 Event's mobile app leveraged the social mobile channel to ask attendees to submit nominations for the next class of celebrated individuals

Figure 17.9 Forbes CMO Summit attendees leveraged their mobile app to drive content through multiple channels, including Twitter, Facebook, and LinkedIn (Twitter example above)

An extension of asking for what you want is leveraging another best practice drawn from social media and online communities to promote attendee engagement—gamifying your event experience and rewarding attendees for performing actions that deliver the most value both to them and for the event. By incentivizing your attendees to engage in the social mobile layer, your event will see a dramatic increase in engagement overall. Through your mobile app and throughout the physical space of your event, you can then in real time further leverage the event attendees' generally natural aptitude for socialization, competition, and achieving status ranks by making the "leaderboard" available for everyone to see (see Figure 17.10).

Over the past few years of working with our clients to gamify their events, we've learned several lessons on how to drive successful healthy competition—as well as what *not* to do. For instance, when you are applying a points system to activities to influence behavior, make sure you understand the specific behavior you are going to drive with the rules you set.

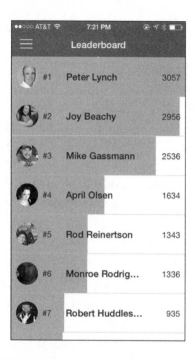

Figure 17.10 DoubleDutch's Partyforce 2014 app leaderboard, an example of how your most actively social mobile attendees can be publicly highlighted at the event

At an event in 2013, one of our clients had an objective to obtain a large photo stream from the first two days so she could create a slideshow for the dinner on the third evening. To encourage attendees to post photos, the event organizers set gamification rules to reward the top attendee in the leaderboard by the end of the second day, and to note that photos in general were worth more. Because the rules were non-specific as to what kinds of photos the event organizer wanted, attendees posted photos of everything—speakers, each other, selfies, even their shoes—just to get points. Also, because only the attendee with the highest points would receive an iPad, the event organizers received several complaints once the top attendee was so far ahead in points scored with non-relevant content that it was virtually impossible to catch up. Key takeaways from this gamification model were twofold; first, ensure the gamification rules you set will drive the behavior you're looking for, and second, if you are going to reward attendees for leaderboard ranking, don't only reward the attendee with the most points, instead randomly select three of the top twenty attendees, thereby incentivizing more people to attempt and make it to the top. Alternatively for multi-day events, reset the leaderboard every day to give everyone a new chance to win each day.

Gamifying an event is a personal endeavor—the event organizer needs to understand the attendees' interests well enough to know what content, activities, and asks will resonate with them and prompt desired behaviors. For example, McAfee, the world's largest dedicated security company, wanted to find a new and creative way to increase user participation in the event's mobile app at McAfee FOCUS14. It devised an interesting play on the event's location with the Cyber Kill Chain Game, allowing McAfee to benchmark knowledge across the event community and test attendees on key information that was being taught throughout the event.

Throughout the conference, the event team sent push notifications to attendee devices to let them know when it was time to play the game. In addition to the game itself, attendees were encouraged to participate in other app functions as well to increase engagement, like through the app's live polling feature where attendees could view in real time the aggregate results of what other attendees were submitting.

The McAfee event team leveraged the mobile app in an integrated and holistic way during the event, which created a deeply successful engagement. Game winners were also announced inside of the app as a promoted post as well as on Twitter, which drew the thousands of users back into the app to re-engage every day. As a result of its integrated strategy, the McAfee team was able to generate some of the highest in-app engagement of all of our accounts in 2014 with nearly 200,000 in-app actions.

It's also important to ensure that no matter the gamification model being applied to the event, the organizer recognizes that it's always going to be a learning experience, oftentimes helping you get to know your audience just a little bit better for next time. There truly is tremendous benefit to leveraging a tool like gamification at your event. When executed well, this kind of program can significantly drive attendee engagement both within the event's mobile app as well as offline in the event's physical space, which gets us to what we believe is the most interesting part—data.

Selfishly as a technology provider, we want to collect as much data as possible from in-app behavior to enable us to help our clients understand their attendees and event success as best as possible. Without high enough technology adoption, it will be significantly more difficult to validate event success with the data captured through the digital layer, both because you don't have enough data to be representative of the population but also because the great tools you've invested in will have positively impacted only a small percentage of attendees. It's important to note that adoption benchmarks vary wildly across the spectrum of event types—companies should expect a range from 80 percent adoption at closed-registration corporate events all the way down to 20 percent adoption at the largest public expos and tradeshows.

Driving adoption of social mobile technology at events can be easy; especially once it is integrated as a standard part of the event's marketing campaign. However, all too frequently we see event organizers send a last-minute email to attendees the night before the event encouraging them to download the mobile app. Formalizing the marketing campaign to include when you start talking to your attendees about technology tools to make their event experience as successful as possible is critical to adoption. Including in the pre-event marketing plan specific milestones for when to start the conversation around social engagement at the event will create a great deal of transparency around how your event team is driving adoption and getting your attendees excited. For events that enable the public to register, it's not uncommon to see the mobile app download page be front and center on the event's website (see Figure 17.11).

With many types of conferences, event organizers can choose to make their social mobile tools available to the general public, even those who choose not to invest the time and money to travel to the actual event. Choosing to do so adds a new layer of engagement where the opportunity to connect and learn expands significantly. Opting for an open social mobile experience when appropriate for the event type strengthens the digital experiences for both attendees and non-attending social participants, though there are instances in which keeping the app closed is more beneficial to measure metrics of event success (see Figure 17.12).

Figure 17.11   McAfee FOCUS14, an annual security conference in Las Vegas, prominently placed the mobile app download link in the top navigation for the conference website to drive high-profile adoption

This year the FOCUS mobile app is open to everyone, not just registered attendees and we've made it easy for you to get started. Once you have downloaded the app, watch the short introductory video within the activity feed of the app that highlights the main features. We also created a short user guide to walk you through the various sections within the app. The app has been launched earlier this year so you can get the communication started. Content will be populated as it becomes available so be sure to look and see what's new.

Figure 17.12   McAfee FOCUS14 website content highlighting an open social mobile experience for everyone

It's up to us as marketers, socially savvy business leaders, and executives to embrace and be at the forefront of technology movements and their application and ability to add value to our companies and business models. In doing so, there is no downside; we only stand to deliver better and more relevant experiences to our clients. In the event space specifically, the more prepared companies are to launching data-driven experiences, the better off marketing departments will be in validating and maximizing return to their companies. Digitizing and measuring the event space is just the beginning of an exciting revolution in which technology builds upon and enhances our social experiences—not only at events but also in our day-to-day lives. As technology continues to improve, our ability to leverage the digital layer to enhance the experiences we have in the physical world around us will improve as well, and that pace of change will continue to accelerate. Are you ready?

18

Social Media: from Accessibility to Generation Z

Holly Nielsen, Social Media Leader, IBM

Technology is changing everything we do by increasing the speed at which we do it, and the world of online social media and networking is no exception—fast-moving and fluid, it's an exciting field to be involved in. New applications and platforms are released daily. Thousands of experts write an endless number of articles telling you what you should and shouldn't do, how to make money, how to capture fans, how many times a day to post, and what to say in each and every one of them. It can be intimidating. Some days, it might be tempting to throw up your hands and refuse to play because you don't know who to trust, what's best for your business, what works for your employees and for you personally, which platform you should use, and where and how you should use it.

In the interest of full disclosure, I will say that I'm an IBM employee who's been deeply involved in social media and social networking for 6 years (and loving it) as a natural extension of digital marketing. In that time, I have seen the hype grow around "social" in much the same way virtual worlds took the world by storm years ago. There is some pressure to stay away from the term "social" for this communication phenomenon and new way of connecting virtually. The argument is that "social" sounds shallow and unprofessional, and by extension, something not advantageous for business. Nothing could be further from the truth. The terms social media, social networking, and social business are thrown around and used interchangeably. I'm guilty of it also.

As more of the population becomes digitally savvy, there will be less confusion and more clarity on which term to use when. But to start, I define them as follows:

- **Social media** describes the various platforms and tools that enable social networking to take place and are just the means of two-way communication.

- **Social networking** is a broader term that incorporates the communication that takes place in the social media channels among the connections you have created. Social networking is an all-encompassing term that can include communications, relationships, engagement, community building, and collaboration.

- **Social business** is the broadest term of the three and arguably the most difficult to define because it can incorporate how you communicate, engage, and collaborate, both externally and internally. It is a term that is bandied about recklessly, but just because you use social media doesn't mean that you're a social business, even though it usually includes social networking and social media. IBM, for example, characterizes social business as cultivating trusted relationships and encouraging innovation and collaboration to make people more effective and integrates the three fundamental characteristics of engagement, transparency, and nimbleness.

Social media is just one element of a marketing plan, and it makes sense to define objectives before building a strategy. Each of these is a reasonable objective and might require different channels to achieve:

- Thought leadership
- Sales leads
- Partnership opportunities
- Conversion of leads to sales
- Direct sales? Traffic to your website or blog
- Business for your brick and mortar stores
- Business for your online stores

After objectives are defined, I've distilled what I've learned into a checklist of 15 multilevel questions to answer, prelaunch:

1. What do you want to accomplish; that is, what does social success look like for your brand?

2. How does your social program support your company's business objectives?

3. How will you measure success?

4. Do you have a digital strategy? What is it, and how will your social presence complement it and support it?

5. Who is your audience? What content is going to be valuable to them?

6. Which social media channels are your audience using? Twitter? Facebook? LinkedIn? Google+? SlideShare? What about Pinterest or Instagram? Tumblr? Snapchat?

7. Which social media channels are your competitors using?

8. Which are the top two or three channels your audience and competitors are using that you can focus on first?

9. How are you going to follow who your customers and competitors are following, and listen to the conversations taking place?

10. Are you going to create a blog and can you host your content on your website? Do you have the content and sufficient content creators to support a blog and keep it fresh? Or does it make more sense to focus on placing your content on other platforms?

11. Do you have the bandwidth/resources to support a social networking program?

12. Do you understand the risks of using social media, and do you have a crisis plan for dealing with unhappy customers, trolls, or bad press?

13. Are there other brands or divisions within your company who already have their social channels set up? Can you piggyback onto their efforts and success?

14. Does your plan include increasing the amplification and reach of your social program by encouraging your subject matter experts (SMEs) to build their own social eminence and actively participate?

15. Are you ready to no longer just push content out to your eco-system—clients, prospects, partners, press, and bloggers—but actually build relationships with them?

Marketing, marketing communications, public relations, and even sales are connecting and interlocking in ways as never before. The traditional communications channels have been turned upside down, and I don't think they'll ever be the same. Communications are much less exclusive—the majority of social channels are open to anyone who wants to listen.

I am still chuckling over the experience of a friend who spent quite a bit of time coaching an industry group colleague of hers on the use of Twitter. They spent a couple of hours on it, and my friend was comfortable that her colleague understood it. Yet, when she checked on this person's new Twitter account, she found it locked. So although this person got the mechanics of tweeting—hashtags, following, retweeting, and so on—she missed the underlying principle of it entirely.

And she isn't alone. This concern of oversharing has been voiced many times in my training classes and coaching. When you spend much of your career being cautious about the information that is potentially shared with competitors (which is why there was such cross-traffic from competitors at trade show booths years ago), the open kimono (or showing the inner workings basis of social) is daunting.

I've recently become enamored with how well the concept of digital natives and digital immigrants explains the generational divide apparent in the comfort levels of social adoption. First introduced by Mark Prensky in 2001, in a paper entitled "Digital Natives, Digital Immigrants," he recognized that digital natives "…think and process information fundamentally differently from their predecessors." Digital immigrants, however, "…learn—like all immigrants, some better than others—to adapt to their environment, they always retain, to some degree, their 'accent,' that is, their foot in the past."

My favorite example of the difference between the two was from a meeting last year. Our team spent one-half the day capturing ideas, concepts, work streams, and so on, onto many of those large white easel sheets. (You know the kind.) A digital immigrant grabbed the sheets and said she would take them back to her hotel room and transcribe them into a document. A digital native said that she'd save her the trouble of carrying them back and would just take photos of the sheets with her smartphone and then put them in the recycling bin.

Whether digital native or digital immigrant, the one thing that "everyone" agrees upon, though, is that social has created a dramatic change in marketing and communications strategies and tactics, and also that it's here to stay.

I have several viewpoints of social depending on which hat I'm wearing. As an individual, I love social media. Facebook keeps me connected with my social graph, even with the understanding that my data is the price I pay to use Facebook. I enjoy the connection and interactions with friends, family, friends of family, family of friends, friends of friends, former classmates, former and current colleagues, and people with whom I share common interests.

Twitter is amazing for exposure to so much new and interesting content, and the most real-time news available. LinkedIn enables me to keep current with current and former colleagues, companies I'm interested in, and special interest groups. Plus it enables me to blog and share my interests with those same individuals and groups easily and quickly.

And as the social media lead for two nonprofits, I maintain Facebook pages, and again, love the interaction. But because these are nonprofit pages, Facebook's algorithm changes that penalize pages that don't pay for promotion has resulted in a dramatic drop in all three areas: reach, amplification, and engagement.

As social media channels become more saturated and corporations need to have business plans that actually create a return on investment, I think we'll see that this issue needs to be resolved.

We've had varying levels of success with different platforms and different tactics, which is typical with social. With the exception of what is usually an insensitive faux pas, the cost and penalties for testing with social are low. If a tactic doesn't work, there aren't exorbitant costs or disgruntled clients to sooth. There's just little to no response, which means that it's okay this didn't work. We can check it off and go back to the drawing board for a new idea.

When I started the IBM Accessibility Facebook page, we were one of the first groups to have what we termed "Facebook Expert Hours." I would pick a topic, round up some experts on that topic, and then publicize the date and time of the Expert Hour. Engagement was fantastic with several hundred fans asking questions and liking comments. Unfortunately, Facebook changed the page layout, and fan comments and questions were shunted off to a sidebar, instead of in the white space in the middle, effectively shutting down a successful program for us.

Another program that has been quite successful is a closed group on LinkedIn. The members are all under NDA, so the SMEs don't feel intimidated about the open kimono effect with the information we share. Requiring criteria to join and limiting membership to those individuals who meet the criteria enables us to use the group for multiple objectives: communication vehicle, recruitment tool, and SME exposure. The advantage of LinkedIn for B2B over the other social media platforms is that no one is anonymous. We know who members are, which firms they work with, and what kind of LinkedIn connections they already have.

One of the greatest challenges we have is finding SMEs with the time and interest in being socially active. In theory, it sounds like a good idea, but even with one-on-one coaching, for many it feels like time they just don't have available, and the benefits are not as immediate or obvious as going on a sales call or participating in a seminar or webinar.

Infographics

The exponential growth of social media channels and the popularity of graphics and visuals on those channels have spawned a new visual format on steroids with a new name: infographics.

Googling infographics to get some sense of how many infographics have been created in the last couple years and whether someone has counted or cataloged them returned 14 million results. Yes, 14 million. Seriously.

And the quick survey I took of the links showed that some of them were for multiple infographics.

Wishpond pulled together some eye-opening statistics on the use of graphics in 2014:

- Ninety percent of information transmitted to the brain is visual. Visuals are processed 60,000 times faster in the brain than in text.

- Videos on landing pages increase average page conversion rates by 86 percent.

- Visual content is social-media ready and social-media friendly. It's easily sharable and easily palatable.

- Businesses who market with infographics grow in traffic an average of 12 percent more than those who don't.

- Sixty percent of consumers are more likely to click a business whose images appear in search results.

- Sixty-seven percent of consumers consider clear, detailed images to carry more weight than product information or customer ratings.

I'm sure to no one's surprise, with the exception of tweets about face-to-face events and webinars, we get almost double the engagement on tweets that include a graphic. If the offer is an infographic, I'll usually do a screen grab of the infographic to include in the tweet.

Filter Bubble

When Twitter started sending out daily e-mails on tweets that might be of interest, and Twitter accounts follow, I was reminded of a TedTalk video I watched late last year, and went digging for it to see whether I remembered correctly. And I did. Twitter's new summary doesn't prevent me from following specific tweeters and hashtags, but it seems to be the first step in becoming a gatekeeper by surfacing the content that the Twitter algorithms determine is relevant to me, and is yet another example of the "online 'filter bubbles'" that Eli Pariser talks about in his 9-minute TED Talk. TED summarizes the video this way, "As web companies strive to tailor their services (including news and search results) to our personal tastes, there's a dangerous unintended consequence: We get trapped in a 'filter bubble' and don't get exposed to information that could challenge or broaden our worldview." Eli Pariser argues powerfully that this will ultimately prove to be bad for us and bad for democracy. (A colleague and I tried the Google search experiment where we both searched on the same word, and then compared what we found—and we did not get the same search results—so the online filter bubble is in play right now.)

So in "summarizing" the stories and tweets sent to me in this weekly e-mail, Twitter is perpetuating and embracing the "online filter bubble" that Eli Pariser talks about—deciding for me what is relevant to me, just by serving it up in a weekly e-mail. I subscribe to several social media aggregation e-mails—one of my favorites is from SmartBrief, but aggregating is what they do and it's what I expect of them.

All this makes me wonder where we draw the line in this age of information overload and how we choose between:

- News customized to what you've looked at so far and the news and articles your social network is reading

- News that helps you stretch your mind and your opinions and lets you step out of your clearly defined point of view to learn and decide on your own

I don't have the answers to this—I think it's one of those time-will-tell problems. I do wonder whether they are mutually exclusive, and whether we have to choose one or the other, or whether there is some way to make them both work.

Making Social Media More Accessible

Today's mainstream social media channels are not accessible to all. I spent 10 years in the accessibility field, and the accessibility of social media was an immediate concern, and in fact delayed our venture onto several of the social media platforms. I'm no longer working with that group at IBM, but accessibility is a topic that people become passionate about, and awareness of it (or the lack of it) is something that becomes part of your DNA.

I don't think anyone will argue with this statement: Social media channels enable social networking, a phenomenon fueled largely by user-generated content and the various ways users can connect and share that content.

But when you look at the fact that up to 15 percent of the world population has some type of disability and can be and are excluded from participating in that social networking by inaccessible social media platforms, it's a huge concern.

2014 usage numbers for the top five social media channels are incredible:

- Facebook has 1.28 billion monthly active users.
- Google+ has 540 million monthly active users.
- Twitter has 255 million monthly active users.
- LinkedIn has 40 million monthly active users.
- Pinterest has 40 million monthly active users.
- YouTube has 1 billion+ total users watching 6 billion hours of video per month.

When Denis Boudreau was president of AccessibilitéWeb, a Montreal-based accessibility cooperative, he put together the most thorough presentation I've seen that evaluated the accessibility of the five main social media platforms. (Pinterest is not included.) He evaluated the platforms on the eight most-common accessibility problems:

- Section headings
- Color contrasts
- Labels and form fields
- Keyboard navigation
- Text equivalents for images
- Multimedia
- Language
- Validation

His findings in 2011? All five platforms failed. LinkedIn did the best, at 29 percent.

Because these platforms are available at no cost to users and participation is optional, there isn't the pressure from paying customers or government regulations to make them accessible and inclusive.

There are a few bright areas. The first is that many mobile requirements are the same as accessibility requirements, so generally speaking, the mobile social media apps tend to be more accessible. And second, both the changing technology-related legislation worldwide that is incorporating accessibility requirements and the consumers who are becoming more vocal about access will ultimately put pressure on these social channels to become fully accessible.

As a social media practitioner, I find it unfortunate that we're not building relationships with all our clients, prospects, and partners within social media channels because of the lack of inclusivity. Until mainstream social media channels are accessible, the ideas and insights of millions of people worldwide are not being fully shared. Neither is fully engaged as customers in the business model of the channel, resulting in potential revenue remaining on the table.

Blogging

I think blogging is one of the unsung heroes of social networking, and many people don't even consider it when they think of social. Yet, where else can you create a platform that enables your SMEs to so clearly share their expertise? PR could never provide this depth in an interview with a journalist—the journalist didn't have the time, space, or expertise to dig so deeply. I recently taught a course on blogging and pulled up some statistics that surprised me.

In February 2011:

- More than 156 million public blogs were in existence.

In February 2014:

- 172 million were Tumblr blogs.
- 75.8 million were WordPress blogs.
- Technorati has 1.3 million blogs.

Blogger doesn't release its numbers, and some experts believe it has the largest inventory of blogs.

IBM has many successful blogs that surface SMEs where previously they would have been limited to displaying their expertise at conference presentations. One of my favorites, since I was a contributor for a couple of years, is the IBM Social Business Insights blog. My co-author and I still hold the record for the number of visits to a blog post ("5 New Social Networking Apps: Cool or Creepy") of more than 75,000.

IBM Cloud and IBM Security both have active blogs, with new posts daily, and the posts are ideal for social media sharing—relevant content from experts, excellent graphics, and usually in a compact footprint.

The Future of Social

In our current social environment, I recommend that people manage their digital footprints and periodically search for themselves on the Web, making sure that the information available about them is positive. And before posting information on a social network, asking yourself this question: Is this information you don't want your grandmother or second line manager to see? If so, don't put it out on social channels— there are no guarantees that something thought private will remain private.

In 5 years, 10 years, or 20 years, how will the social landscape look? Will we see a move toward more privacy spreading across the globe, such as the European Union (EU) precedent of Article 12 of the Directive 95/46/ EC, enacted in 2014 that enables anyone to request the removal of their information from the Web?

Or, will Generation Z (born either in the late 1990s or early 2000s, depending on which source you reference and already used to having their every moment documented and shared on social platforms) create a future in which digital privacy no longer matters or exists? Will being off the social grid to live disconnected from public utilities and government systems be as difficult as it currently is now?

19

Enterprise Social Media: Science Versus Art

Christopher David Kaufman, Senior Consultant for Mobile and Social Business Strategy, Oracle

"There is nothing more difficult to plan, more doubtful of success, note more dangerous to manage than the creation of a new order of things…. Whenever his enemies have the ability to attack the innovator, they do so with the passion of partisans, while the others defined him sluggishly, so that the innovator and his party alike are vulnerable."

—Niccolo Machiavelli, the *Prince*

The opening quote is also the first paragraph to the book *Diffusion of Innovation* by sociologist Everett Rodgers. It seems apt because it is the social media manager that the enterprise has placed at the center of innovation for business processes, new opportunities, and setting up a new way to represent a company's brand or message to the public today. And yet, at every multinational corporation, there is a person who stands between every conversation about your company and every one of your company's customers. They are the innovators trying to inspire the stale corporate message of trying to sell more of brand Y to consumer X. As social is slowly merging with Big Data, they are also slowly being measured by tiny but important equations.

Before beginning with innovators and equations, let's start with Machevilli. Machevilli was certainly not aware of today's social media, though he clearly understood networks and messaging…. Today's unsung heroes of social media fit the description of innovator; they are the undervalued and often misunderstood social media managers or directors. They are the quintessential throat to choke when things go badly. And their sole purpose in life is to avoid drinking, at least to the extent that they would never accidentally flick a wrong finger, which would have them posting their inner thoughts of depravity to the corporate Facebook account. So they keep posting at near sobriety, despite the costs to their souls to continually pump out the sanitized corporate messages to as many people as possible via every sustainable social network that will listen. But they have a curious advantage.

I was one of those people and know many still. I can attest that they constantly challenge the status quo with new ideas to push "innovative" campaigns through social networks despite being forced to push the corporate drivel. Though they might not succeed every time, they are the cool ones in corporate. They have the cool projects that at any given time combine the three hottest innovative segments in technology: social, mobile, and location-based services inside their next social media marketing campaign.

But in the end, despite being the social media manager at large companies, these innovators' hip take on marketing, ultimately their lives, are tied to one equation. Of course, there are many marketing equations that businesses use to measure the effectiveness of any specific campaign: churn, customer lifetime value, and so on. The most important in terms of social media is understanding what n is. N is the brand's community on any social network.... Of course, most social media marketers hope that "n" grows. In fact, that is the prime directive of most marketing social.

Right now, in offices all around the world, these social media managers, also known as the unsung innovators, are staring at the equation $n = x$. Figuratively, x is the number of followers the brand has on any social network N. X can equal likes, follows, shares, favorites, or 1+.... In the end, its $n = x$. Right?

Before I continue, there is a philosophical argument hidden behind this equation. Some might say it's just $n = x$, a numbers game of reaching more people. Others suggest it's not about brands and numbers of people reached, but rather $n = me$. That is to say that the ultimate focus of the social media manager is that one-to-one engagement you probably have already been reading about, possibly already in the pages of this book.

How do we manipulate the messaging so it's not just $n = x$ but $n = me$, being that "me" is a special wondrous magical connection that happens when employees are empowered to deliver genuine, individually crafted narratives and honest conversation to present an organic brand-focused engagement. Blah, blah blah…. Well, I will not name names, but although it's true, you need to understand your brand's personality and how to message that. The $n = me$ people do not have the complete equation any more than the $n = x$ people.

For your information, you cannot scale one-to-one conversations with brands that have 1–3 million followers… just saying….

So before we break down the equation more, let's focus on the prime directive: increase n. Because even the $n = me$ people want more me people. Not personally me, but you get the idea.

So how do we expand the pie? I would presume almost every chapter in this book is about either $n = x$ people, $n = me$ people, or some mystical combination thereof. Well, to innovate and to be the innovator, we need to "lean in" and not necessarily the Sheryl Sanberg way. But rather, if you continue reading this chapter, you will understand that social media is for innovators, focusing on innovations, directed at messaging innovators. Hang in there, it will get clearer.

First, social media is generally broken down by owned (your FB post), earned (user-shared post), and paid (sponsored) types of campaigns. Generally, these campaigns are not one or another but rather a mix of paid promotion, social share incentives, and managed social channels pushing out the messaging. This mix will get even more muddy with PR releases and general television, radio, and movie trailer promotions to such an extent that the charts and graphs showing what is working and not working increasingly become more murky. The key is to move the right messaging through the right social networks at the right time and place. It is the hope that by moving the "messaging product" through social networks repeatedly or by reaching new networks that "n" will grow.

Now if you read anything on enterprise social media, it will appear that the prime directive in social media departments is focusing on two things: engagement and growth. Remember $n = x$ or $n = me$? Growth of the brand advocates or increases to their engagement is not that simple nor actually that different, despite what most VPs of digital or uber social media gurus tell you. Now although that appears to differ from our original objective of just growing "n," it is not. And although the social media managers or directors may be measured on engagement, in the end they will hang their hats on growth. You are going to have to just trust me on this…. Because that is a constant; every social media manager knows this is going to happen. Engagement can plummet with the swipe of Mr. Zuckerberg's pen in twisting how feeds are disseminated. Growth, unless you leave Facebook, Instagram, and Twitter and move all your content to MySpace…growth is the metric you want your bonus tied to.

Most important, it is believed that growth equals revenue. And now that the VP of marketing, the CMO, or head of communications has bought that fancy social media cloud monitoring and engagement application, it is time to see it return some profit.

Although there are ways to tie social to revenue directly via technical means, it does not differ greatly in terms of technology than paid search keywords or banner ad tracking. So although we could go into the tying of social identity to revenue (another chapter in this book entirely), most marketers know that its a numbers game, only a percentage will click or buy, so you can tweak the percentage to click or tweak the size of the pie.

In social, especially real-time, after you laid down your cash, paid messaging can be tweaked only so much. I know of teams that tweak e-mails like a gaggle of fanatical monks on ancient Sanskrit, but social has so many variables, and a lot of messaging tweaks come during the small windows of opportunity within the paid promotional ad flights. Otherwise the biggest tweaks come mostly at the end of a campaign during a post-mortem. Sure, you may reorganize your content calendar or kill an out-of-control bidding run, but the boost you get when you run paid media will generally cloud what is going on in your organic posts, earned shares, as you will have various traffic drivers coming from those owned, earned, and paid objectives.

And that's the real problem about "n." Who and what is "n?" How and why does "n" grow or not grow fast? Not just growing a community, but how, who, why, and in what ways do we try to move the needle to develop and measure larger and larger communities. And is there a difference in a community that exists around a brand, other than that they like or follow the brand?

So many gurus, social media mavens, or just your average social media manager continue to apply various ways to understand how or why n = x exerts different forces at different times. What are the differences in their "n" and another "n" community or branded network site?

The social media manager basically looks at how "n" is growing and how others are growing their "n." Or, worse, the social media manager's boss is e-mailing him how some other brand is doing it via *The New York Times*, or worse, Mashable!

Now that all social media managers are listening to their communities, they may have already seen there are differences inside it. Besides the obvious such as the username or avatar graphic, which provide often an entertaining mix of real- and super-powered personalities, many social media monitoring cloud applications do barely an adequate job of providing age, gender, and location. There are multiple reasons for this, but that's for another chapter in another book. Suffice to say, these three metrics are sometimes added with sentiment analysis, an even more poorly measured metric than age or gender. Sentiment is actually loved by the C-Suite (CEO, CMO, and COO) but ignored by many a social media manager. Simply put, "That movie was sick!" can mean different things depending on who said it, where it was said, in response to what, and where it was said.

Finally, the social media manager will have two other metrics to decipher n: conversation history and follow/followers. Each social media platform will have various bells and whistles that shape those metrics into various scores or charts, or snapshots. Many newer tools are adding themes to the history of the listened to user, for example. These "themes" are primarily grouping of word clouds based on high frequency terms.

But the majority of cloud-powered Big Data prepackaged tools provide basically these metrics: conversation history, follow/followers, gender, age, location, and sentiment.

But is that the state of the art of solving "n?" Does it involve pushing out messaging to those willing or able to watch, listen, or read either by paying to promote it in a network or hoping for incentivized offers so those who like the brand will share the message among their social networks? Is the high-tech hope and keenly focused Big Data cloud-powered fire hoses sucking up every public utterance from blogs to Vines that might lead a consumer to ultimately click Like or Follow?

Well, yes and no, because there is a combination of old research and new Big Data tools that are providing a competitive edge to the lone social media manager staring at that letter n and hoping it grows x times.

Surprisingly, the research does not just go back to pre-Instagram, or pre-Facebook days. The research goes back to pre-Internet. In fact, when you realize you are studying how messages move through social networks, you can travel all the way back to just before the second World War.

And this brings us back to our quote of the Prince. A series of studies that broke the most ground were embodied in the book *Diffusion of Innovation* by Everett Rodgers. You may query if you are so inclined, to ask your social media manager, "What are your thoughts about Everett Rodgers?" and sadly few consultants or for that matter social media managers or gurus know about his work. But you have this book, so let's provide a brief overview how real social scientists dealt with how and why n persons move innovative messages x times.

Diffusion of Innovation: Moving Messages Through Social Networks for Social Media Campaigns

You may not know this but social media is the science of moving messages through human complex systems. As such, much of the last 75 years of social research bears tremendous value to those trying to move messages through Facebook or SnapChat.

The model presented in Rodgers' book suggests that the way an innovation or new idea spreads or is adopted is that individuals known as innovators generally less than 3 percent of a targeted population introduce the new idea to early adopters. Then the early adopters, who consist of less than 15 percent of the population, introduce the new idea to a broader majority. These majorities are represented by either the early majority or the late majority, which each constitute less than

35 percent each. And finally the last group to adopt a new idea is the laggards, which generally take up less than 17 percent.

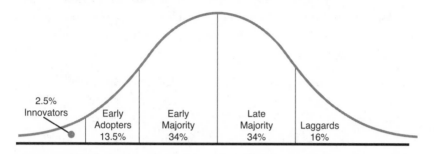

Figure 19.1 Normal distribution curve of innovativeness (Source: Wikipedia.org)

Let' look at the key characteristics. How do you know a social media innovator from an early adopter? They are the information seekers. They are generally mass media mass consumers. And most important, innovators and early adopters are status-aware and status-motivated. In social, they are the first ones in any social network or social mobile application.

Now although the innovator and early adopter are sometimes lumped together, the innovator is characterized by being venturesome, and the early adopter is characterized by what Rodgers' calls "respect." Where the innovator seeks risk, the early adopter seeks the respect that comes with being in a central position of their associated social or communication networks. They are going to introduce the "innovation" to the early majority, so they act in many ways as a gatekeeper or curator of innovations. What Gladwell called "mavens," but we're skipping Gladwell and going to the real source…while the innovators will be the first to play in the new social app or social network. The early adopters are often the first to analyze and present the innovation to their network.

The early majority and the late majority are the middle, simply put. They are both in terms of the normal distribution and in terms of risk, respect, and connectedness the norm. Although the early majority can be characterized as the deliberators. Rodgers writes, "Be not the first by which the new is tried, nor the last to lay the old aside," is the definition of the early majority. The late majority are the skeptics. They must see the innovation around them to such an extent that to ignore it would be to be feel left out. So, again, in social, the early majority are the ones who see the growth of some app, some media, or some network and jump on. The late majority, that's your cool uncle joining Instagram or your wacky cousin joining Facebook a few years ago. Certainly not first, or second type adopters, but they are not the last either.

Finally, we have the laggards. They are the traditionalists. They hold on to the old way and old ways of doing everything. They are not stupid or lacking of style, but in terms of adopting new messaging, memes, technology, or social applications, they are the last guy to join Facebook. Note, an innovator in physics may be a laggard in Snap-chat. These types are not part of a personality test in terms of who and what they are learning and absorbing across many different types of ideas and processes.

What's interesting here is these five types were not defined in the days of AOL or even MySpace. These types of message carriers were defined more than 70 years ago. In fact, when this model was defined, its core insights actually stood up to this day. Rodgers talks about how diffusion moves as an S curve. What he is talking about is that the new innovation or new idea moves slowly through innovators and then to adopters. These early adopters are the "threshold" where the S curves up dramatically as the early majority adopts the new idea (see Figure 19.2). It maintains its strength of adoption through the late majority, and it is not until the laggards adopt that the early adopters or innovators begin to drop off and begin their cycle of adopting a new innovation. Thus, you get an S curve on its side—and more grandmas on Facebook.

Now Rodgers looked at this all the way back to studies on hybrid seeds used in the 1930s. But we can see it quite reliable with Google Trends. The best example is when you take a look at the search traffic of two words: orange and annoying. Some of you already know what I am talking about. But let's look at each word separately. What we see is that seasonally the word orange spikes in November and December of every year. If you choose hot dogs, you would see the same spike but in July.

So when you see the phrase "Annoying Orange," you will see the S curve. You don't see it in the word annoying or the word orange. Annoying does not have a seasonal lift, but orange does, and so do hot dogs and many other things. See Figure 19.3. So what happened here?

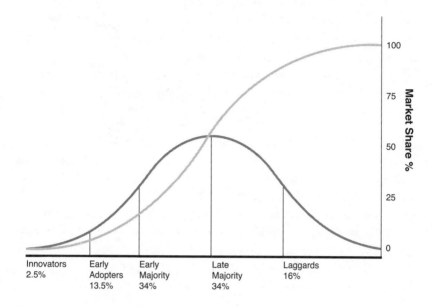

Figure 19.2   S curve of adoption

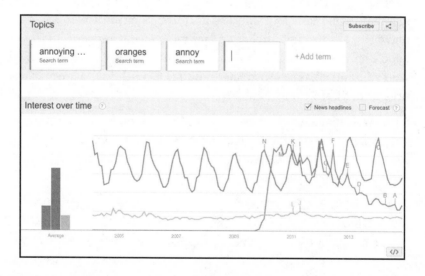

Figure 19.3   Google Trends for orange, annoying, hot dogs, and annoying orange for the years 2008, 2009, and 2010

What happened is that hot dogs and oranges are not innovations, not anymore. They do get talked about, and cultural lifts affect their rise in the consciousness of any network from various influences. In fact, external or exogenous forces often create what I call "J curves". So rather than a small set of individuals moving a message to a larger network set, the J curve is just a group of mass media outlets talking about something in parallel that generally lifts a topic or innovation to high levels of adoption. Government propaganda is such an example, say for vaccinations.

But here with the annoying orange, we have a video series that started out on YouTube that no one knew about. Some YouTube innovators began to follow it; early adopters identified and shared it; and broader adoption moved like an S curve to the early and late majority. In the case of the annoying orange, the S curve will be less S-like due to mass media. If this were a true "viral" event, the adoption would appear even more like an S. But as mass media and social media merge, and TMZ and MSNBC blur their lines, so this will become harder to find the distinctions on occasion.

Suffice to say, if you look at any trend to see if it is manufactured or organic, look to see if there is an S curve or a J curve. If mass media is pushing it, there is no gradual uptake or threshold. Just a gradual adoption as the message gets pushed not through personal interconnected networks, but through broadcast and mass media network outlets. A good example is a movie. Try looking at the spikes for "Die Hard." It won't die and it has returned hard multiple times—and not once in any organic or viral S curve nature.

So we now understand the who of what is moving messaging through our social networks and the what to observe in a message through our social networks. Let's now use Diffusion to get to the when an innovation is ready to become diffused.

How a diffusion of innovation, as Rogers describes it, is exactly what our social media manager of a consumer brands is trying to do in social media. Innovation is an idea, practice, process, or object that is perceived as new by an individual or group. But to understand what Rodgers was talking about, let's look at the key characteristics that move a new idea through a social network.

First, we look at which communication channels the message will travel, basically how the messages move through the network. This can be face to face at conferences or front porches or via telephone or instant messaging or geotagged posts. Some social networks have "structured lists," featured content, and other structural influences that shape how or who will see or hear a post or message.

Next, we must consider the time as a quality of the rate of the speed of the adoption. Not all adopted ideas happen overnight, but their adoption may still follow the classic S curve that occurs over time when the innovation spreads through interpersonal networks. We see in the Annoying Orange example it may take months before the early majority even knows that an innovation exists.

Finally, the social system is the set or structure of the interpersonal connections that are engaged in a joint activity or issue that the innovation addresses. These social systems can be farmers, villagers, or friends on a social network like Flickr. The way an image post moves through Tumblr is different than the way an animated gif moves through Flickr. The makeup of the social network is sometimes defined by the initial adopters and the structure of how the social network responds to the messaging content.

There are diffusion elements that help or hinder the spread of new ideas as well:

- **Relative advantage**: This may seem to just address what Roger and other social scientists initially looked at: hybrid seeds and insecticides or antibiotics. But there has been work in terms of personal advantages as well: Coupons, offers, and other brand affinity programs require processes that promise some advantage. I will share more about this in the case studies below. There is also the element of respect or notoriety. If the innovation is crass, nude photos of a female celebrity, for example, this might resonate within a social network such as Reddit, but not a mommy blogger's network.

  This brings us to the compatibility with existing values of the social network.

Does the new idea work as a new idea within that network? Rogers talks about the campaign to get South American villagers to use boiled water and its complete failure. The villagers' values did not support the idea of imaginary bugs too small to see that could then kill anybody. Often the message could be innovative, but the target network does not see it as an innovation. Try selling a *Die Hard 5* premier night with Bruce Willis to a classic movie auteur social network; nobody bites? However, try selling it to those mommy bloggers who remember Bruce Willis from his "Moonlighting" television show; it's a wildfire!

- **Simplicity of use and trial-ability**: How easy is the new idea to consume and can the new idea, messaging, or product or service be experimented on? The idea to spread must be innovative and be a simple-to-understand concept. Also, can the new idea, messaging, or product or service be recreated? Being told that a cool new product exists is not as impactful as seeing it work: Seeing it work in person or in some way enabling the usability of the innovation is more effective than reading a paragraph about it. Which social media campaigns work the best? Ones where you "like" a photo or create a photo of yourself in with the brand mascot? The one where you share a picture or the one where you travel to a museum made of up pictures from your social network?

Figure 19.4 illustrates a matrix to show how simplicity and innovation are intertwined.

The y-axis starts at 1,000 and goes up to 1, and the x-axis starts at 1,000 and goes out to 1. The z-axis splits the difference and pinpoints the viral nexus toward the outer reaches.

The idea here is to find concepts that are simple and comprehensible. As we saw in the Google Trends charts, oranges and annoying are simple and comprehensible. But neither are viral because they lack any innovation. It is not until you combine orange with annoying that you gain the innovation. This can be seen with moose and swimming pools (see Figure 19.5). Separate, they are both understood and comprehended. But combined they are viral. That is the nature of social media; the goal is to create simple and easily digestible messaging that is innovative and thus hopefully totally unique to the network.

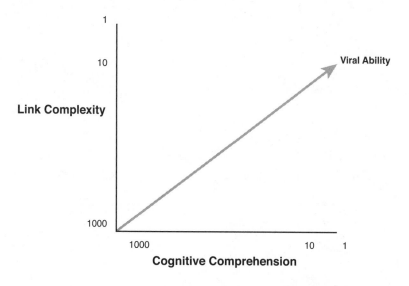

Figure 19-4 Link Complexity is the degree of Centrality of Cognitive Comprehension

If it takes too long to understand, or is well known, it does not spread. If it is easily understood, and well known, it does not spread because there is nothing innovative. Thus, to be spread virally or in an S curve, it must be easily understood and not well known.

If no one can observe the results, it does not move. What decades of social science showed was that the results of a new idea must be observable beyond the enclave of the innovators. Sounds obvious, but its not. Many times, innovators will adopt new ideas. But because the network is not porous or the structure, timing, or advantage do not resonate outside, the innovation fails to be adopted by early adopters. It is critical that the innovation creates some kind of visible or tangible result for the user outside of the innovation. Visible results lower the uncertainty and stimulate more peer discussion around the new idea or innovation.

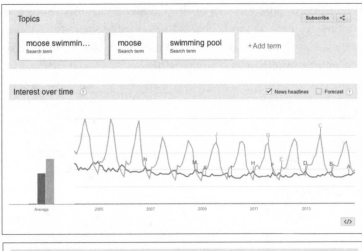

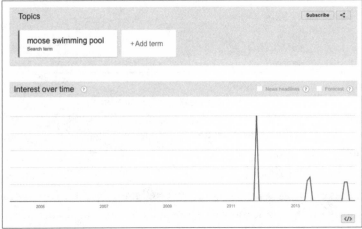

Figure 19.5 Google Trends for moose and swimming pools for years 2009, 2010, and 2011

I covered the essence of a 400-hundred page tome in about a dozen paragraphs. And we still have the n = x versus the n = me people, a throat to choke, and only a limited set of metrics to measure "n" with. How does the social media manager or director use the science of Big Data, to grow "n," or, for that matter, how does the manager get a better idea to develop innovative campaigns that deliver better results within this paradigm of diffusion of innovation?

Targeting the right individuals based on brand affinity rather than brand status in terms of value resonances…. For example, getting Justin

Bieber to tweet about your product may get it noticed, yet is that the right network to sell Viagra? Probably not. Targeting innovators but not realizing that the innovation is something the network no longer values is a real issue. To give you a more concrete way to understand, I present two case studies. Both are real, though the names and corporations have been changed to protect the innocent.

Digital Data Agency: Studio Television Shows "Compatibility with Existing Values"

Big Digital Data Agency

The Problem: A television network saw that each of its television shows had more than 1 million Facebook followers. What's the problem? Who were they and why did they like the various TV shows? More important, what was the defining characteristic that they liked about the show? Did they like the actor or actress in the show? Were the followers old? Young?

Facebook enables aggregate metrics, but those are limited to age brackets and gender. In terms of buying, you can select age, gender, location, and an affinity of brands. Affinity brands are brands the target user likes as well.

So could our understanding of types of adopters bring greater results in expanding the messaging through social networks? Is there a better way to define who the engaged enthusiastic brand ambassadors are and target unique messaging to segments?

The customer: Studios are unique corporate animals. They pump out multimillion dollar products every month on the theatrical side and on the television side push out seasonal products and product updates to their established brands on a regular basis. They have millions set aside to target social networks, including Facebook, Instagram, Google+, Twitter, to name a few.

Their need to establish a movie's or TV show's credibility is early in production and continues as the movie or television show hits the screens.

Process: As the contract director of social media, I took a Big Data approach. I used a third-party data aggregator Lookaka and collected the data around three major TV shows. The data was provided by scanning the Facebook user IDs of public pages of Facebook. This provided a data set of affinity brands. Lookaka provided the top 100 affinity brands associated with each TV show. This enabled the studio to see that among their fans liking the show, they also liked brands in shopping, beverages, and other media.

Discovery solution: The idea that brand ambassadors are solely defined by their characteristic of Liking a brand is limited. Individuals as diverse as fans of any movie franchise or television show are all unique individuals. The needs of why some one watches a television show are different from show to show and from person to person.

Could the data from the affinities provide greater insight? How can what people like help provide insight into whether the message is compatible with their values? How does finding this resonance vibrate within a television show work?

Solution: So what if we combined certain affinities together? For example, what if we did this for one television show we saw that they liked the young actress on, a Facebook page titled "I f#cking love science," an "I love puppies Facebook page," and another cartoon-based sitcom FB page. Through trial and error, and some gut instincts, we took a look at over a dozen high-ranking affinities and combined them into two-pair sets.

One pair set was the lead actress and puppies Facebook pages the television show fans liked. This merge of television show Facebook likes, puppies Facebook likes, and actress fan Facebook page likes totaled 80,000 people. So of the 1 million likes for the show, we found that 80,000 also liked the actress page and puppy page. We also combined a science page and a primetime snarky cartoon show page's likes. In this second set, we found a total of 60,000 who liked the television show, the bawdy science Facebook page, and the primetime cartoon show.

The critical test was to see if the two sets overlapped. If people just randomly like each show and everything on Facebook, then these sets we created would not be mutually exclusive and provide little insight.

It turned out that they were. In fact, we saw that when we compared the two sets of Facebook IDs from the two groups of affinities, we had less than .3 percent overlap. Meaning, out of a combined 140,000 fans, there were only 30–45 users who liked both sets of Facebook pages.

Implementation: What we concluded was that fans of the show like the show due to different thematic attractors. Despite liking the show, there were also different demographics. We did a random sampling of the two sets looking at 20–30 Facebook IDs in both the actress-puppies set and the science-cartoon set.

What we uncovered was that we had found that the actress and the puppy page likers were made up of Millennial females that like the show. We found that the science and cartoon likers were made up of Generation-X males. Looking at the random sampled sets of their conversations uncovered that the Millennial females liked and identified with the "finding herself" actress and the Generation-X males identified with the male sarcastic slackers supporting cast.

Up to this point, the television network had been messaging fans as a homogeneous whole: "Fans of TV Show Brand X."

Then we looked at those segments and targeted the most active on Facebook. Two key characteristics of innovators are venturesomeness and outgoingness. This shows up online as activity in multiple conversations, likes, favoriting, or first to opt-in to campaigns. The second characteristic is value-resonance or some specific reason they liked what they saw in the show's multiple thematic attractions. An example would be innovators/early adopters who are creating or curating content that the community finds value in. So creating an animated gif of them and a TV show character is one example.

Results: Testing the hypothesis of these groups was significant and mutually exclusive. We had the network buy three sets of ads: one directed to the active Millennials females, one directed to the active Generation-X males, and one to an active control group they normally target as homogenous blob of fans. We found that the targeted groups provided a 20 percent click-through rate via earned over the control group. Typical CTRs are at best in the 1 percent range.

Note: If you're a Facebook advertising sophisticate, you know you can buy ads based on likes of other brands. So you could have bought ads for those who liked puppies? But why? Or, you could buy ads for those who like science? But how would you communicate that or even guess that has anything to do with your brand?

So what that meant was by targeting early adopters or those with early adopter characteristics and by ensuring that the message contained values that resonated with the target, we could get to their social networks and earn click-throughs from the early adopters, friend network at a significant boost over the control group of "brand likes" at a significant multiple compared to the control group.

Social Score Matrix	Thematic Attractors	Simpsons	PRIZM/Affinity SpongeBob / AngryBirds	PRIZM/Affinity Skittles/ Call of Duty	PRIZM/Affinity Oreo/Marvel	PRIZM/Affinity StarWars/S.Park	PRIZM/Affinity CocaCola/EllenG
Oct 1, 2012							
Core Demo Groups			13-17 Social Savvy	18-24 Cartoon Gamers	25-34 Pulp Fictioners	35-44 GenXhausted	45-64+ Family Safe
Size Rank			5 (largest)	3	2	4	1 (Smallest)
Buzz Change			▲	4 5 (largest)	▼ 2	3	1 (Smallest)
Potential Audience			.7M	3.5M	.9M	2.2M	.1M
Live Ratio			0%	0%	0%	0%	0%
	Technology		3	4	1	2	4
	Immersion		2	1	3	3	2
	Escapism		4	3	4	1	1
	Quality		1	2	2	4	3
Action List			Cartoon Alarm TW backgrounds	Simpson WebGame	Simpson Create Comic	Simpson Meet God	Calendar pop-in

Figure 19.6   Thematic attractor matrix based on life of PL-esque movie

Following is an example of where the social network platform did not take diffusion issues into consideration.

Process: What happens when a company does not focus on early adopters, value resonance, or how receptive the social network is to a presumed innovation, but instead focuses on community of likes or the hype of influencers?

Discovery solution: There is a story I cannot confirm nor deny. But after leaving the studio contract work to work for an interactive gaming company to run social media, I knew of another social media campaign that my friends at a studio were working to deploy.

Solution: This campaign used another platform. This platform, rather than focusing on data, focused simply on grouping people around sharing an offer actively online. The platform offered incentivized coupons or giveaways to those who share the coupons or giveaways. Thus, they had a 1 million+ member community of people looking for coupons. Those that signed up were regularly offered "deals." They marketed these coupon seekers as "influencers."

Studios often get new media companies to provide services at under cost if the new media company can use the "win" on its web page or as a case study. This was one of the scenarios. The new media company offered a "prebuilt" community of influencers. This seemed ideal, as the studio did not have to spend to build a community out. The studio spend would be only approximately $20,000–$50,000 for the entire deployment.

Implementation: Just before the movie premiered, the community offers went out to the "highly energized" prebuilt brand influencers/ ambassadors. These offers should have resonated within this movie community. Two weeks went by, and when the project manager reported the number of shared or earned users that the community garnered with their coupon offer, the number came back not as expected.

Results: The response was two, as in two people among the hundreds of thousands offered to click to redeem a coupon on the shared link. In shock, the senior executive was heard saying, "I could have taken a roll of thousand dollar bills and walked the sidewalks handing out money and gotten a better response."

That company that had sold its solution of pre-built community of influencers is no longer in the external "influencer" business of spreading or diffusing messages in social networks. It is now focused on using employees to spread social media messaging for primarily internal corporate communication. Good move.

Basics steps on Implementing an Innovation Diffusion-Aware Social Media Campaign

To recap, moving messages through social networks is not a new science. It is quite old and has been heavily researched and studied. Depending on the standard metrics of your social media monitoring and engagement system, it is just scratching the surface at the opportunity to target innovators in which to move innovative messages.

The social media manager must understand that even in a unique vertical community, subnetworks or smaller communities exist, and their value resonance will have an effect at how rapidly a message moves through their personal social network.

There are three basic tools of the modern social media marketer:

- Segment the target into affinities around themes.

- Measure and test message resonance based on those thematic attractors, inside the subnetworked segments.

- Understand the real equation is not n = x or n = me, but rather, N = CX / Me.

See what I did? I brought it all back!

Conclusion: N = CX / Me

Consumer experience: No large social media department can scale one-to-one conversations to millions of followers. So no, N = Me is just not a scalable solution. On the flip side of that equation, N = X or growth-focused campaigns cannot reach greater numbers if they treat each target as a generic homogenous blob of brand likes.

The key to moving messaging at scale through human complex systems is utilizing data. First, one must segment innovators, and then test out those thematic attractors who resonate within those segments, and deliver unique consumer experiences to each based around what those innovators can absorb or comprehend quickly. This provides value as in the status of being creative, cool, funny, touching, or smart, not in terms of attracting the late majority or laggards, but by delivering the equation programmatically via N =CX / Me so that those innovators discover and create observable instances of their own innovations to their own networks.

This is the goal of the new social media managers: Understanding that they have the power and the data to create unique messaging to individuals at scale. And that providing unique experiences not only requires technology, but that it also requires a bit of book smarts as well.

Just because Facebook, Twitter, Vine, and YouTube are digital creations of the twenty-first century does not mean that decades of social science do not provide insights as well. And so, the science is that the true innovators are those who learn how innovations are adopted and spread.

20

Real-Time Marketing That Customers Actually Want to See from Brands: Stop Trying to Be Like Oreo and Start Trying to be Bloomberg

Charlie Treadwell, Director of Global Social Media, Symantec

The world has changed. Today's digital marketing environment shifts in the blink of an eye, and successful marketers can ride these shifts in real time, responding to customers at the crest of breaking news cycles and the pivotal moments of trending topics. At Symantec, we fine-tune this strategy by creating the content that overlaps our brand's goals with our customers' interests.

Customer-centric content delights and adds value at every stage of the customer life cycle. Relevant content that aligns with customer interests is key to an effective content marketing strategy because it is more likely to be read, clicked, shared, and engaged with.

The "sweet spot" for a brand is found when brand goals overlap with customer interests (see Figure 20.1). This can be during a breaking news story, trending topic, industry event, or even fun pop-culture event.

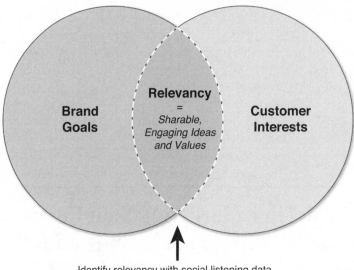

Identify relevancy with social listening data.

Figure 20.1 Relevant content is revealed when a brand's goals overlap with ever-changing customer interests.

The world we live in today is an assault on all our senses. The deluge of data and information overwhelms us. My friend Michael Brito, author of *Your Brand, The Next Media Company: How a Social Business Strategy Enables Better Content, Smarter Marketing, and Deeper Customer Relationships*, talks regularly about the tunnel vision people have when something happens in their lives. When you try to decide whether to buy your son the Xbox or the PS4 his birthday, billboards and stories on the news suddenly jump out at you. Because we know customers' interests are constantly shifting, effective content creation, listening to customers' questions, and rapidly responding can increase brand relevancy over time.

We live in a world with a 24-hour news cycle (see Figure 20.2). This means a story can break, peak by reaching maximum awareness, and begin the decline toward "old news" in 48 hours or less.

Symantec has always been a leader in social media listening (see Figure 20.3). That's not just my opinion as the director of Social Media today. That was my opinion of Symantec when I was leading the Social Media Insights team for Cisco.

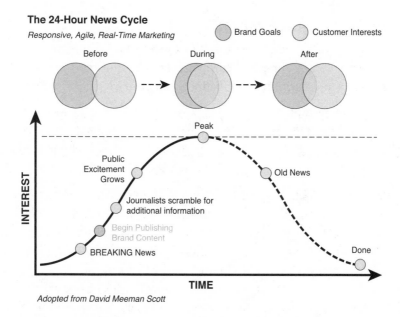

Figure 20.2 The 24-hour news cycle as defined by David Meerman Scott, author of *The New Rules of Marketing and PR* (Credit: David Meerman Scott)

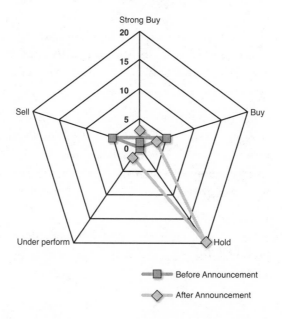

Figure 20.3 Shifting investor preference on SYMC shares within 24 hours, pre-announcement split between sell and buy, post-announcement near-unanimous hold

Effective Rapid Response

By now, you might be aware that on October 9, 2014, Symantec became the most recent technology company announcing the monumental decision to split itself into two distinct publicly traded companies.

What publicly traded company or Investor Relations team wouldn't want to see this type of real-time quote from investors? "Post split, you have two companies, one focused more on cash flow and one focused more on revenue. So, put together, can it help revenue? I think it can."

Some of the insights are seemingly obvious, and you might wonder what we do with this type of information. When you make a decision whether to task an entire organization to create new content, reach out to the media or talk to analysts and investors, sometimes knowing when not to do something is the key differentiator that frees up your resources to focus on creating content that answers the questions people are asking. For example, some Norton Security customers asked the question, "What does this mean for Norton?" We quickly updated our messaging and created a new blog post for Norton customers addressing those questions.

Even better, who doesn't want to see their company go from a split recommendation of BUY and SELL to a nearly unanimous HOLD overnight? Talk about bringing disparate ideas together and changing people's opinions.

Here's the thing that the inner data geek in me gets excited about. Symantec made our announcement at 1 p.m. PST on October 9 and by 7 a.m. on October 10, our AR, HR, PR, IR, marketing, sales, and support teams all had a detailed report analyzing online conversations from each of their respective target audiences.

So how did we possibly turn a report like this around in such a short timeframe and without the legal capability to disclose the analytics team prior to the announcement? How would we see specific questions from our customers, partners, employees, investors, and analysts?

Listening to Your Customers in Real Time

I'd like to shed a little light on the magic woven by Erling Amundson, senior manager of Social Insights, and his world-class team at Symantec. We have a global social media listening and insights team with two primary centers of excellence located in China and India. The growing number of significant cybersecurity stories in the media have enabled us to refine our real-time insights process to drive content strategy at lightning speed. Our primary goal is to create what Jay Baer calls *Youtility*: marketing so good, people would pay for it.

When Symantec began preparing to launch our Security and Information Management announcement, we analyzed the real-time questions Erling's team provided before we made the announcement. The first report gave us an insight of our key target audiences' opinions and questions, but it also gave us a benchmark pre-announcement and post-announcement (see Figure 20.4).

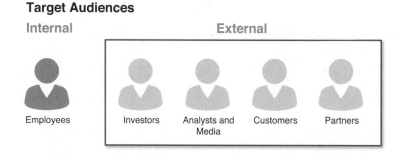

Figure 20.4   Top target audiences for communications during the announcement to split the company

If you've ever heard me speak, you know that I'm a strong believer in starting your strategy by defining your audience and then listening to and capturing the questions they ask. Today, Google is still the number one place where B2B decision makers start when they begin their buying process, and Google now focuses on providing answers to questions, not just keywords. Try it by typing in: **What time does the sun set in Phoenix?**

I'm not going to share the entire report, or what we did with the insights, but I can give you a peek. Analysts were abuzz during the speculation and the announcement (see Figure 20.5). Here's what one said: "It's nice to see the board make a decision that makes sense for the company and investors."

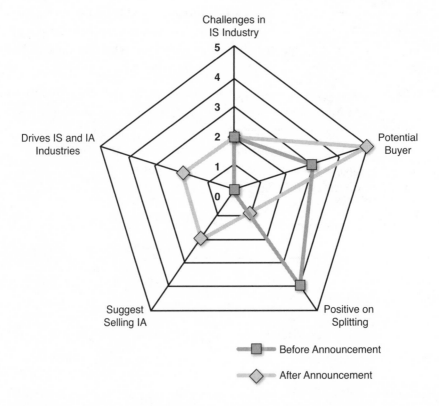

Figure 20.5 The 24-hour shift in commentary from financial and industry analysts

Setting Up the Team and Processes to Create Content in Real Time

After all, if 64 percent of B2B buyers think your content really matters and it impacted on their purchasing decision (source: 2013 B2B Buyer Behavior Survey), what's the impact of not having relevant, up-to-date content available at the moment your customer needs it?

Start with your customer, define your audience, and stay focused. Ignore the bright shiny objects and stay true to your content strategy.

Where do you find customer questions? In social media, of course!

Stock and Flow: Follow This 80/20 Rule When Creating Content

Seventy-eight percent of marketers say that their biggest challenge with content is "creating original content" and that they don't have enough time to do it (for more information, see the 2013 B2B Content Marketing Benchmarks, Budgets, and Trends).

The first emotion that's going to consume your entire body when you try to launch a real-time marketing program will be the feeling of complete panic. Remember that dream when you were in high school in the front of the class—you didn't do your homework, and for some Freudian reason you were in your underwear? That's the fear of not being prepared. And most brands are not prepared to share relevant content with their customers when a real-time opportunity reveals itself.

At Symantec, we created a Stock and Flow content strategy, following the magic ratio of 80/20, or 80 percent stock and 20 percent flow. That's another way to say 80 percent of your content for a real-time campaign should be content you already created, or content someone else already created. Don't be afraid to share someone else's content during your real-time campaign. I don't recommend sharing your competitors' content, but I do recommend sharing content from people that influence your customers or content that creates value for your customers—content so good, people would pay for it. We call this "marketing as a service (MaaS)." And don't forget to thank someone when she shares your content or replies when she has questions or snarky comments. Yes, reply to those people too, but don't stoop to their level. Take the high road, or the unexpected road, and surprise them. You'd be surprised how a "Thank you so much for your comment!" response can convert a troll into a brand advocate.

The concept of stock and flow is one borrowed from economics and supply chain management. In theory, you want to have a stock of products in your warehouse to meet spikes in demand and have a flow of new content to ensure you can react to seasonal preferences (see Figure 20.6). Think of the difference between milk and the insane amount of pumpkin spice (insert product) goods that show up on the grocery store shelves in October and November. The truck delivering the goods to the store carries both, but the store inventory manager knows exactly how much he needs of each and when to increase the seasonal or flow products.

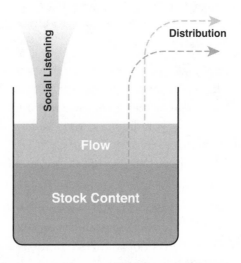

Figure 20.6 Content inventories need evergreen stock content to repurpose and constant inflow of flow content to keep the topics fresh and relevant. Social listening and search trends are an excellent source of flow content.

In real-time marketing, *stock* is the durable stuff; it's the content you produce that is as interesting in 2 months (or 2 years) as it is today (for example, white papers, videos, infographics, and even blog posts). It's the evergreen content, as in content with a long shelf life, that will always be relevant but might not be relevant until that moment when your customer gets tunnel vision and notices it or starts seeking it out. Think Xbox or PS4 during the holidays.

Flow is the real-time feed. It's the stream of daily and hourly updates that reminds people you exist (for example, breaking news, trending topic, throwback Thursdays, industry events, or even fun pop-culture event). We find flow content from listening posts throughout the brand that enable the content team to function as a news room. Our content strategists constantly consume relevant information from as many sources as possible and craft content to answer customer questions— content that pulls customers in by attracting them with great, relevant, real-time content. Social listening is one of the most-effective and real-time ways to do this, but don't underestimate the value of search, Google alerts, news feeds, Flipboard, your PR team, and all your employees who should know they can send you something if they spot a trend emerging.

Stock is a pillar of social editorial calendar planning, inclusive of campaign priorities and evergreen thought-leadership content. Flow is reactive; it's jumping into the social conversation in real time. When a real-time marketing opportunity reveals itself to you, stock content is how you insert your brand story in a relevant way into the news cycle.

Building the Team and Giving It the Tools It Needs to Respond in Real Time

When preparing for a real-time marketing opportunity, we need to prepare for an event in which we don't know when it's going to happen, or what the topic is going to be. To do this, we borrow a concept from the Lean Startup model. In the traditional marketing model of 20 years ago, we could see our destination and had a clear path if not a straight line to get there. This is what I refer to as the "Known-Known quadrant," as shown in Figure 20.7. We know what we need to build and we know how much time we have to get it done.

Today marketing requires us to be agile, nimble, and flexible. You have to "float like a butterfly and sting like a bee" (Muhammad Ali aka Cassius Marcellus Clay, Jr.). Marketing is now complex and dynamic. Many marketers have begun to adopt Agile Scrum as a methodology for campaign planning. I've been trained and certified as an Agile Scrum Master and manage my team with my own variation of Agile Scrum. Agile works in the world of the Known-Unknown. In this case, you know one of two things: either what you need to build or how quickly it needs to get done.

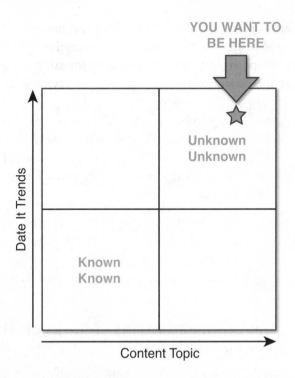

Figure 20.7 A four-quadrant grid used to identify the proper content development model—in this case, waterfall—when the date and the topic are known, or agile when neither the date or topic are known. This can also be referred to as "just-in-time content development."

In real-time marketing, we need to go a step further and venture into the outer limits. Boldly go and enter the quadrant of the Unknown-Unknown. In this treacherous and mysterious realm, you're accepting that you have no idea what you need to create and no idea when you have to get it done. If this doesn't scare the crap out of you, you've got a pair of brass ones, and I want you to come work for me. Few managers will give you the air cover to step out onto this thin layer of ice. If you can find that manager, you're in the right place to begin a real-time marketing program.

In the Lean Startup model, you're not only admitting that you don't know what you're building, but also when it needs to be delivered. You're also admitting that you might need to pivot your strategy and have the decisiveness and confidence to do so quickly. My favorite quote for moments like these comes from the magnanimous and always entertaining Mike Tyson: "Everyone has a plan until they get punched in the mouth." Preparation and planning are not the same thing, and don't be fooled by the false confidence you'll get from having a plan.

We've cultivated a team that enables us to feed that stock-and-flow content model. For each of our brands, Norton and Symantec, there's a social strategist responsible for defining the overarching objectives, goals, strategies, and tactics. This person leads the team.

Then there's a content strategist who is responsible for knowing the target audiences and finding the relevant overlap between brand goals and customer interests. Actively seeking out the content that's most relevant to our customers and interpreting our social listening and insights data, this person needs to be an excellent creative and analytical person who also writes and creates the content calendar of tweets, blogs, and updates.

Then there are the fearless community managers. The most critical thing you can do for these people is to empower them by giving them the tools and confidence they need to roll with the punches. We put these folks through improv training with Second City. Because good ideas come from an effective team, we put the whole team through the improv training because great ideas also come from collaboration, ideation, and iteration. These guys know that I have their back, no matter what happens. They absolutely have to know this at all times. Our infamous Justin Bieber tweet is an example of this.

The Justin Bieber tweet was an early example of where we struck gold before we actually knew what we were trying to create. This was a critical moment in our evolution in which we saw a great idea, went for it, and realized we needed to pivot our strategy. In January 2014, when the Biebs was having some personal challenges, and the Grammy's were trending, I asked my community manager at the time, Allen Kelly, to keep an eye out for a *relevant* opportunity to create a real-time campaign—in this case, a simple tweet with an image of text.

Allen came up with the idea on a Saturday and sent me a text message while I was at lunch with my wife Allison asking, "Do you think this is a good idea?" It read, "ALERT: If someone sends you a link to download the latest Bieber single, DON'T DO IT! It's a link to download the latest

Bieber single." See Figure 20.8. I handed the phone to my wife to gain some distance from the idea, and she laughed out loud, and I replied back, "Go for it!"

Figure 20.8 Norton Security's satirical Justin Bieber Alert from January of 2014

This story not only generated more earned impressions than we had seen to date, but we also had customers running back to us that had been detractors for years. We saw comments like, "I'm on my way to Best Buy right now to purchase your product" or "I uninstalled your free trial; will you ever forgive me?" Word of mouth leads to loyalty and ultimately sales. We saw an 18 percent spike in online sales for the 48 hours following this tweet.

I also received a notification from our legal department because we created significant risk for the brand by using Justin Bieber's name without his permission. We weren't using him to pitch a product but rather to comment on a current news story. Luckily my manager,

LaSandra Brill, and her VP, Alix Hart, both had my back. No one got fired or sued.

Another critical role I've mentioned already is our social listening and insights team. This is our crack team of researchers who leverage social listening and other tools to capture conversations, trends, and, most importantly, questions of our target audiences in real time.

That's the basic makeup of the social media real-time marketing team: social strategist, content strategist, community manager, insights analyst, and a VP that's got your back. Don't forget the last part, or you might find yourself in a precarious position and will be updating your résumé in the near future.

For stock content, Symantec has invested in a world-class content team of writers, designers, journalists, and a video production crew. All are unmatched in their ability to create quality content on a consistent basis as well as possess a rapid-fire turnaround flow of content when needed.

Don't Forget Search!

Seventy-eight percent of B2B buyers still start their journey with search, and that number is growing the last time I checked. This means you absolutely need to optimize your content for search. Social content is beginning to have a higher search rank, and social shares are factored into Google's algorithms. Don't be afraid to spin up a paid search campaign in Google if you see people searching for answers to specific questions they have. If you have a great video, blog post, or infographic that could help them answer that question, why not put it at the top of the search results? They'll thank you for it, share it with their friends, and probably buy your product out of the primal urge for reciprocity.

Who Wants ROI, When You Can Get Reciprocity?

The Rule of Reciprocity was one of the core concepts I adopted in my social media strategies when I was a community manager at Cisco in 2009. I first read about this concept in Bob Cialdini's book *Influence, The Science of Persuasion* (@RobertCialdini). Many of you that have been in sales and marketing for the past 30 years might already know about this book. I was 3 years old when the first edition was published, so give me a break for just getting around to reading it. The second chapter dives into the concept and power of reciprocity. "People are more likely to give in to a request, if they have first received an unexpected gift, either tangible or intangible."

Next time someone asks you to quantify the ROI of your social media program, ask him to quantify the ROI of the holiday cards he sends out every year. He'll be completely stumped. We're all still trying to understand how you measure the impact of this type of marketing, how we know social is linked to advocacy, which drives word of mouth, and ultimately sales. You can bet when I figure it out, that I'm going to write a book about it so that you all can stop trying to answer the ROI question and get back to doing good work.

21

Bonus Chapter

WARNING: Do not waste your time reading this chapter if you already know how to make your videos go viral!

When we were putting together *How Companies Succeed at Social Business,* we tried to chronicle how successful practitioners are putting their social business strategies to work. We didn't talk much about the social media tools themselves, because social business isn't about the tools—it's about the people.

However, as a bonus, we wanted to highlight best practices around optimizing one tool in particular that we believe will continue to become more and more significant for growing human connections on-line: video.

So we asked ourselves who we could get to talk not only about the *power* of video, but also someone who can tell us how to become *pros* at video. That person is Erik Qualman, author of *Socialnomics* and YouTube super-hero #1. Erik not only knows a lot about how to become a star on YouTube, but he also has an incredible track record to prove it. And as it turns out, Erik is a really nice guy as well.

We hope you enjoy this bonus chapter on becoming a pro at YouTube by Erik Qualman.

—Shawn Santos

How to Become a Pro at YouTube

Erik Qualman, author of *Socialnomics*

YouTube is the second largest search engine in the world. The explosion of mobile is also increasing the power and omnipresence of video. By 2017, two-thirds of all user consumption on mobile devices will be

---

video. More than 100 hours of video are uploaded to YouTube every minute. This is a global phenomenon—80 percent of viewers are outside the United States.

I learned how powerful YouTube can be for a business first hand. As a result of loyal viewers, my social media video series is the most watched of its kind in the world. The first video, "Social Media Revolution," is the one that truly changed the game for me. Since then, I've failed, learned, and succeeded over the years with online video, and you can, too.

One of the top questions I receive after giving a keynote speech on digital trends, reputation, or leadership is, "How can we make a viral video?" But that is the wrong question to ask. If you go into video production with the end goal of making a viral video, you are certain to fail. The correct question is always, "What kind of video can we produce that will provide value to the viewer?" The viewer makes things go viral, not you, the producer. There are some things we can do as producers to help give our videos a chance to go viral, which I discuss in this chapter, but you always must start with the viewer in mind. When it comes to our digital world, we always need to think outward looking in, rather than our historic *Mad Men* approach of inward looking out.

Another question I am often asked is, "What compelled you to make the first 'Social Media Revolution' video?" The reason I produced the first video was simply as a tool to help explain social media, especially to small business owners and executives who weren't digital natives. As laughable as it seems now, not everyone understood the power of social media. This was at a time when Myspace (remember it?) was bigger than Facebook. Many brushed off social media as simply being "something that teenagers do." I was having a difficult time convincing people that social media was the next big thing for everyone. So, I decided to do two things: write the first edition of my best-selling book *Socialnomics* and produce a complementary video.

I'd seen a great video called "Shift Happens," produced by Karl Fisch and Scott McLeod, on changes in education. I decided that I needed to make something like this but completely centered on social media. I've produced many videos since this time and even own my own production arm (Equalman Productions) that develop videos for some of the top brands in the world. Disney has even come calling.

What follows are some key insights. I put the first video on a YouTube channel labeled Socialnomics09 rather than Socialnomics. The reason was that I wanted to test to see if it would work properly before putting it onto my primary YouTube channel. Well, did it work! I received hundreds of thousands of views in days. The problem this created was that I needed to keep it on this channel (Socialnomics09). YouTube will not allow you to move videos and their views to another channel—the number of views starts at 0 rather than at 200,000. Hence, I've been stuck with putting all my videos on Socialnomics09. I've since discovered that this has happened to many people I know. So, my first piece of advice is to test everything on your main channel because viral can truly happen overnight, and you don't want to be pinned to a test channel.

"Going viral" is not a strategy. However, here are five key steps you can take to give your videos a *chance* at going viral:

1. Good music: Unless your video is of a cute baby or an extraordinary kitten, the music you select will be critical to its success. In various countries, YouTube's Content ID program enables you to use copyrighted music. As a quid pro quo, a pop-up window displays during your video listing the song title and artist and enables users to click through to purchase the song. YouTube and the music label then share the revenue from the sale.

   My advice is to find successful viral videos that are similar to the one you want to produce, and determine what music they are using. You may seriously consider using the same music because it has proven to be successful and the music owner isn't blocking it.

   Keep in mind that your idea will not be new. As of the writing of this book, every minute there are 48 hours of video being uploaded to YouTube. Review videos similar to what you want to do, and take note of what is working and not working for these particular videos.

YouTube's Content ID program can be a bit frustrating because often music labels and musicians can change their minds on when and where their music can be used. Hence, you may have three videos that use the same music and they all have 4 million views, but then one day one of them has an error message saying the music is owned by EMI. Also, they may not work in every country. If you truly want to play it safe, either go through the steps of obtaining the rights or use royalty-free music.

2. Short and sweet: Definitely keep your video under 5 minutes, preferably to 1 minute or less. In *Enchantment*, author Guy Kawasaki displayed data from research firm Visible Measures showing that 19.4 percent of viewers abandoned a video within the first 10 seconds, and by 60 seconds 44 percent had stopped watching. Lead with your most eye-popping content to gain and hold viewer attention. Don't build to a crescendo that may never be viewed.

3. Viewer is king: Only viewers make videos go viral. Yet, often we produce videos from the vantage point of what we want to get out of them. This approach is wrong. We need to constantly ask the questions, "Am I providing something of value for viewers? What do they want to get out of it?" If you have to include your brand, then make the mention short and preferably at the end of the video.

4. Other purpose: Don't produce a video simply hoping that it goes viral. Produce a video with a clear purpose in mind. For example, you may produce a video for your sales team so that it can use it when it presents to the board. If it goes viral because you adhered to the first three suggestions, it's a bonus! If it doesn't go viral, no problem; it is still a great tool used by your team.

5. Share: When people ask for your original file so that they can use it in their presentations or for other purposes, share it. Sure, there will be a few who do so with malicious intent, but they will be in the minority. The majority will be adding distribution points

and beacons for your great work. They may make the video into something cooler than you ever dreamed of as well. Also, understand that YouTube data shows that videos often require a tastemaker to provide the crucial tipping point. In a well-known TED talk, YouTube showcased several popular videos that were dormant for months until a tastemaker like Jimmy Kimmel blasted it out to his legion of followers.

Guided by these five maxims, I produced several videos explaining the power of social media. Viewers pushed these viral, becoming the world's most viewed social media videos. Remember that making a viral video is not a sound strategy—making a video that provides value to the viewer is.

20 Tips to Be a Video Star

All of us will be on video, whether it is simply for a conversation with the family via video or if we are interviewed by a national media outlet. Because these videos will be archived forever, it is important for us to put our best face forward.

Whether marketing a product or service, promoting a personal or professional endeavor, or simply sharing an event with friends, at some point you will be filmed and uploaded to YouTube, Vimeo, Facebook, or even national television. It could be for a family reunion or for *The Ellen DeGeneres Show*. Whatever the situation, the following tips can help you be prepared to put your best face forward.

Following are 20 tips to help you look like a professional:

1. Relax your face: This actually starts with the rest of your body. Make sure your hands aren't balled up and your shoulders aren't scrunched. Some people find it helpful to give a little self-massage on the temple and neck. Also, rubbing your palms together to generate warmth and placing them onto your closed eyes is another trick to help relax your face.

2. Smile: Specifically concentrate on raising your cheekbones. This will naturally give the illusion to the camera that your eyes are sparkling.

3. Focus on yoga-esque breaths: Deep and slow. This breathing technique can help relax your face and body and also help prevent you from talking too fast.

4. If being interviewed, do not use normal nonverbal cues like nodding your head: This is different from a normal conversion. If you nod, it appears as if you are a "know it all" and are impatient for the question. It conveys to the audience that you already know the answer. This is a difficult habit to break, so you may not get it right the first few times you are on camera; but with a little practice, it will become second nature.

5. When possible, use a good microphone: They are cheap, so go out and buy a good one.

6. Make sure the light is in your face and not behind you: Natural light is best at dawn and dusk. If you can shoot during these periods, it will make you look your best.

7. Have good posture: Stand up against a wall and have your shoulders and the top of the back of your head pressed firmly against the wall and slowly walk away from the wall keeping this posture intact for the camera; feel free to go back to slouching after the lights go off!

8. Overemphasize everything: Your words, excitement, volume, gestures, eyes, and so on. Do not shout as if you are scolding a misbehaving dog (see #2 about being relaxed), but you need to project as if you are on stage performing a play. The first time I saw Magic Johnson being interviewed, I thought why is he shouting instead of talking in his normal voice? Then I found out the first few times I saw myself interviewed that if you are talking in your normal tone, you come across as drab and unexcited. If the bubbly Magic Johnson has to take it up a notch to look excited on film, then we all need to!

9. Be concise: If you are filming your own video, make it less than 2 minutes. If you are being interviewed, answer the question with your most powerful statement first. If it appears the interviewer wants more, then you can go to the second and third most powerful points.

10. Sit on your tails: If you are wearing a suit jacket, tuck the tails of your coat under your behind and place your sitting bones firmly on them. This will give a nice line on your shoulders.

11. Makeup: If offered HD makeup, accept it. I know this will be tough for guys at first; but if you do not have it, you can look tired, shiny, and old on HD. If you are at home, apply base makeup with a brush—this can dramatically reduce shine and lines. If you are like me and do not have base makeup lying around, use a cotton swab to go over your face quickly to at least remove the oil and dirt.

12. Hydrate: Make sure to drink plenty of fluids beforehand. Have water nearby in case you need it. Avoid ice and sugary drinks. Sparkling water with lemon is the best.

13. Spend the majority of the time looking into the camera: The camera is your audience. If you are on Skype or FaceTime, do not watch your little image in the corner. Look into the camera. If you are being interviewed, ask the interviewer where you should place most of your eye contact. When you get on the television show *Ellen*, make sure you know where the various cameras are and "work" each camera. If speaking on stage and you are being recorded, ask the cinematographer where you can and can't walk to be in the light and in the frame still. Make sure you play to the camera for your major points of emphasis; you can use these for your highlight reel later.

14. Before you begin speaking: A good trick is to hum the Happy Birthday song and then immediately say, "The rain in Spain falls mainly on the plain."

15. Wear clothes that you are most comfortable in: Wear what you feel you look the best in, but do not wear things that would distract (for example, a large broach, a crazy tie, dress with a puffy/flowery design near the top). If you are comfortable, you will be confident. For David Cameron, this might be a suit with a blue tie; for Garth Brooks, it might be jeans and an open-collared black shirt. Try to be consistent in what you wear on videos; this makes you more memorable. Think Johnny Cash (the man in

black), Tiger Woods (red shirt on Sundays), Richard Simmons (exercise tank top), Mark Zuckerberg (hooded sweatshirt), and so on.

16. If you feel like you have a frog in your throat: Eat some cantaloupe because this provides soothing lubrication.

17. Be yourself: The previous tips help you put your best face forward, but you also need to make sure you are yourself on the camera. This can be difficult. Some speaking coaches say do not use your hands, but then I paid close attention to the one of the best speakers in the world, Jim Collins (author of *From Good to Great*), and he definitely uses his hands. The difference was that every movement had a purpose. Hence, the use of his hands assisted his delivery rather than distracted from the message. If you are going to move, move with a purpose. If you are used to speaking with your hands, then speak with your hands. If you speak with your hands, try to make sure you raise them up so that they are in the frame of the camera; the worst thing is for a finger to be occasionally flying in and out of the frame. If the video is showing only your head, try to lower your hands so that they have less of a chance to fly into the frame randomly. Never have your hands block your face unless you are demonstrating being ashamed.

18. If you're filming someone else, help them with these steps: Make them a star and they will shine brightly on you!

19. Have fun!

20. Do post-mortems. The beautiful thing about video is you can review it. Act as if you are the head coach of the New England Patriots and review video to get an advantage. How many UMs do you say? Are you slouching? Do you look better with your glasses on or off? Do you say "like" or other "pet" words too often? What little quirks do you have (dropping your head, slouching your shoulders, turning your back to the audience, shifty eyes)? Review these and put them into the notes section of your phone. Review the top three quirks you have the night before giving a presentation and before you go on stage, review them so that you work on them.

Some of the best people you can learn from are Benjamin Zander, Dan Heath, Jim Collins, Tim Sanders, Guy Kawasaki, and Andy Stanley.

Case Study: Grand Rapids Lip Dub

Video can be powerful if approached correctly, and sometimes, it can even go viral. Let's look at one of these cases, where a focused, well-planned, and well-executed effort produces remarkable results: The Grand Rapids Lip Dub.

Situation: After *Newsweek* wrote an article, "Dying City," in early 2011, the people and businesses of Grand Rapids, Michigan, were in a strong state of disagreement. A trio of residents in this west Michigan City decided it would get the word out to the contrary; their town was flourishing.

Action: They took to the streets, literally. The storyboarded idea was to put together a "lip dub" video that showcased the beautiful downtown of Grand Rapids and its cultural multitude of enthusiastic citizens.

They solicited local businesses for financial and resource support. They ended up with more than 20 sponsors of varying participation levels, covering the $40,000 production budget. The final video involved a shutdown of the downtown to Grand Rapids and approximately 5,000 people lip synching to a cover of Don McLean's "American Pie."

Results: The video went viral, reaching 4.2 M views on YouTube in the first 4 months, cracking the top 10 for most viewed video in the world at the time. This includes hundreds of thousands of Facebook likes/shares to date. Also, the project received huge coverage across traditional media outlets and blogs, greatly increasing their message and reach.

A conservative estimate would put the total media impressions at approximately 15 M to date when you add in the video views, articles, social reach and blogs. Utilizing an average CPM of $20, you could easily say they received approximately $300,000 worth of media impact on their $40,000 investment (15M * $20 / 1000 = $300,000). And keep in mind that the final video is more than 9 minutes long, which is a lot of 30-second commercials.

The global reach and impact of this campaign resulted in its creators (Jeffrey Barrett, Rob Bliss, and Scott Erickson) forming a new agency entitled Status Creative.

Here's a link to the final video: http://bit.ly/GranRapLD

Key Learnings: Although it can be somewhat intimidating to produce for the uninitiated, video has had transformative effects on how people expect to consume content, how value is conveyed, and what entertains people online. If approached correctly, the impacts of video on your business can be transformative as well. I hope that after reading my chapter, you will walk away with a high-level understanding of the following points, and use them to produce video like a pro!

- Reach and exposure in social media can be achieved with much less investment than traditional media or Internet display ads.

- Creative and entertaining executions are in demand by consumers and will be rewarded by being shared within the social sphere.

- Community outreach can be powerful; there are masses of proud citizens who are willing to contribute for a town, a product, or an industry.

You will become a relic if you don't embrace the power of video. Do as I did to grow the success of my business when it comes to YouTube: Fail fast, fail forward, and fail better. And, remember, it's not about you, your company, or your brand; it's about viewers. Viewers determine your success or failure, so be certain to develop your videos from the outside/in instead of from the inside/out.

About the Authors

Shawn Santos is Director of Solution Design for ServiceSource. There, he helps leading technology companies optimize recurring revenue streams by providing strategic and operational business analysis, in conjunction with the design of SaaS and managed services solutions for complex global opportunities.

At TSIA, he had responsibility for the global program portfolio, and was credited in this role for building the industry's first and only social business research and collaboration group for technology services, with members spanning Cisco, NetApp, Microsoft, Bentley, BMC, VMware, Yahoo!, HP, IBM, Xerox, Oracle, and many other brands.

Previously, Shawn held management positions at Agilent Technologies and for leading wine consultancies Enologix and Global Vintage Research. Shawn obtained his undergraduate degree in molecular and cellular biology from the University of California at Santa Cruz, and has completed post-graduate work at both the University of California at Berkeley and University of Pennsylvania's Wharton School of Business.

In 2008, he founded Hope Animal Network, a community-driven non-profit advancing animal welfare in developing countries.

Connect with Shawn
LinkedIn: bit.ly/LI-Santos
Twitter: @ShawnSantos

Cory Edwards is head of Adobe's Social Business Center of Excellence. He is responsible for the company's social business operations and integrating social media into the way Adobe does business. He and his team consult with and train departments across Adobe to define and measure their social strategies. Prior to Adobe, Cory was director of social media at Dell.

He has a B.A. degree in public relations from BYU and an M.B.A. degree from the W.P. Carey School of Business at Arizona State University.

Connect with Cory
LinkedIn: bit.ly/LI-Edwards
Twitter: @coryedwards
Blog: bit.ly/Blog-Edwards

Sara Del Grande is a global operations leader with a passion for improving customer experiences with technical services. She has more than 25 years of experience in Silicon Valley working both behind the scenes in IT at first at Apple Computer and then Cisco to her current role with direct responsibility for customer experiences with the Cisco front-line contact center: The Customer Interaction Network. Sara holds a B.S. degree in business administration—marketing from San Jose State University.

Connect with Sara
LinkedIn: bit.ly/LI-Sara
Twitter: @SaraDelGrande

Gloria Burke is the chief knowledge officer ("CKO") at Unisys and is responsible for the development of the company's Enterprise Social Business strategy and supporting social culture adoption initiatives. Gloria also leads the visionary team responsible for the evolution of Inside Unisys, the company's social intranet environment that hosts its authoritative knowledge base and collaborative work spaces. Gloria also serves as Global Portfolio Leader for the Unified Social Business Practice at Unisys

She is a published author and a frequent blogger on social technologies. Gloria was named by *Information* *Week Magazine* as #2 of the Top Ten Social Business Leaders of 2013 and was also recognized in this list in 2012.

Connect with Gloria
Email: gloria.burke@unisys.com
LinkedIn: bit.ly/LI-Burke
Twitter: @GloriaBurke

Shar Govindan is director of Social Learning at Bentley Systems and on the team responsible for conferences, social media, special interest groups, user groups, and communities. He has coauthored several technical publications including *Social Boom* (FT Press, 2011) and *Computer Modeling of Water Distribution Systems* (AWWA, 2012). Shar served as a co-chair of TSIA's social media round table, on Constellation's Future of Work research panel and on AWWA's Engineering Modeling Applications Committee. Shar has a master's degree in environmental engineering from the University of Connecticut and project management mastery from Stanford University.

Connect with Shar
LinkedIn: bit.ly/LI-Shar
Twitter: @SharGovindan

David Shimberg's career has been a journey of leadership, business development, marketing, and technology. His experiences as a technology executive, an

entrepreneur, an author, a public speaker, a sales team manager, and an advisor provide him with unique depth and perspective.

David currently serves as the director of BMC Software's Global Services marketing team responsible for the group's strategic marketing and communications.

David co-authored *Client/Server and Beyond—Strategies for the 21st Century.*

Connect with David
LinkedIn: bit.ly/LI-Shimberg
Twitter: @DavidShimberg

John Ragsdale is vice president of technology and social research for the Technology Services Industry Association (TSIA). Ragsdale drives TSIA's technology research agenda, delivering insightful, thought-leadership research and analysis on the most pressing business issues facing service leaders, enabling them to better plan and execute their service strategies. Prior to joining TSIA, Ragsdale spent six years at Forrester Research as vice president and research director, covering CRM, knowledge management, self-service, and multi-channel technology.

In 2012, Ragsdale released his first book, *Lessons Unlearned: 25 Years in Customer Service,* which chronicles his career inside the customer service industry.

Connect with John
LinkedIn: bit.ly/LI-Ragsdale
Twitter: @John_Ragsdale
Blog: bit.ly/Blog-Ragsdale

Nestor Portillo has worked for the gamut of top-notch high-tech companies (Siemens, IBM, Microsoft, Wang, to name a few) and although his skill set is vast, his greatest professional expertise revolves in the worlds of international business development, social media, influencer/advocates management, audience marketing and customer experience.

Nestor's work has been recognized by *Forbes, Mashable, Marketing Professional, Business Insider,* and *ZDNET* as industry best practices. Currently he works for Cisco leading the worldwide online community, blogs, and influencer programs business for the Digital Strategy team in the Cisco marketing organization.

Connect with Nestor
Twitter: @nportillo
LinkedIn: bit.ly/LI-Nestor
Web: bit.ly/Web-Nestor

Jerome Pineau has been a software architect, entrepreneur, sales engineer, technical evangelist, community manager, marketing director, and social media strategist—all in the same lifetime. Jerome drove strategy and implementation of social customer care for the Autodesk Global Customer Support Division, led product marketing at Sprinklr.com, and as director of Social Strategy Consulting at Lithium.com, helped some of the world's largest brands stay profitable, competitive, and relevant in the digital era.

These days, at www.bigdigitalumbrella.com, he puts his extensive international experience in technology, digital strategy, and product marketing to work for brands he loves.

Connect with Jerome
Web: jeromepineau.com
LinkedIn: bit.ly/LI-Jerome
Twitter: @JeromePineau

Lewis Bertolucci is head of social media at Humana, Inc., and has more than 10 years' experience in the dynamic, heavily regulated healthcare industry. He has exp-

erienced the full spectrum of social media's evolution and has built a scalable social media program across Humana from the ground up. Lewis is also responsible for their Enterprise Social Network of over 40,000 associates that has become the fuel for Humana's cultural and social business transformation. Humana's ESN has been recognized by ReadWriteWeb, Mashable, Altimeter Group, Forrester, TechTarget, Gartner, CiteWorld and The Community Roundtable.

He's created an online lifestyle magazine, hyper-local online magazine newsstand, and mobile lifestyle app. Lewis is also an active public speaker, having spoken at Idea Festival, Social Media Marketing World, Social Media Success Summit, Social Media Explorer, and PR Daily / Ragan Communications.

Connect with Lewis
Twitter: @Lewis502
LinkedIn: bit.ly/LI-Lewis

Regina Estes led the Internet & Support Services group with Xerox North American Services Strategy until her retirement in 2012. She has 30 years of experience

in customer support and service with expertise in knowledge management, post-sale support strategies, and customer self-service solutions. Regina holds a Master of Business Administration degree in project management.

Connect with Regina
Email: raestes@epbfi.com
Twitter: @restes88

Sandra Puglisi manages the Customer Tools and Social Media team on the Xerox.com site. The last 3 years she has focused on customer

experience and development of the social media strategies within the support organization. Sandy has a Bachelor of Science degree in project management and business management.

Connect with Sandra:
Email: Sandra.Puglisi@xerox.com

Lynn Llewellyn is ServiceNow's senior director—Knowledge Management where she is responsible for the Knowledge Management program, Information Development, internal Technical

Training, Customer Experience, including the Social Media Support team. Before joining ServiceNow, Lynn worked for 17 years at Legato, EMC, and VMware Canada.

Connect with Lynn
Twitter: @lynnllewellyn2
Email: lthomson90@hotmail.com

Genevieve Gonnigan
is the former social care manager at Infor, the world's third largest enterprise software provider. Genevieve is currently a principle consultant for i.Am Personal Branding and Reputation Management Consulting Services. She is also a board member of Healing Hands Healing Hearts, Inc., a not-for-profit organization providing mentoring and career preparedness programs for Chicago's inner city youth.

Connect with Genevieve
Twitter: @ms_genevieve

Michelle Koysta is a
digital communications leader focused on social media and community engagement with 14 years of communications experience, including 8 years defining digital and social media strategies. Michelle is currently a customer success executive at Hootsuite. In 2009, she launched the award winning @BlackBerryHelp Twitter account, an early pioneer in dedicated customer service handles on Twitter.

Michelle is a frequent public speaker at digital and social media conferences and an active participant in the Canadian social media industry.

Connect with Michelle
Twitter: @michellekostya
LinkedIn: bit.ly/LI-Kostya
Web: michellekostya.com

Caty Kobe helps
companies go beyond surface-level connections and buzzwords to find solutions that benefit everyone involved. Listed as one of the top 100 most social customer service professionals, Caty is a fearless customer advocate, a devoted leader, and an all-around do-gooder. She's a community management practitioner, an avid tweeter, and an occasional blogger and webinar speaker.

Connect with Caty
Twitter: @catykobe

Françoise Tourniaire
is the founder of FT Works, a consultancy firm that helps technology companies create and improve their support operations. She has more than 20 years' experience as a support and services executive. She is a co-founder of ChurnSquad, a boutique service organization focused on helping vendors assess, monitor, manage, and reverse their churn rates while maximizing revenue expansion.

She is the author of *The Art of Software Support, Just Enough CRM*,

Collective Wisdom: Transforming Support through Knowledge, and *Selling Value*.

Connect with Francoise
Twitter: @FTtalks
Web: FTWorks.com

Annie Tsai is the chief customer officer of DoubleDutch. Prior to Double-Dutch, Annie was the chief customer officer and then chief marketing officer at Demandforce, Inc.

(acquired by Intuit in 2012).

In 2014, Annie was recognized as being one of the 50 most influential CMOs in social media on Forbes.com. In 2013, she published *Online Marketing for Small Businesses* and has been writing a blog focusing on business and customer experience management at anniesaid.com. Annie holds a B.A. from the University of California at Berkeley.

Connect with Annie
Twitter: @meannie
LinkedIn: bit.ly/LI-Annie
Web: anniesaid.com

Holly Nielsen is the U.S. Social Media Leader for IBM Global Technology Services (GTS) and chief blogger at Hooked on Social

Networking. In her spare time, she serves as social media lead and executive member of TEDxSanJoseCA and

as a manager for One Brick. Holly holds a business administration degree with a concentration in marketing from California State University, Chico, and was awarded a social media innovation patent through her work in IBM Research.

Holly is a tireless advocate for the poor and hungry, especially those One Brick helps, as well as rescuing animals.

Connect with Holly
Twitter: @HollyNielsen
Blog: bit.ly/Blog-Holly
LinkedIn: bit.ly/LI-Holly

Christopher David Kaufman is asked by corporations to do one thing: ease their pain points by using creative cutting-edge appli-

cations by applying the social dynamics of communities and crowds via social, mobile, and enterprise-wide technologies. Christopher combined his degree in human complex systems (UCLA) with his work for 15 years of creating software, building communities, and marketing consumer packaged goods and entertainment properties.

He is currently working on a textbook about the science and academic research on how messages move through human complex systems.

Connect with Chris
Twitter: @HumanComplexity
LinkedIn: bit.ly/LI-Chris
Blog: bit.ly/Blog-Chris

Called a Digital Dale Carnegie, **Erik Qualman** is the author of *Social-nomics*, which made Amazon.com's #1 Best Selling List for the United States, Japan, UK, Canada, Portugal, Italy, China, Korea, and Germany. His 2012 book *Digital Leader* helped him be voted the second "Most Likeable Author in the World" behind *Harry Potter* author J.K. Rowling.

Erik has performed in 42 countries with Coach, Sony PlayStation, National Restaurant Association, IBM, Facebook, SCG Thailand, ADP, Starbucks, M&M/Mars, National Retail Federation, Cartier, Bertelsmann, Raytheon, Chrysler, Small Business League, Home Furnishings Association, Montblanc, TEDx, Polo, UGG, Nokia, Google, AutoTrader, and others.

Erik has had the fortune to share the stage with Al Gore, Julie Andrews, Bill O'Reilly, Jeff Bezos, Howard Schultz, Brett Favre, Tony Hawk, Sarah Palin, Jose Socrates, Alan Mulally, and many others of note. Erik is listed as a Top 50 MBA Professor and sits on several company boards. His work has been highlighted on 60 Minutes, in *The New York Times*, *WSJ*, *Mashable*, *USA Today*, ABC News, *Financial Times*, *Forbes*, *Fortune*, CBS News, and *The Huffington Post*.

Fast Company lists Professor Qualman as a Top 100 Digital Influencer. He has an MBA from the McCombs School of Business.

Connect with Erik
LinkedIn: bit.ly/LI-Erik
Twitter: @equalman
Web: equalman.com/

Charlie Treadwell leads a global team responsible for social media branding, campaign activation, communities, social listening and insights, social selling, and  social support. He joined Symantec in 2013, and immediately embarked on the process of redefining paid, owned, and earned media, in the context of social media. As a certified agile scrum master, Charlie used tried and true methods of agile to transform Symantec's existing social media program into an agile marketing team. Charlie listened to customers' key questions with real-time insights, driving content strategy and responsive marketing at the speed of social.

Connect with Charlie
LinkedIn: bit.ly/LI-Charlie
Twitter: @ctreadwell

Esteban Kolsky is a customer strategist with 25+ years of experience in technology, customer service, communities, social media, online and offline market-  ing, CRM, and enterprise strategy. An early pioneer in community-based customer service, feedback management, and using social channels for customer service, he helps clients develop and implement strategies that create win-win relationships with their customers.

Connect with Esteban
Twitter: @ekolsky
Web: estebankolsky.com

Index

service-level agreements (SLAs), 132
ServiceSource Chatter campaign,
  MyOfficeRocks, 13–14
sharing information, 209–220
  implementing social media programs,
    212–215
  implementing social media tools, 218
  measuring impact of social media program,
    219
  social media revolution, 210–212
  social media tools, 215–218
SLAs (service-level agreements), 132
smartphone penetration of operating systems,
  271
SMEs (subject matter experts), Enterprise
  Social Business Transformation, 74
social businesses
  approach to consultants, 117–126
  challenges, 177–193
  defined, 1–2
  developing strategy, 25–35
  NeverSeconds blog, 2–5
social care, 221–230
  cross-functional social teams, 227–230
  identifying evangelists, 223
  multigenerational gap, 223–226
  training, 223–226
social customer care initiatives, 171–174
social experience management, 174–175
social media
  accessibility, 292–294
  customer activity continuum, 29–30
  future, 295
  infrastructure, 47–48
  knowledge management, 210–212
  marketing plans, 285–295
  programs
    science *versus* art, 297–316
  technical support channels, 129–136
  tools, 215–218
Social Media Advanced Guard committee
  (Unisys), 96
Social Media Center of Excellence (Adobe),
  48–53
  enablement, 50–51
  governance, 49
  innovation, 53
  measurement, 51–52
social metrics, 188, 190
social network engagement, Enterprise Social
  Business Transformation, 89–92
Social Sentiment programs, 57–69
social support myths, 257–265
  communities are an add-on support,
    258–260

community go/no-go decision, based on
  ROI analysis, 263–265
small support communities are not viable,
  261–262
social support, B2B environments, 195–207
  blog management, 202
  creating a strategy, 197–199
  global support, 201
  high-level corporate plans, 205
  implementation of strategy, 19–201
  listening streams, 203–204
  recognizing need for change, 196–197
  understanding and meeting customer needs,
    195–196
social-by-design business journey, 43–44
social-sharing widget, Bentley's LEARNserver,
  109
socialization of organizations, 101–116
  Bentley Be Social Award, 106–107
  blogs and videos, 108–109
  challenges and management support,
    103–104
  innovations, 109–115
  internal enterprise social growth, 107–108
  millennials as ambassadors, 105–106
  transition from business technical to
    business social, 101–103
Special Interest Groups (SIG), virtual, 112
speed of social spread, 182–184
Sprinklr, 174–175
state of technical support, 127–144
  benchmarking customer communities,
    136–144
  social media channels, 129–136
Stock and Flow content strategy, 323
stock, real-time marketing, 324
strategies
  advocate programs, 16–25
  developing social business, 25–35
  Unisys, Enterprise Social Business
    Transformation, 76–79
structure of community teams, 245–248
subject matter experts (SMEs), Enterprise
  Social Business Transformation, 74
Symnate Security Response blog, 44–45

T

teams
  community, 243–256
  real-time marketing, 325–330
technical support, 127–144
  benchmarking customer communities,
    136–144
  social media channels, 129–136
Technology Services Industry Association
  (TSIA), 127–144